ANTHONY TROLLOPE
AND HIS CONTEMPORARIES

A study in the theory and
conventions of mid-Victorian fiction

Anthony Trollope

and his contemporaries

*A study in the theory
and conventions of
mid-Victorian fiction*

David Skilton

Longman

LONGMAN GROUP LIMITED
London
*Associated companies, branches and representatives
throughout the world*

© Longman Group Limited 1972

First published 1972

ISBN 0 582 50022 2

Printed in Great Britain by
Butler & Tanner Ltd, Frome and London

CONTENTS

ACKNOWLEDGEMENTS

I am grateful to the present editor and librarian of the *Spectator* for access to their editorial records; the editor and proprietors of the *New Statesman* for permission to consult the marked file of the *Athenaeum* in their possession; and Mr J. Gordon Phillips, Archivist of *The Times*, for his kind work on my behalf in finding the authorship of numerous articles in that newspaper from its Editorial Diaries.

I also wish to thank Dr Tony Tanner, Mr Hugh Sykes Davies and Dr Raymond Williams for their advice and encouragement at various stages in the preparation of this work.

D. J. S.

NOTES ON REFERENCES

Abbreviations

Autobiography   Anthony Trollope, *An Autobiography*, ed. F.
                   Page, Oxford University Press, 1950
Letters   *The Letters of Anthony Trollope*, ed. B. A.
                   Booth, Oxford University Press, 1951
Bibliography   M. Sadleir, *Trollope: a Bibliography*, Dawsons
                   of Pall Mall, 1928; repr. 1964
Commentary   M. Sadleir, *Trollope: a Commentary*, 3rd edn,
                   Oxford University Press, 1945; repr. 1961
Critical Heritage *Trollope: the Critical Heritage,* ed. D. Smalley,
                   Routledge, 1969

The Palliser novels are quoted in the Oxford Trollope edition, ed.
M. Sadleir and F. Page, 1948–54; other novels in the World's Classics
series where available. All references to Trollope's novels are also
given by chapters, numbered cumulatively, regardless of volume
divisions, so that (for example) chapter 1 of volume 2 is called chapter
19, where volume 1 has 18 chapters.

In chapters 1 and 2 of this work, where chronology is important,
each review quoted is detailed by date, volume and page numbers
on each appearance. In chapters 3 to 6, each review is only cited in
full on its first appearance in each chapter.

INTRODUCTION

This book aims at being rather more than a study of Anthony Trollope. Although his fiction deserves a great deal more critical attention than it has yet received—and the present study is in part a contribution to Trollopian criticism—the underlying purpose of the following chapters is to utilize the vast amount of information that mid-Victorian periodical criticism presents, in order to examine the critical background against which Trollope and the other novelists of the day worked. From this evidence, a clearer picture can be gained of some of the conventions which partly controlled what the novelists wrote and how they were read. A novelist who defies a literary convention, of course, is still writing with reference to it, while his ignoring it could also be a significant fact about his work.

Despite our ever-growing acquaintance with mid-Victorian criticism of the novel, the subject requires far more attention. There have been a number of invaluable studies of individual periodicals, and a considerable amount of work on the best-known critics involved, such as G. H. Lewes and R. H. Hutton. But there are almost insuperable difficulties to such work. The large variety of literature that came under review makes a detailed analysis of a given journal's criticism practically impossible, while the examination of an individual critic's work is bedevilled by the anonymity of much of the best criticism. Thanks to the pioneering surveys of such scholars as R. G. Cox, J. D. Jump, R. Stang, A. B. Wilkinson and K. Graham, a great deal is known in general terms about Victorian reviewing, and novel criticism in particular. Nevertheless there remains a need for further detailed studies in depth.

Ideally, what is required in a study of a given body of review material is that each critical statement should be examined in several different contexts. First of all, that of the critic's other judgments, including those on other works by the same author, and (ultimately) the critic's religious, social and critical assumptions and beliefs. Next there is the context of other critics' pronouncements on the same work, as well as the contemporary critical and intellectual atmosphere, of which the given critic's whole system of thought is part.[1] Then there is the context of the development of the author's whole *œuvre*, and finally that of the historical circumstances of his publication and popularity.[2]

The focus of the present study is the fiction of Anthony Trollope, and the aim is to examine and re-examine in these various contexts, a significant portion of what was written about it in his day in the British Isles. The result of a multifaceted study is not only to gain a clearer view of Trollope's career and reception, but to expose more distinctly certain critical problems of central importance in the age, and various aspects of the social and literary scene in which all novelists of the day wrote. Thus, while the present study examines Trollope's reception in some detail, and concludes in an original analysis of his fiction in relation to its age, there are insights gained into general mid-Victorian critical problems which transcend the limits of Trollopian studies alone. This is an examination of the principles of mid-Victorian criticism rather than a study of Trollope's popularity as such, and the main stress is therefore on the how and the why of what is said (which, in a broad sense, belong to the critical language of the day) rather than on the degree of approval expressed by individual critics for individual books.

Chapter 1 analyses Trollope's reception more or less chronologically, paying most attention to the establishment of his reputation in the early years, and to the period of his greatest public success in the 'sixties. It is shown how the critics collectively built up an 'image' of the author's work, how this image affected their attitudes to his later productions, and what different sorts of popularity he enjoyed in the 'sixties. Critical recognition of Trollope only came with *Barchester Towers*, whereafter he could be seen by many readers only as the author of the Barsetshire novels, although an intellectual minority hoped that such a book as *Orley Farm* showed that a truly great new novelist had appeared. Chapter 2 sets the critical demand for

[1] A particularly original way in which the literary background can be studied through an analysis of literary references and mentions in book reviews, is demonstrated in the case of Swedish literature in the 1950s and during the late nineteenth-century rise of Scandinavian modernism, by K. E. Rosengren, in his *Sociological Aspects of the Literary Scene*, Stockholm 1968.

[2] The debt of any student of Trollope to Sadleir's account of the publication of each book in his *Bibliography* is too extensive to be acknowledged at every point.

tragedy in the novel, and the accusation that Trollope 'lacked imagination', in the context of the current status of prose fiction, and of rival theories of imagination in the 'sixties. The hatred of realsm that is often met with is shown to be an expression of a widespread fear of advancing materialism. Chapter 3 examines a moral dilemma which was central to Victorian criticism, of how, granted the need to portray vice in fiction, it was possible to write moral fiction at all; and a religious, anti-materialist solution is analysed at length. Chapter 4 shows how critics frequently made conflicting demands of 'truth to life' and social respectability and delicacy, and how they thus placed the author in a series of impossible 'double-bind' positions. It is seen that there were certain more or less understood conventions of the novel that were at least partly designed to overcome such problems, and an approach to various of Trollope's novels through the reviews, shows these conventions in action, revealing how at different times he obeys, defies or gently stretches the conventions concerned. Chapter 5 is an investigation of a strangely neglected subject—the Victorian demand for 'depth' in characterization. Some of the implications of this demand are that different methods of characterization were assumed to be necessary for male and female characters, and that there coexisted in the period both a representational and an expressive theory of art in novel criticism, in which 'romantic' and 'classical' attitudes blend. The central thread of this chapter is an analysis of Richard Holt Hutton's important theory of characterization, and the assumptions about mimesis which underlie his criticism. Drawing on the conclusions already reached in the earlier chapters, the final chapter now examines Trollope's own writings on the novel, exposing a stronger polemical aspect of his *Autobiography* than it is usually thought to possess, and showing how far his descriptions of his own writing process tally with his contemporaries' assumptions about it.   The book ends with an analysis of the distinctive features of Trollopian realism, and its relation to its age, so that Trollope's fiction is reassessed in the light of the earlier findings about its contemporary critical and historical context.

The bibliography of contemporary British articles and reviews on Trollope constitutes a far more extensive list than any so far published. Some eighty-nine hitherto unpublished attributions are definitely established.

A wide selection of twenty-six periodicals has been used in the present study. As well as the Benthamite *Westminster*, it includes what Mark Pattison dubbed '[t]hose venerable old wooden three-deckers, the *Edinburgh Review* and the *Quarterly Review*', and also his 'three new iron monitors, the *Fortnightly*, the *Contemporary*, and the *Nineteenth Century*'.[3] With the Baptist and Congregationalist *British Quarterly Review*, the Unitarian *National Review*, the Establishment *Church Quarterly Review*, and the Catholic *Home and Foreign Review*, a wide range of religious opinion is represented, while the old Whig and Tory rivals, the *Dublin Review* and the *Dublin University Magazine*, add an Irish perspective. The closest attention, however, is paid to *The Times*, and to four weeklies, the *Academy*, the *Athenaeum*, the *Saturday Review* and the *Spectator*. Trollope himself speaks of the *Saturday*, the *Spectator* and *The Times* as having the greatest critical weight with the public,[4] and they certainly contained much of the best criticism of his fiction, even though the *Spectator* only rose to excellence under the joint ownership and direction of Meredith Townsend and Richard Holt Hutton from 1861, while the standard of novel criticism in *The Times* fell off drastically after Eneas Sweetland Dallas left the paper in 1865. The lively Conservative *Saturday* and the soberer Liberal *Spectator* largely divided the weekly political market, and of the purely literary weeklies which attempted a complete coverage of new books, the *Athenaeum* remained distinctly old-fashioned during the 'fifties and 'sixties, while the *Academy* was a new journal of the 'seventies, devoted to consciously modern literary reviewing.

These weeklies plus *The Times* give a balanced view of literary opinion in the period, as it concerns an author like Trollope, who wrote for an educated middle- and upper-class public. Most of the comment found in other journals could be duplicated from the five chosen papers. Besides, mid-Victorian critics of the novel cannot in general be said to have profited much from the greater length available to them in the quarterlies, where the frequently very long articles are often more impressive for their extent than their brilliance.[5]

It is no longer necessary to apologize for taking a serious interest in Trollope's fiction itself, but the particular value of using it as the focus for a study of mid-Victorian criticism of the novel is less obvious. In the first place Trollope's career spans a crucial age of transition in

[3] 'Books and critics', *Fortnightly Review* (ns) xxii, Nov. 1877, 659–79, p. 663.

[4] *Autobiography*, pp. 192 and 269.

[5] It is unfortunately impracticable to give many references to Donald Smalley's *Trollope: the Critical Heritage*. Because Professor Smalley has to extract from many of the articles, passages are often omitted which are essential to the present study. Moreover, Trollope's less important work, especially his shorter tales, called forth much of the best criticism, and this Professor Smalley has not had space to represent.

novel-writing, criticism and periodical publishing, stretching from *Dombey and Son* to beyond *The Portrait of a Lady*, seeing the rise of self-conscious, late-Victorian literary ideals, and continuing from the age of the Newspaper Tax, through the heyday of the monthly magazines, and the full-flowering of weekly criticism after the repeal of the Newspaper Tax. Meanwhile the dominant mode of novel publication shifted from publication in parts, to serialization in magazines. But the greatest value of Trollope is that he was so apparently 'average', so much, it seems, the 'voice of his age'. A liberal-conservative, a conforming but not devout member of the Church of England, a man eminently practical to the point of philistinism, an author who more than any other satisfied the mid-Victorians' obsession with seeing their own social and domestic world 'mirrored to the life', and finally *the* fashionable novelist *par exellence* in the 'sixties.

Curiously, his general conformity to everyday, middle-class ideals —the fact that he was not a Brontë or a Meredith, a Miss Braddon or a Miss Broughton, or even a Dickens for that matter—means that certain critical issues stand out unusually clearly. When, for instance, we find him condemned for immorality, we are forced to examine the grounds of complaint more closely than would be necessary in the case of his more scandalous contemporaries, and hence to reassess both Trollope's apparent conformity, and our understanding of the critics' moral standards.

The range of his fiction is important too, from the comfortable clerical world of *Barchester Towers* to the Irish famine in *Castle Richmond*, from the delicate miniature of *Rachel Ray* to the savage, all-embracing satire of *The Way We Live Now*, and from the mediocre circulating library fiction of *Marion Fay* to the near greatness of *Orley Farm* or *The Last Chronicle of Barset*. We see the reviewers confronted by the problem of whether or not to regard him as a great novelist, and of how to establish in the first place what constitutes greatness in a genre in which they are still not at home, critically speaking. There is one type of examination, incidentally, to which Trollope's reception does not lend itself, and that is the impact of criticism on the course of individual novels, since, with the exception of *Framley Parsonage*, he invariably completed his books before publication began, unlike Dickens, Thackeray and others. Here again, our attention is necessarily directed to more strictly critical topics.

One aspect of Trollope's reputation that can find no place in the present study is his fame as a writer of travel books. *The West Indies and the Spanish Main, North America, Australia and New Zealand*

and *South Africa* all received widespread and serious attention in all quarters, as the observations of a fluent, intelligent and practical man, who had wide experience in public administration. Although this second sphere of literary fame bears very little on the present subject, it does illuminate one aspect of his fictional output, and that is his compulsion to communicate to his readers about people and places with which they were not familiar. Hence the *Tales of All Countries* and *Harry Heathcote of Gangoil*, or—when the traveller's experience was more effectively absorbed into a well-structured novel—the Australian scenes of *John Caldigate* and the Italian scenes in *He Knew He Was Right*. Probably no novelist famous for writing about the country life of his homeland was ever better acquainted with so many different parts of the world. This aspect of his work shows how wrong it must be to ignore his practical, anti-sentimental stance as a writer. In his own day, his fictional vision too was of more than trivial interest, whatever some twentieth-century readers might think of it.

This is not to say that Trollope's fiction is uniformly good. Some is distinctly weak, and written, upon occasion, on demand:

> I feel, with regard to literature, somewhat as I suppose an uphol-sterer and undertaker feels when he is called upon to supply a funeral. He has to supply it, however distasteful it may be. It is his business, and he will starve if he neglect it. So have I felt that, when anything in the shape of a novel was required, I was bound to produce it.[6]

It seems clear that Trollope sincerely underestimated himself as a novelist. Then and now his readers too have tended to take him less seriously than at his best he deserves. The question of how his image as a writer was originally established by the critics, and how it affected his whole writing career, is the subject of chapter I.

[6] *Autobiography*, p. 356.

I

THE ESTABLISHMENT OF TROLLOPE'S REPUTATION

The earliest novels

At the peak of his popularity, Trollope became one of the most fashionable novelists of the Victorian age, but his rise to fame was slow. Although his first novel was published as early as 1847, he received very little intelligent critical attention before *Barchester Towers* appeared ten years later, and it was not until the 1860s that he could command a really large public, and demand correspondingly high prices from his publishers.

In his *Autobiography* Trollope would have us believe that his first three novels passed practically unnoticed in the press.[1] There were in fact at least thirteen notices of *The Macdermots of Ballycloran*, the first of them, alone.[2] Yet neither it nor its two successors attracted much serious attention, and such reviews as they did get are, like the novels themselves, more important in view of what came after than interesting in their own right. The story of the publication of *The Macdermots of Ballycloran* is confused, not to say shady. It seems that Trollope's publisher Newby tried to pass off this unknown writer's novel as a new book from the pen of Anthony's mother, the well-established and popular Mrs Trollope herself.[3] But even this confusion as to authorship failed to make the novel a success.

---

[1] *Autobiography*, pp. 75–9.
[2] See L. O. Tingay, 'The reception of Trollope's first novel', *Nineteenth Century Fiction* vi, Dec. 1951, 195–200.
[3] L. O. Tingay, 'The publication of Trollope's first novel', *TLS* no. 2822, 30 Mar. 1956, 200. Tingay's case is supported by the printed slip for the *Macdermots* in the Cambridge University Library catalogue, which originally names the author as Mrs Trollope, and has later been altered in pen.

To display the low quality of some of the minor criticism of the period, it is worth looking briefly at three or four of the notices of Trollope's earliest work. These represent the dead-level of periodical criticism of the period, against which the achievements of the best reviewers can be measured. It is instructive to see just what sort of reception an unknown new writer had to be content with. Once *Barchester Towers* had been published, however, and the better critics had devoted to Trollope the sort of attention calculated to place him and to define his achievements in the public mind, the less able reviewers could follow the lead and give fairly adequate accounts of his work. But before this, the notices of Trollope's books were usually most unsatisfactory, as H. F. Chorley's reviews in the *Athenaeum* will illustrate.

Henry Fothergill Chorley, who reviewed *The Macdermots of Bally-cloran, The Kellys and the O'Kellys* and *La Vendée* for the *Athenaeum*, was a prolific journalist in a variety of fields. An unsuccessful novelist,[4] and for a long time a friend of Dickens and Mendelssohn, he was for nearly forty years his paper's chief music critic, but to his chagrin he was also allotted a great deal of 'inferior literature' to review.[5] He shows little power of judging the literary value of a new work, not distinguishing, for example, between the high quality of the *Macdermots*, and the undoubted failure of *La Vendée*. Having an almost morbid fear of vulgarity in both life and literature,[6] Chorley goes to extremes even by mid-Victorian standards in requiring his fiction to be an utterly anodyne and delicate amusement, and he judges new novels almost entirely in terms of how pleasant or unpleasant they are. Consequently he prefers the *Kellys* to the *Macdermots* 'because although not more powerful, it is less painful'.[7] The *Macdermots* he dislikes as an example of the outmoded, pathetic genre of Irish fiction, distasteful in its 'dull domestic misery', and he advises Trollope to concentrate on happier subjects, since 'he seems to possess a vein of humour . . . which, if duly reined in (our caution is not needlessly prudish), might win him success among those who prefer "the quips and cranks" of Mirth's crew to the death-spasms of Crime and Sorrow'.[8] In all his criticism, and in his notice of *La Vendée* in particular, Chorley liberally displays the heavy use of extract and quotation that is the greatest vice of the reviewers of the period—and something at which, his biographer notes without irony, he was

---

[4] Under the pseudonym 'Paul Bell'.

[5] H. G. Hewlett, *Henry Fothergill Chorley*, 1873, ii, 2.

[6] 'Henry Fothergill Chorley' (anon), *Temple Bar* xl, Dec. 1873, 93–101.

[7] *Athenaeum* no. 1081, 15 Jul. 1848, 701.

[8] *Athenaeum* no. 1020, 15 May 1847, 517.

'more than ordinarily gifted'.[9] Fortunately his inflated style and his overwritten kind of criticism—'individuality . . . degenerated into mannerism', as the *Dictionary of National Biography* happily terms it—was going out of fashion about this time, and Chorley himself now disappears from this record of Trollope's reception, until in 1867 he is once more allotted a minor novel by an unknown author: this time Trollope's anonymous *Nina Balatka*.

The *Spectator*[10] is far more sensitive to matters of technique in its notice of the *Macdermots* than Chorley is. Although the reviewer considers the plot '*too* natural', too spare for a full-length novel, and stretched out with 'needless minutiae', he commends Trollope's 'natural' characters, which are 'without much of book exaggeration: they are human in their vices, not mere abstractions of unalloyed folly, weakness, or virtue'. This reviewer finds the final catastrophe of the *Macdermots* 'not so much painful as uninteresting'. 'The persons are too coarse and sordid', he explains, ' the incidents too low, to inspire much sympathy.' His is an interesting critical reaction because, denied a conventional response to a stock fictional type of character, he does not in fact know how to respond at all. The reader, he claims, cannot feel any real interest in the characters 'either as gentry or peasants, because they belong to neither'.

Nevertheless this reviewer has already discerned in Trollope's first novel several of the qualities that will occupy critics throughout his whole career: his paucity of plot; his detailed preoccupation with everyday life; and his efforts to excite the reader's sympathy and interest for characters who are essentially ordinary, or who do not belong to the established literary types of sympathetic characters. The objection on this last score is not only socially revealing about mid-Victorian criticism in general, but attacks the very basis of Trollopian realism. The charge of coarseness reappears frequently when Trollope's interests range too far down the social scale for his sensitive critics. Most important of all, the critic's dilemma when faced with Trollope's particular brand of realism is already apparent: the truth to life is skilful, perceptive and exact; but it does not necessarily make for great literature in the eyes of the mid-Victorian critic because for the very same reason it can also be considered too ordinary—not 'imaginative' or 'intense' enough. Reproduction, it is felt, may belie creativity. 'With much knowledge . . . of men as they are . . . and skill in nicely marking their traits', the *Spectator* decides, 'Mr. Trollope fails from want of largeness and imagination'.

The notice of the *Kellys* in *The Times* of 7 September 1848,

[9] Hewlett, *Henry Fothergill Chorley*, ii, 3.
[10] xx, 8 May 1847, 449.

the first of a large number of reviews of Trollope, is noteworthy mainly because the novelist characteristically represents it in his *Autobiography* as even more effectively biting than in fact it was. Nevertheless, it was a sarcastic attack on his 'coarseness', and very far from favourable.[11]

From the point of view of the contemporary critics, *The Warden* too belongs to the very earliest stage of Trollope's career, before he was discovered, since most reviewers, like their readers, respond more readily to a novel when they already have a fairly clear image of its author and his work in their minds. The novel never achieved what Trollope calls 'the essential honour of a second edition' in its original form, and his profit from it was small: 'Indeed,' he writes, 'as regarded remuneration for the time, stone-breaking would have done better.'[12] Nevertheless *The Warden* does mark the beginning of the recognition that Trollope had 'powers far above the average as a writer of fiction',[13] even if full appreciation of the novel was only granted retrospectively. T. H. S. Escott is frequently inaccurate in his book on Trollope, but he is surely right when he records that although *The Warden* opens the Barchester series, it 'did not complete its growth into world-wide favour till that series had advanced some way'.[14]

In a favourable though unperceptive review in the *Athenaeum* of 1855,[15] the novelist Geraldine Jewsbury commends this 'clever, spirited, sketchy story, upon the difficulties which surround . . . the administration of the charitable trusts in England'. Far from objecting to the deliberate intention of the book, she regards it as marred by too little preaching, by 'too much indifference as to the rights of the case'. It is interesting to see how this critic is hampered because the author is still a relatively unknown quantity. She has not yet isolated the essential characteristics of Trollopian realism, and the initial assessment of this, his first novel to meet with any success at all, suffers accordingly. The *Spectator* in its review, however, outlines Mr Harding's position far more sensitively, pointing out that even if Trollope condemns the abuse, 'the whole tenour of the feeling of the narrative is the other way'.[16]

After seven years, it is just becoming possible to treat Trollope seriously, as a significant new novelist. Fuller critical acknowledgement of his powers now follows, and, eventually, his popularity.

[11] *Autobiography*, pp. 77–8. See *Critical Heritage*, p. 557.

[12] *Autobiography*, p. 98.

[13] *Leader* vi, 17 Feb. 1855, 164–5.

[14] *Anthony Trollope: his work, associates and literary originals*, 1913, p. 103.

[15] No. 1422, 27 Jan. 1855, 107–8.

[16] xxviii, 6 Jan. 1855, 27–8.

Trollope discovered

The reception of *Barchester Towers* must be examined at some length, since it is now that Trollope's reputation is established, and the terms in which he will be considered for most of his life laid down.

The *Spectator*, most sensitive in its reception of *The Warden*, misjudges *Barchester Towers*,[17] calling it too diffuse for satire, and finding in it (surprisingly) only characters that are 'rather abstractions of qualities than actual persons'. Meanwhile H. St John in the *Athenaeum*[18] contents himself with the most general of comments on the effectively 'dramatic' construction of the novel, and the 'infusion of romance [which] gives lightness and brightness to the ecclesiastical picture'. The young *Saturday Review*, however, now prints its first review of Trollope,[19] and is from the beginning more critical and intellectual about him than the ageing *Athenaeum*, long gone into a critical decline. The *Saturday*'s comments must be quoted at length as perhaps the earliest example of what came to be accepted as the standard 'definition' of the Trollopian world:

> Such a conflict [as that between Dr Grantly and Mr Slope] is a hard matter to describe. It is necessary to make it lively, and yet real—to give characteristic touches, and yet escape vulgarity—to handle theological disputes without bitterness, injustice, or profanity. Considering the dangers he runs, Mr. Trollope's success is wonderfully great. The theologians, unlike most theologians in novels, are thoroughly human, and retain the mixed nature of ordinary men; and, what is more, they are described impartially. The author is not a party writer . . . He sees and paints the follies of either extreme. Then, again, he has the merit of avoiding the excess of exaggeration. He possesses an especial talent for drawing what may be called the second-class of good people—characters not noble, superior, or perfect . . . but still good and honest, with a fundamental basis of sincerity, kindliness, and religious principle, yet with a considerable proneness to temptation, and a strong consciousness that they live, and like to live, in a struggling, party-giving, comfort-seeking world. Such people are so common, and form so large a proportion of the betterish and more respectable classes, that it requires a keen perception of the ludicrous, and some power of satire, to give distinctness to the types taken from their ranks by the novelist. Mr. Trollope manages to do this admirably; and though his pudding may have the fault of being all plums, yet we cannot deny it is excellent eating.

[17] xxx, 16 May 1857, 525–6.
[18] No. 1544, 30 May 1857, 689–90.
[19] iii, 30 May 1857, 503–4.

This passage displays one of the views of Trollope most commonly
held during his lifetime, defining as it does the Trollope of the Barsetshire Chronicles, who remained—and still remains—for many people
the 'true' Trollope. It is from now on the standard by which reviewers
judge his work, and can serve to guide or to mislead them at different
times, opening their eyes to the qualities of a *Small House at Allington*,
while blinding them to the virtues of a *Miss Mackenzie* or a *Way We
Live Now*. Henceforth where subject-matter and the novelist's view
of the world are concerned, such a definition as that quoted above
is usually taken as the Trollopian norm: with results that make an
interesting study in the power of a reader's expectations over his
perceptions.

E. S. Dallas in *The Times* of 13 August 1857 welcomes the freshness
and vividness of both *Barchester Towers* and *The Warden*, and the
'curious and interesting' side of social life they reveal. But he takes
Trollope to task for 'pandering to a very morbid curiosity' in the
public by descending to personalities in his satire about Tom Towers
and the *Jupiter*; although, as Trollope claims in his *Autobiography*,
he was 'living away in Ireland at the time' and had not then even
heard the name of anyone on *The Times*.[20]

There are very few known articles on Trollope by his great novelist
contemporaries, and the anonymous review of *Barchester Towers* in
the *Westminster Review* of October 1857 is one of them—even though
there has been some doubt at times which of his great contemporaries
it should be attributed to. In 1909 M. Buxton Forman named
George Eliot, and this attribution was generally accepted until G. S.
Haight recently refuted it from conclusive documentary evidence
which proved the author to be George Meredith.[21] Meredith is
generous, recommending those 'few' novel readers 'who have not
yet made acquaintance with Mr. Trollope' to get *The Warden* and
Barchester Towers at once, for even if Trollope does neglect 'the
emotional part of our nature', Meredith recognizes that here is 'a
caustic and vigorous writer, who can draw men and women, and tell
a story that men and women can read':

Mr. Trollope has satisfactorily solved a problem in this production.
He has, without resorting to politics, or setting out as a social

[20] p. 99. I am grateful to J. Gordon Phillips, Archivist of *The Times*, for
providing the attribution of this and numerous other articles, from the paper's
editorial diaries.

[21] *Westminster Review* (ns) xii, 594–6; M. Buxton Forman, ed., *George
Meredith: some early appreciations*, 1909, p. 43; G. S. Haight, 'George
Meredith and the "Westminster Review"', *Modern Language Review* liii,
Jan. 1958, 1–16. Later in the same article in the *Westminster*, incidentally,
Meredith reviews his own *Farina*.

reformer, given us a novel that men can enjoy, and a satire so cleverly interwoven with the story, that every incident and development renders it more pointed and telling. In general our modern prose satirists spread their canvas for a common tale, out of which they start when the occasion suits, to harangue, exhort, and scold the world in person. Mr. Trollope entrusts all this to the individuals of his story.

Later in Trollope's career younger writers were not often to pay him such worthwhile compliments: and Meredith's champions, James Thomson and W. E. Henley, were less magnanimous than their master.

Trollope was not yet fully established, however. In his book on *Novels and Novelists from Elizabeth to Victoria*, published in 1858, John Cordy Jeaffreson could still devote a mere thirteen lines to Trollope:[22] that is one-third of the number he gave Charlotte Yonge, for example, and put Trollope on a level with very minor figures like Samuel Lover and Dudley Costello. But an important *succès d'estime* seemed to be growing up for the author of *Barchester Towers*. In 1859 Trollope's brother Thomas Adolphus, domiciled in Florence, received a letter from Elizabeth Barrett Browning containing 'generously appreciative criticism' of *The Three Clerks* from the writer and her husband,[23] while Anthony himself was given warm praise for the same novel from his great idol, Thackeray.[24] Trollope was also joining Thackeray as favourite novelist of Cardinal Newman, who told a correspondent on 8 October 1858 that he had found the opening of *Barchester Towers* so amusing that 'after I was in bed last night, I am ashamed to say, I burst out laughing, and, when I woke in the middle of the night I began laughing again'.[25]

From the time of *Vanity Fair*, novel-writing in Britain had been, and continued to be, dominated by two giants. 'It is now Dickens and Thackeray, Thackeray and Dickens, all the world over', wrote David Masson in 1859,[26] echoing an earlier opinion of 1851: '. . . the two writers throw into relief each other's peculiarities . . . [T]hey are, in some respects, the opposites of each other'.[27] Quite apart from the

[22] ii, 396. The dearth of novel criticism in book form in the period can be judged from Jeaffreson's statement that this (to us) very slight work was '[f]avourably treated by the critics, . . . raised me in the esteem of literary workers, and increased the number of my readers'. See his *Book of Recollections*, 2 vols, 1894, i, 163.
[23] T. A. Trollope, *What I Remember*, 3 vols, 1887–89, ii, 188.
[24] In a letter of 28 Oct. 1859; see *Autobiography*, pp. 137–8.
[25] *The Letters and Diaries of John Henry Newman*, ed. C. S. Dessain, vol. xviii, Nelson, 1968, p. 482.
[26] *British Novelists and Their Styles*, p. 234.
[27] *Ibid.*, p. 237. Part of this section of Masson's book is rewritten from his anonymous article '*Pendennis* and *Copperfield*: Thackeray and Dickens',

quarrels in which the two became involved, the literary world and
the general reading public seem to have been divided into rival fac-
tions, so that, said Masson, 'there is no debate more common wherever
literary talk goes on, than the debate as to the respective merits of
Dickens and Thackeray'.[28] The young James Hannay for one, would
hold, around 1848, that to praise either was to dislike the other;
and although he later contributed a score of articles to *Household
Words* and half-a-dozen to *All the Year Round*, he continued as
a devoted Thackerayan to undervalue Dickens in print.[29] Hannay's
adherence to Thackeray was partly a matter of approving the more
'gentlemanly' author, just as the distinction Masson draws between
the two novelists is based on Thackeray's use of the language of a
classically educated university man.[30] Thus a thoroughly university
publication like the *Anti-Teapot Review* could take it for granted that
its readers would agree in considering Thackeray 'the greatest and
most perfect English writer and humourist'.[31]

On this map of the literary world, Trollope is early placed firmly
in the neighbourhood of the Thackeray pole—precisely where he
would wish to place himself. The *Spectator*, for one, describes him as a
'club man',[32] and in general he is socially approved by the critics,
even the fastidious *Saturday* naming him as 'one of the few popular
writers of the day who always write as a gentleman and a man of
sense and principle should write'.[33] Moreover, after *Barchester Towers*
the critics are beginning to think of him in terms of potential greatness,
as 'among the illustrious living writers of fiction whom we are able
to count off upon our fingers',[34] and as a possible rival or successor

---

North British Review xv, May 1851, 51–89, itself partially repr. in *Thackeray:
the Critical Heritage*, ed. G. Tillotson and D. Hawes, Routledge, 1968,
pp. 111–28. Throughout this earlier article, Masson sustains the picture of
fiction as dominated by these two great novelists.

[28] *British Novelists and Their Styles*, p. 235.

[29] See G. J. Worth, *James Hannay: his life and works*, University of Kansas
Press, 1964, pp. 35–6, 67–8 and 107. See also Hannay's *Course of English
Literature*, 1866 (repr. from the *Welcome Guest* of 1859), esp. p. 321.

[30] *Thackeray: the Critical Heritage*, pp. 111–12.

[31] i, May 1864, 5.

[32] Review of *North America*, xxv, 7 June 1862, 635–6.

[33] Review of *North America*, xiii, 31 May 1862, 625–6.

[34] Review of *Doctor Thorne, Leader* ix, 29 May 1858, 519–20. It is unfortunately unlikely that the editor, G. H. Lewes, was the author of this perceptive and favourable review, or indeed that he was in any way responsible
for it, since, writing to W. B. Rands about the *Leader*'s review of Bagehot's
Estimates of Some Englishmen and Scotchmen (ix, 6 Feb. 1858, 140), Lewes,
Rands says, claimed at that time to be 'no longer responsible for the literary
matter [in the *Leader*], and was even anxious to have it known that he was
not'. See *Contemporary Review* xxxiv, Feb. 1879, 621, under one of Rand's
signatures, 'M.B.'. Nevertheless the three notices in the *Leader* of *Barchester*

to Thackeray, who is in the mind of one *Saturday* critic when he declares *The Three Clerks* to contain 'scenes from family life more true, more pathetic, and more skilfully sustained than any which can be found except in the writings of novelists whose fame is no longer doubtful'.[35] A comparison of *The Three Clerks* to *Pendennis*, for example, is very pertinent, inasmuch as the London of the former novel is recognizably the same city as that of Pendennis's less aristocratic haunts; and inasmuch, too, as Trollope is at his most didactic. He is preaching warnings against the corruption of the world, and portraying and debating the aspirations and snares of youth, in what is after all a *Bildungsroman*. Each novel, of course, also concerns the development of a writer, and draws significantly on autobiographical material.

The Three Clerks, praised by the Brownings and by Thackeray, was also held by some important critics, notably in the *Spectator* and the *Leader*,[36] to be superior to both *The Warden* and *Barchester Towers*. Despite this, and although considered by the author 'certainly the best novel I had as yet written',[37] it failed to make a lasting impression on the general view that critics held of Trollope's work, and therefore never provided them with the same secure frame of critical reference as *Barchester Towers* already had. This was presumably because *Barchester Towers* was reinforced first by *Doctor Thorne*, and then by the phenomenally popular *Framley Parsonage* and *Small House at Allington*. Even if some critics took *Barchester Towers*, *The Three Clerks*, *Doctor Thorne* and *The Bertrams* to be all of equal importance at the time they appeared, there can be no doubt that when they came to look back on Trollope's work in later years, they saw *Barchester Towers* and *Doctor Thorne* loom larger, magnified, as it were, through the later Barsetshire novels.

Already in 1857 the habit of reverting to Barsetshire as the standard of judgment had started. The *Saturday Review*, for instance, which first set out the definition of the Trollopian norm, finds *The Three Clerks* less satisfactory than the two previous novels,[38] and reverts to praising the world of *Barchester Towers* once more. From now on, to many people, Trollope remains essentially the author of the *Chronicles of Barsetshire*.

Towers, *The Three Clerks* and *Doctor Thorne* from May 1857 to May 1858 show a consistency of thought and of high quality, that would suggest the same author throughout.

[35] iv, 5 Dec. 1857, 517–18.

[36] xxx, 12 Dec. 1857, 1300–1, and viii, 19 Dec. 1857, 1218, respectively.

[37] *Autobiography*, p. 111.   [38] iv, 5 Dec. 1857, 517–18.

Trollope's appeal in the late 'fifties and early 'sixties was his un-pretentious 'truth to life', although even at the peak of his popu-larity around *The Small House at Allington*, we find ever-growing complaints that truth alone is not enough, and that some 'elevation' or 'idealization' of subject-matter is essential. There is a steady stream of these complaints, as different critics at different times look in vain for religious message, social prophecy, poetic concentration, or an aesthetic self-awareness. Eventually the clamour only dies down because many of the reviewers become indifferent about him towards the end of his career. But in the late 'fifties there were few dissident voices. The review of *Doctor Thorne* in the *Leader* best expresses the prevalent favourable opinion:

> . . . the scenery, the personages, the incidents are pure English, and such as might have occurred last year; indeed, by a casual allusion or two, Mr. Trollope has impressed a sort of contemporary actuality on his scenes. Several of the constituents of modern English society are represented with striking force and fidelity; the factitious aristocracy of birth and wealth, the self-made aristo-cracy of brain and will, and the true aristocracy of simple faith and honest worth are contrasted in no forced, conventional manner, and in no grudging or envious spirit.[39]

For its part the *Saturday Review* praises the truth to life of the Woodward family in *The Three Clerks*: 'These girls are like real girls. They have the strong and the weak points of young women in real life';[40] while the *Athenaeum* describes the same novel in terms of the most extreme literal realism: 'His characters all stand upright on their feet, as real men and women should; his scenes, for their vivid lifelike reality, might have been transferred from actual occurrences; the speeches set down for them might have been spoken . . .'[41] To the *Leader*'s critic, *The Three Clerks* might serve for the Civil Service as a 'mirror set in a paper frame',[42] while the *Spectator* commends 'that close observation of human manners, and of human nature as modified by human manners in this middle of the nineteenth century, which form the author's distinguishing characteristic'.[43] All in all, the critics agree that 'English society [is] faithfully and powerfully pictured' in the novels of 'this sturdy and healthy "realist," Mr. Anthony Trollope'.[44]

The critics did find faults, however, particularly in his plots. Geraldine Jewsbury thought that *The Three Clerks* had 'nothing

[39] ix, 29 May 1858, 519–20.   [40] iv, 5 Dec. 1857, 517–18.
[41] No. 1574, 26 Dec. 1857, 1621.
[42] viii, 19 Dec. 1857, 1218.
[43] Review of *Doctor Thorne*, xxxi, 29 May 1858, 577–8.
[44] Review of *Doctor Thorne*, *Leader* ix, 29 May 1858, 519–20.

like a consecutive plot',[45] and the *Saturday* felt that it invited the reader's attention to 'wander' too widely,[46] while the *Leader* considered the 'conduct of the story . . . careless, not marching straight on'.[47] It was Jewsbury again who complained that the 'love affairs of Frank and Mary drag' in *Doctor Thorne*, so that the novel is damaged by repetitions.[48] The *Leader* said the book fell down on 'constructive ingenuity'.[49] The *Saturday Review*, often severer in its criticisms than its contemporaries, castigated Trollope not only for his 'carelessness' in controlling his 'languid' plot, but also for apologizing weakly for being unable to solve the problems that arose from his story, instead of fulfilling his 'duty' as a novelist by actually solving them.[50] Trollope himself, looking back in his *Autobiography*, rightly considered the plot of *The Bertrams* 'more than ordinarily bad',[51] and Newman thought the third volume 'a dreadful fall off . . . deplorably bad'.[52] The *Saturday* objected to Trollope's 'episodical sketches' and 'the temerity with which he shoots those odd fragments into the body of his tale',[53] and Geraldine Jewsbury supposed the weakness to be due to the exigences of the three-volume form. In particular, she said, 'Mr Trollope uses his traveller's journal too lavishly'— a judgment it would be hard to fault. The plot, one must agree with her, is 'the least part of the business'.[54] It was, however, practically only Eneas Sweetland Dallas who fully understood how profoundly unimportant a conventional plot was to Trollope.[55]

In mid-Victorian terms, the damaging thing about the critics' objections was that since it was assumed that a well-constructed plot was necessary to a novel, it naturally followed that a novelist was being slapdash in not providing one. While it is probably true that Trollope found enormous difficulty in turning out a conventional mid-Victorian plot, and so was making a virtue of necessity, it is perfectly clear that his rejection of contrivance and suspense in his stories was central to his fictional method.[56] Nonetheless the slightness of his plots is also the basis of the constant attacks he suffered from as early as *Doctor Thorne* right up to the end of his life, for hasty writing, overproduction, and lack of correction. In 1858 the *Saturday Review*

---

[45] *Athenaeum* no. 1574, 26 Dec. 1857, 1621.
[46] iv, 5 Dec. 1857, 517–18.
[47] Review of *Doctor Thorne*, ix, 29 May 1858, 519–20.
[48] *Athenaeum* no. 1597, 5 June 1858, 719.
[49] ix, 29 May 1858, 519–20.
[50] v, 12 June 1858, 618–19.   [51] p. 126.
[52] Letter of 2 Oct. 1862, *Letters and Diaries*, xx, 284.
[53] vii, 26 Mar. 1859, 368–9.
[54] *Athenaeum* no. 1639, 26 Mar. 1859, 420.
[55] 'Anthony Trollope', *The Times*, 23 May 1859, 12.
[56] See chapter 6 below.

warns him that he risks missing 'the position to which he is un-
questionably capable of rising', because of 'the rapid multiplication
of his progeny'.[57] Significantly it is only four days later that Edward
Chapman, presumably with this review fresh in his mind, writes
to Trollope to reject *Brown, Jones, and Robinson,* giving as his
reason that 'there is a strong impression abroad that you are writing
too rapidly for your permanent fame'.[58] The *Saturday* critic is so
typical of his contemporaries in his analysis, that it will suffice to
follow his enumeration of the supposed effects of overproduction on
Trollope's novels. In the first place, mere 'mechanical skill' replaces
'what constituted the value and promise of his style', and although
'clever', *Doctor Thorne* shows 'a diminution in the life and point'
which characterized *The Warden* and *Barchester Towers*. There is
much description which must be admitted to be good, the critic
continues, but which [Trollope] with proper pains might have
written much better'. In fine, the weaknesses of plot and language
result from 'carelessness'.

The terms of condemnation are conveniently vague. The charge of
irresponsibly mechanical and slapdash work is the easiest complaint
a critic can raise at any time in Trollope's busy career, because
the diagnosis can be as non-specific as the critic cares to make it.
Just what does constitute 'the value and promise' of Trollope's
style in *Barchester Towers* can go unexamined, while a diminution
in 'life and point' sounds sufficiently damning to require no elucidation. This is certainly not to say that a critic is necessarily wrong
to object to the speed at which Trollope was pouring fiction on to the
market, but the issue seems normally to be prejudged from the rate
of publication of his novels, rather than from the novels themselves.
There is bound to be a similarity between the different novels of so
profuse a writer, and in the case of Trollope the resemblances are
obvious. Lacking new positive points to raise, then, the critic is
easily tempted back into another attack on rapid writing. And the
critics' problem was a real one, for in the thirteen years of his greatest
success, from 1857 to 1869, the *Athenaeum* published no fewer than
twenty reviews of Trollope, the *Saturday Review* twenty-two plus
two other articles, and the *Spectator* twenty-four. At a certain point,
one might conjecture, the originality if not the quality of the criticism was bound to drop off.

As yet the complaint is not so much want of ability as lack of
attention to the highest artistic aims. But very soon, as time passes,
and Trollope continues unreformed, the critics round on him for lack
of 'imagination', as though angry with him for fascinating them

[57] Review of *Doctor Thorne*, v, 12 June 1858, 618–19.
[58] Letter of 16 June 1858, *Commentary*, p. 178.

for so long and so often with such mundane amusements. The difference between the early criticisms and the more damaging attacks he was subject to in the 'seventies[59] is that in the late 'fifties and 'sixties Trollope is writing a kind of fiction which is fundamentally in tune with what the public and most of the critics want. In the 'seventies this is no longer true. The critical differences are no longer underpinned by a basic agreement on aims. Furthermore, his sales and prices were falling in the 'seventies, and he was therefore more vulnerable to adverse press notices than in the late 'fifties, when his popularity was growing year by year. The period in which the reviewers begin to attack him is the time of his phenomenal success in the 'sixties, when he scarcely needed to worry. This explains why he did not trouble to say anything significant about press attacks in his *Autobiography* once he was established, until the adverse notices of *Lady Anna* and *The Prime Minister* in 1874 and 1876 coincided with an alarming drop in the price he could expect from a publisher.

Another complaint which is frequently heard from the time of *The Warden* onwards concerns Trollope's habit of addressing the reader directly, and discussing his characters and the conduct of his story. The storyteller as self-conscious manipulator was perhaps out of fashion for the reason suggested by Geoffrey Tillotson and Donald Hawes in the introduction to their volume on Thackeray in the *Critical Heritage* series:

> What Forster was objecting to [in his review of *Henry Esmond* in the *Examiner* of 13 November 1852] was in part something that was rarer in nineteenth century literature than in eighteenth century, something that can truly be called by the much misused term 'classical'. The great and perhaps final difference between the romantic and the classical is that between writing in which the writer is felt to be palpitating with earnestness and writing done with seeming coolness, at arm's length, as it were, distanced, and enclosed in calm.[60]

The whole issue is much more obtrusive in the case of Thackeray than Trollope, because no reader can mistake that 'it was during the progress of his commentary that Thackeray mainly constructed his authorial personality'.[61] As I show in chapter 6, the role of Trollope's narrator is more easily overlooked, and consequently it has been underestimated, and even ignored altogether. Neverthless it is an essential role of mediation in any of his novels. It is not safe to assume, as many nineteenth-century critics did, that all his so-called 'authorial intrusions' are superfluous excrescences, and even

[59] See *Commentary*, pp. 311–13.
[60] *Thackeray: the Critical Heritage*, 1968, p. 14.
[61] *Ibid.*, p. 14.

less that they are so much actor's 'gag', needed to pad out a thin tale to three-volumed corpulence, as, for example, the *Leader* assumes on reviewing *The Warden* and *Doctor Thorne*, and the *National Review* in its comments on *Barchester Towers*.[62] Some of the first-person comments of Trollope's narrator, however, are surely misjudged, and there is a central critical problem in the need to reconcile Trollope's apparently perfect fictional illusion, with the ever-felt hand of his narrative persona. A solution to this problem is also offered in chapter 6.

Reviewers also objected to Trollope's habit of including passages in which he leaves the main stream of his story to branch off into a little lecture or pamphlet, on some subject more or less arising out of the fictional situation at that point in the novel, such as the organiza- tion of the Civil Service, or the comparative abilities of village post- men. Naturally critics attributed this habit to the need to expand to three volumes. At best, in fact, these discursions are general state- ments of social or moral principles, which enable the reader better to judge or understand the characters' conduct, or the course of events. At worst, they are almost entirely irrelevant to the rest of the book, as direct comment, underlying principle, or analogy. A blatant example is the aside in *The Three Clerks* on the classing of ships 'A1', in which I can find no possible relevance.[63] The *Leader* administers frequent rebukes on the subject of digressions, but it is characteristically the *Saturday Review* which takes the subject up with the greatest vigour:

> Subjects are introduced into it which should find no place in a novel. One whole long chapter is a mere pamphlet on the merits and demerits of the Civil Service . . . A writer of fiction must not leave off story-telling and commence a dissertation on the English Constitution. Supposing a serialist did this, what would the public say?[64]

The *Saturday* has a double objection. As Merle Bevington frequently points out in his book on the paper, it is more interested in questions of fact than the appreciation of fiction.[65] So it is more concerned about whether the subjects raised in this way can get a sufficiently serious airing in a novel, than about whether artistic unity is preserved. It fears that many readers probably 'omit the intercalated pamphlet altogether', so that the novelist's teaching, even if it is good, is lost.

[62] vi, 17 Feb. 1855, 164–5; ix, 29 May 1858, 519–20; and in 'Mr. Trollope's Novels', vii, Oct. 1858, 425, respectively.

[63] Chapter 44, World's Classics, p. 524.

[64] Review of *Three Clerks*, iv, 5 Dec. 1857, 517–18.

[65] M. M. Bevington, *The Saturday Review 1855–1868*, Columbia University Press, 1941.

The religious questions raised in *The Bertrams*, the paper remarks, 'are not subjects to be adequately discussed in two or three pages of a romance, and if they are not to be discussed, they ought not to be started'.[66] At this point the *Saturday* has already embarked on the long series of attacks it is to mount throughout the period of Trollope's greatest popularity, on his social, moral and religious ideas, and his notions on love and marriage.

The West Indies and the Spanish Main—'that which, on the whole,' Trollope records, 'I regard as the best book that has come from my pen'[67]—was his only book to be greeted with almost unqualified panegyric. He himself tells in the *Autobiography* of the reception of the work in *The Times*: 'The view I took of the relative position in the West Indies of black men and white men was the view of the *Times* newspaper at that period; and there appeared three articles in that journal, one closely after another, which made the fortune of the book.'[68] There appear to have been two very long articles on 6 and 18 January 1860, both by Eneas Sweetland Dallas, whom Trollope does not name in his *Autobiography*, as he seems to have quarrelled with him later:

> I afterwards became acquainted with the writer of those articles, the contributor himself informing me that he had written them. I told him that he had done me a greater service than can often be done by one man to another, but that I was under no obligation to him. I do not think that he saw the matter quite in the same light.[69]

Relations between the novelist and this critic were to remain stormy, for the critic whom Trollope rebuked for receiving a bound manu-script from an author 'as an acknowledgement for a laudatory review in one of the leading journals of the day',[70] seems to have been the same Dallas, whom Dickens had presented with the manuscript of *Our Mutual Friend*.[71]

Dallas did indeed express himself favourably in his two long reviews of the *West Indies*. 'We looked for amusement only from Mr Trollope,' he wrote in the first article, 'and we are inveigled into instruction. . . . [W]e have to thank him for a most valuable contribution to our books of travel.' Others had already anticipated *The Times*'s praise,

---

[66] vii, 26 Mar. 1859, 368–9.
[67] *Autobiography*, pp. 128–9.
[68] *Ibid.*, p. 130. [69] *Ibid.*, pp. 130–1. [70] *Ibid.*, p. 264.
[71] See F. X. Roellinger, 'Dallas in Trollope's Autobiography', *Modern Language Notes* lv, June 1940, 422–4. See also *Commentary*, pp 304–7, for an account of yet another quarrel between Trollope and Dallas, over the latter's suggestion to bring out *The Vicar of Bullhampton* in the *Gentleman's Maga-zine*, and not *Once a Week* as agreed.

and the *Spectator, Athenaeum* and *Saturday*[72] all for once agreed in lauding this 'important blue-book in the agreeable disguise of a popular work from Mudie's'.[73] Eighteen months later Trollope met Carlyle under the most gratifying circumstances, as G. H. Lewes reported in a letter to Thomas Adolphus on 5 July 1861:

> Yesterday Anthony dined with us, and as he had never seen Carlyle he was glad to go down with us to tea at Chelsea. Carlyle had read and *agreed* with the West Indian book, and the two got on very well together; both Carlyle and Mrs. Carlyle liking Anthony, and I suppose it was reciprocal, though I did not see him afterwards to hear what he thought.[74]

With such encouragement as this, it is no wonder that the author retained a special affection for this book. And it marked a turning-point in his career too, by giving him a new esteem and self-confidence in his dealings with his publishers: 'I at once went to Chapman & Hall and successfully demanded £600 for my next novel.'[75]

In the reception of these first successful books, the main lines of Trollopian criticism for the next decade or more have been laid down. The critics' image of Trollope as the writer of *Barchester Towers* is firmly established: the humanely humorous portrayer of everyday reality, who is most at home making gentle fun of the clergy. Largely because of his compelling truth to life, he raises important questions as to the moral and social responsibility of the novelist. His style is lively and unusually readable, but he is careless and writes too fast. Nevertheless he promises to take a place in the front rank of English novelists.

This promise he is never destined to fulfil, and much of the critics' later dissatisfaction is born of his refusal, as they see it, to make a bid for immortality by writing more slowly. One of their chief problems is what original things they can find to say about an author who publishes so frequently. Hence their complaints of hurried work. Yet—equally exasperating perhaps—he never fails to reach a high standard in his work.

The characters of the *Athenaeum* and the *Saturday Review* in their Trollope criticism, as they remain for the next decade, are already established: the former usually critically lightweight, glowing alternately warm and cool in its appreciation; the latter heavy, moral, serious, and legalistic, and aware of its position as a moderate Conservative paper written by educated gentlemen for educated gentlemen. The

---

[72] *Spectator* xxxii, 12 Nov. 1859, 1166–7; *Athenaeum* no. 1671, 5 Nov. 1859, 591–3; *Saturday Review* viii, 26 Nov. 1859, 643–5, and 3 Dec. 1859, 675–6.

[73] Review in the *Spectator*.

[74] T. A. Trollope, *What I Remember*, 3 vols., 1887–89, ii, 305.

[75] *Autobiography*, p. 131.

Spectator undergoes a change of ownership and direction, and after its highly variable reviewing of early Trollope, becomes in the 'sixties his most consistently intelligent critic, under the control of its new literary editor and co-proprietor, Richard Holt Hutton. On the other hand, by the mid-'sixties *The Times* had fallen off drastically in its critical quality from the high standard set by Dallas. Meanwhile the *Leader* stops publication, and the *Reader* soon appears. But whatever may befall Trollope's critics, he himself is now entering on a period of almost unparalleled popularity.

The despot of the lending-libraries

In 1859 we find Trollope demanding and getting £600 for *Castle Richmond* on the grounds of his confirmed reputation—half as much again as the £400 he received for *Doctor Thorne* or *The Bertrams*. Then, in October 1859, when he had only been working on *Castle Richmond* for a couple of months, Thackeray commissioned *Framley Parsonage* from him for the new *Cornhill Magazine*, offering him for the first time £1000, and an important place in the establishment of the most successful periodical venture of the 'sixties with this, his first serial fiction. He was now secure on the high plateau of his popularity, which endured for most of the decade. Financially on the upgrade for eight or ten years, he could command £2500 for *Orley Farm* and for the Small House, £3,000 each for *Can You Forgive Her?* and the *Last Chronicle*, and £3,200 for *Phineas Finn* and *He Knew He Was Right*.[76] He never, however, attained the £3,600 that Thackeray received for *The Newcomes*.[77]

Michael Sadleir describes Trollope in these years as 'the unchallenged leader of contemporary novelists, the despot of the lending-libraries, and the acknowledged interpreter of the mentality and sentiment of the England of the day',[78] and already in 1859 Dallas had dubbed him 'the mighty monarch of books that are good enough to be read . . . the Apollo of the circulating library'.[79] This extreme of popularity with public and publishers alike lasted into the late

[76] See Sadleir's *Bibliography* for details of the publishers' agreements.

[77] 'I have signed and sealed with Bradbury and Evans for a new book in 24 numbers like Pendennis—Price 3600£ + 500£ from Harper and Tauchnitz.' Letter of June 1853, *Letters and Private Papers of W. M. Thackeray*, ed. G. N. Ray, Oxford University Press, 4 vols, 1946–47, iii, 280. Thackeray is the aptest comparison on the point of prices, since it is clear from Trollope and his critics, as well as from his association with the *Cornhill*, that he was aiming at the same public. As far as the *Cornhill* was concerned, '[t]he largest payment made for a novel was £7,000 to George Eliot for "Romola." ' See *George Smith: a memoir*, 1902, p. 114.

[78] *Commentary*, p. 298.

[79] 'Anthony Trollope', *The Times*, 23 May 1859, 12.

'sixties, and was briefly revived by the hugely successful *Eustace Diamonds* of 1871 to 1873.

The *Cornhill Magazine*, the instrument of Trollope's rise to fame, was founded by the publisher George Smith, with Thackeray as editor. It was a remarkable achievement. The idea of using novels as the basis of a periodical, with a big name to attract the public, was not new, of course. *Bentley's Miscellany, Household Words* and *All the Year Round* were obvious precedents, dependent on Thackeray's great rival and aimed at a correspondingly different readership. What was new about George Smith's magazine was that it promised to combine the sales attraction of serial fiction with the sort of serious articles hitherto confined to the heavy quarterlies. Moreover, it offered all this at the low price of a shilling, the price of a serial part of a novel alone, or of the cheapest monthly magazines.[80] In fact *Macmillan's Magazine* was planned about the same time, and succeeded in coming out two months earlier at the same low price. It never achieved quite the quality that the *Cornhill* sustained, however, and in any case it made fiction less of a speciality,[81] while the list of serial novels in the *Cornhill* is dazzling.[82] George Smith writes that the first number of his magazine sold 'no less than 120,000 copies',[83] and the later average sales under Thackeray's direction were around 85,000.[84]

These were boom years in periodical publication, and numerous monthlies were set up in imitation. Such were *Temple Bar* (1860), *The Argosy* (1865), *Belgravia* (1866), and *Tinsley's Magazine* (1867), all of which were on the lighter side of the *Cornhill*. Meanwhile there were other journals competing for the same public too, such as the *St James's Magazine* (1861), *London Society* (1862), and Trollope's *St Paul's Magazine* (1867). Yet none of these came near to threatening the pre-eminence of the *Cornhill*. Even if it did rather decline in sales later under the editorship of Leslie Stephen (1871–82), the *Cornhill* went on to achieve an even higher intellectual quality.[85]

[80] See L. Huxley, *The House of Smith Elder*, 1923, pp. 89–90, and *George Smith: a memoir*, p. 106. The main facts about the founding of the *Cornhill* are in P. Smith, 'The Cornhill Magazine—Number 1,' *Review of English Literature* iv, Apr. 1963, 23–34.

[81] See A. J. Gurr, 'Macmillan's Magazine', *Review of English Literature* vi, Jan. 1965, 39–55.

[82] See Huxley, *op. cit.*, pp. 92–3.

[83] *George Smith: a memoir*, p. 113.

[84] See G. N. Ray, *Thackeray: The Age of Wisdom, 1847–1863*, Oxford University Press, 1958, p. 299. In the fourth of his *Roundabout Papers*, of June 1860, Thackeray himself gives the circulation as over 100,000 (*Cornhill* i, 759).

[85] See O. Maurer, 'Leslie Stephen and the *Cornhill Magazine*, 1871–82', *Texas Studies in English* xxxii, 1953, 67–95.

Clearly there could be no better way to success than through the medium of this unique magazine.

For *Framley Parsonage,* which opened the *Cornhill Magazine's* first number, enjoyed a tremendous vogue. Many people would have agreed with Mrs Gaskell when she wrote to George Smith on 1 March 1860: 'I wish Mr Trollope would go on writing Framley Parsonage for ever. I don't see any reason why it should ever come to an end, and every one I know is always dreading the *last* number. I hope he will make the jilting of Griselda a long while a-doing.'[86] The *Saturday Review,* which did not quite approve of so popular a phenomenon as Trollope had become, nevertheless described his popularity in the strongest terms:

> The author of *Framley Parsonage* is a writer who is born to make the fortune of circulating libraries. At the beginning of every month the new number of his book has ranked almost as one of the delicacies of the season; and no London belle dared to pretend to consider herself literary, who did not know the very latest intelligence about the state of Lucy Robarts' heart, and Griselda Grantley's flounces.[87]

The *Saturday* is balancing here carefully between respect for the book's success, and contempt for its popularity. 'It seems a kind of breach of hospitality to criticise *Framley Parsonage* at all', the notice goes on:

> It has been an inmate of the drawing-room—it has travelled with us in the train—it has lain on the breakfast-table. We feel as if we had met Lady Lufton at a country house, admired Lord Dumbello at a ball, and seen Mrs. Proudie at an episcopal evening party. How is it possible, after so much friendly intercourse, to turn round upon the book and its leading characters, and to dissect and analyse them as a critic should?

This curiously Victorian dilemma sometimes makes a reviewer merely enthuse uncritically over a book, like Dixon or Jeaffreson in the *Athenaeum,* or—the other side of the same coin, perhaps—cast scorn on it because of its very popularity, as the *Saturday* is inclined to do.

William Hepworth Dixon, editor of the *Athenaeum,* refers to 'the hundred thousand readers who have followed with breathless eagerness the loves of Lucy Robarts and Lord Lufton, and who have gossiped and cried over Mark and Mrs. Mark, as though they had been

[86] *The Letters of Mrs Gaskell,* ed. J. A. V. Chapple and A. Pollard, Manchester University Press, 1966, p. 602.
[87] Review of *Framley Parsonage,* xi, 4 May 1861, 451–2.

living personal friends',[88] and from now on there can be no doubt as to Trollope's popularity, although some journals—and the *Saturday* in particular—often stand back to wonder whether the size of his captive audience really reflects his literary worth. For instance, the *National Review* of January 1863, which surely exaggerates when it estimates his readership at over a million, concludes that he achieves his popularity *because* 'he never attains to the dignity of an artist'.[89] Even the *Saturday*, though, cannot dispute his importance either as a fashionable phenomenon or as a social chronicler: 'Mr. Trollope has, in fact, established his novels as the novels of the day, and his is the picture of English life which, for a brief space at least, will be accepted as true by those who wish to see English life represented in fiction.'[90] It is the society of Barsetshire that the readers most want, as Hepworth Dixon makes clear: 'We expect the Dean, the Archdeacon, and the Bishop, with Tom Towers and the *Jupiter*, whenever we take up a story by Mr. Trollope, as we expect our nuts to be brought in with the wine, and the dear old jokes to occur in the dear old places of the Christmas pantomime.'[91] The nuts, the wine, and 'the dear old jokes' from the pantomime make the modern reader think more of Dickens than of Trollope; but for a short spell, Trollope obviously enjoyed a comparable status as a part of English family life, although the centre of gravity of his public lay further up the social scale than Dickens's. In any case, Trollope certainly ranked as a social institution at this time. *Lloyd's Register of Shipping* records two vessels named the 'Lily Dale' in the 'sixties,[92] and in 1862 when the *Spectator* attacked the new organ of the High Church party, the *Church and State Review* (a periodical of 'placid English ecclesiastical bigotry . . . well adapted to the ruminant clergy'), it could aptly dub it 'The Plumstead Episcopi Review'.[93]

In a review of *The Small House at Allington* in the *Athenaeum*, John Cordy Jeaffreson gives a highly coloured picture of the effect of monthly publication on the original readers:

'The Small House at Allington' has already been as thronged with interested visitors as Strawberry Hill the ten days before the sale! . . . and now that it has come before the public complete in two beautiful volumes, with Mr. Millais's illustrations retained, . . . those who have taken it in monthly fractions will go over the ground

[88] Review of part one of *Orley Farm*, *Athenaeum* no. 1741, 9 Mar. 1861, 319–20.

[89] Review of *Orley Farm*, xvi, 27–40; p. 32.

[90] Review of *Rachel Ray*, xvi, 24 Oct. 1863, 554–5.

[91] Review of part one of *Orley Farm, loc. cit.*

[92] Of Bideford (1865) and Miramichi, New Brunswick (1867). See *Lloyd's Register of British and Foreign Shipping* for 1866 and 1870.

[93] 'The Plumstead Episcopi Review', xxxv, 7 June 1862, 627–8.

again with something of regret, recognizing the old landmarks
where the story broke off, leaving them hungry and impatient at
the month's pause . . . [M]any readers . . . would have rashly
offered to forfeit three weeks in the month, if they might thus have
learnt the progress of the story a little further ahead . . . [T]here
has been as much speculation whether Lily Dale would marry
Johnny Eames, as about any 'marriage on the *tapis*' (as the *Morn-
ing Post* phrases it) in any town or village in Great Britain.[94]

The *Saturday Review* thought serial publication must be trying to
such a 'non-sensational writer, who does not rest his interest on
playing bopeep with a secret' like the sensational writers the paper
so disliked.[95] Yet the public was insatiable, and both the *Spectator*
and the *Athenaeum* express dismay at the title of the *Last Chronicle*:

Even the present writer has found the loneliness very oppressive
since he was told that he was never again to meet almost the best
known and most typical of his fellow-countrymen again, and has
indulged some rash thought of leaving England for ever . . .

[T]he fortunes of these inhabitants of Mr. Trollope's county of
Barsetshire obtain such a thorough hold on the interest of readers
that they are anxious to hear more about them, more even than
Mr. Trollope is willing to tell . . .[96]

For many critics Barsetshire remained the ideal everafter, and there
is even nostalgia for it in a reviewer who remarks in 1880 that
'[m]any readers will probably consider it a merit that the political
element is less prominent in *The Duke's Children* than in many of
Mr. Trollope's later novels'.[97]

An occasional critic can be found granting Trollope the very highest
artistic status, as J. Herbert Stack did in 1869, when he praised his
unity and harmony above those of Dickens and Thackeray.[98] It was
usual, however, to take a lower, though still sympathetic view. A
typical example is General Sir Edward Hamley's review of *North
America*.[99] Trollope, says Hamley, is

[94] No. 1900, 26 Mar. 1864, 437–8.
[95] Review of *Lotta Schmidt and Other Stories*, xxiv, 21 Sept. 1867, 381–2.
[96] *Spectator* xi, 13 Jul. 1867, 778–80; and Geraldine Jewsbury (anon),
Athenaeum no. 2075, 3 Aug. 1867, 141, resp. These sentiments are echoed by
the *London Review* of 20 Jul. 1867 (repr. *Critical Heritage*, p. 299) and by
Mrs Oliphant in *Blackwood's* cii, Sept. 1867, 276–8.
[97] *Nineteenth Century* viii, Aug. 1880, 340.
[98] Mr. Anthony Trollope's novels' (sgd), *Fortnightly Review* (ns) v, 1 Feb.
1869, 188–98; p. 196.
[99] *Blackwood's* xcii, Sept. 1862, 372–90. General Sir Edward Hamley, a
close friend of Frederick Locker-Lampson, was a notable example of 'the
succession of soldier contributors' Blackwood recruited; see A. I. Shand, *Days
of the Past*, 1905, pp. 218 and 247.

among the most amusing and popular of our novelists, and is
certainly one of those with whom the great majority of novel readers
can most fully sympathise. His plots are easy to follow, and depend
on the most ordinary and probable circumstances for their interest;
yet that interest is quite sufficient to produce earnest attention to
the processes and anxiety for the result.

Moreover, continues the General, the characters are 'so like the
personages of daily life' that any reader can enjoy 'that cheap and
pleasurable triumph of criticism which consists in discovering a
remarkable resemblance between characters of the fiction and persons
of his acquaintance'. If nothing else, this passage should warn one
not always to apply too literary a sense to the Victorian word 'criticism', when used about the novel.

Even the *Saturday Review* sometimes deigns to praise Trollope's
fiction, but in the most condescending fashion:

> Commonplace in subject, but neither vulgar nor mean, pure in tone,
> but not in the least degree noble or enthusiastic, it is essentially
> the literature of the moral and respectable middle-class mind—
> of people too realistic to be bothered by sentiment, too moral to
> countenance the sensationalism of crime, and too little spiritual to
> accept preachments or rhapsody for their daily use. It is the litera-
> ture of the careless out-of-door summer life which does not want
> to be stirred by strong emotions of any kind, and for quiet winter
> evening family reading, which must not have them. And it is safe.
> The most careful mother need not make a pioneer excursion among
> Mr. Trollope's pages in quest of naughtiness forbidden to her
> daughters; and yet few young people . . . will call those pages
> slow . . .[100]

At this time of his great popularity, Trollope's fiction satisfies the
demands of a broad spectrum of middle-class readers.

This is not to say that all his novels were equally successful. *Castle
Richmond*, which came out in May 1860 when *Framley Parsonage*
had been running for five months, encountered, Trollope writes,
'what, in hunting language, we call a cropper':

> *Castle Richmond* certainly was not a success. . . . The girl herself
> has no character; and the mother, who is strong enough, is almost
> revolting. . . . [T]he story as a whole was a failure. I cannot
> remember, however, that it was roughly handled by the critics
> when it came out; and I much doubt whether anything so hard
> was said of it then as that which I have said here.[101]

The critics did dislike Lady Desmond, however. The *Saturday* pro-
tested at the book's 'monstrosities . . . [which are] unpleasant to the

---

[100] Review of *Lotta Schmidt and Other Stories*, xxiv, 21 Sept., 1867, 381–2.
[101] *Autobiography*, pp. 175 and 156–7.

reader, and cannot be justified by any principle of artistic propriety',[102] while Miss Jewsbury in the *Athenaeum* shrank from 'the contempt and indignation she inspires', from her attempts to rob her daughter of her lover.[103] Yet perhaps the novel that was received with the least enthusiasm was *The Belton Estate*, of which Trollope himself wrote, 'It . . . will add nothing to my reputation as a novelist.'[104] The weeklies could find no redeeming features, only deficiency in spirit, humour, life and story. The *Athenaeum* reported that 'the verdict of the periodical readers was, we believe, unfavourable'.[105] *The Belton Estate* was the first novel to be serialized in the new *Fortnightly Review*, from 15 May 1865 to 1 January 1866, and despite its shortcomings, the *Spectator* almost regretted its passing when faced with its successor: '[W]e fear that the Fortnightly will lose greatly by substituting it even for one of the least effective of so keen and humorous a novelist as Mr. Trollope. *Vittoria* is a tale of the *manqué* Italian Revolution of 1849, by Mr. George Meredith, an author hitherto known as a novelist of some ability and a rather low ethical tone.'[106] The reception of *Miss Mackenzie* was also uniformly disappointing. The *Reader* was typical in deriving no 'amusement or instruction' from it, and finding 'photography' of 'the least romantic personages and the least romantic sections of society' dull, if not downright objectionable.[107]

Rachel Ray, on the other hand, provoked mixed reactions. The *Spectator* perceptively demonstrated how much of the novel's humour derived from narrative viewpoint,[108] while the *Saturday* predictably scorned it as marketable triviality for young ladies.[109] George Eliot, to whom Trollope had sent a copy of the novel,[110] replied in rather conventional terms calculated to please Trollope, yet with much more praise than mere *politesse* would have required. As one of the very

---

[102] ix, 19 May 1860, 643–4.   [103] No. 1699, 19 May 1860, 681.

[104] *Autobiography*, p. 196. Compare, however, Browning's comment on the novel in a letter to Isabella Blagden: 'I like that much: it is the only novel of Anthony's that I have read of late years: very unpretending, but surely *real*, and so far a gain. Miss Braddon's I stop my ears to.'–19 Aug. 1865, *Dearest Isa: Robert Browning's Letters to Isabella Blagden*, ed. E. C. McAleer, Nelson. 1951, p. 221.

[105] No. 1997, 3 Feb. 1866, 166 [Wilberforce].

[106] xxxix, 3 Feb. 1866, 136. A year later, on the paper's notice of the completed novel, Meredith wrote bitterly to Swinburne, 'I see the illustrious Hutton of the "Spectator" laughs insanely at my futile effort to produce an impression on his public.' 2 Mar. 1867, *Letters*, ed. W. M. Meredith, 1912, i, 189.

[107] v, 27 May 1865, 596.

[108] 'Mr. Trollope's caricature: Rachel Ray', xxxvi, 24 Oct. 1863, 2660–1.

[109] xvi, 24 Oct. 1863, 554–5.

[110] On 18 Oct. 1863, *Letters*, p. 138.

few comments on Trollope's fiction by any of his great novelist contemporaries, it must be quoted at length:

> I am much struck in 'Rachel' with the skill with which you have organized thoroughly natural everyday incidents into a strictly related well-proportioned whole, natty and complete as a nut on its stem. Such construction is among those subtleties of art which can hardly be appreciated except by those who have striven after the same result with conscious failure. Rachel herself is a sweet maidenly figure, and her poor mother's spiritual confusions are excellently observed.
>
> But there is something else I care yet more about, which has impressed me very happily in all those writings of yours that I know—it is that people are breathing good bracing air in reading them—it is that they [the books] are filled with belief in goodness without the slightest tinge of maudlin. They are like pleasant public gardens, where people go for amusement and, whether they think it or not, get health as well.[111]

The reception of four of the major novels of the 'sixties—*Orley Farm, Can You Forgive Her?, The Claverings* and *Phineas Finn*— was divided in a most significant fashion. There were no reports of the sort of fashionable acclaim for them that greeted *Framley Parsonage* and the *Small House*, and no records of particularly vast sales (although *The Claverings* must have been widely distributed in the *Cornhill*). Yet they all received very respectful attention from the better critics, and we can infer that they had a minority appeal to a smaller public. *Orley Farm* was his first, not very successful, venture into monthly part issue, with separate publication of the two volumes at eleven shillings each (a shilling above the normal price) in December 1861 and September 1862 respectively. The first volume went unsatisfactorily, and Trollope wrote to Frederic Chapman from Cincinnati asking, 'Who the deuce buys the first volume of a book? As far as I can hear the novel is as well spoken of as any I ever wrote. I fear we made a mistake about the shilling.'[112] Certainly *Orley Farm* was well spoken of, but the discrepancy between the reviews and the sales was more than a matter of the odd shilling.

Again, Trollope and his reviewers concurred that the story and 'moral' of *The Claverings* were good, but as the author wrote, he was 'not aware that the public ever corroborated that verdict'.[113] In this case, attention must have been diverted from it in serial because of a six-month overlap with the part issue of the *Last Chronicle*, while the first book edition came out between the two separately published

---

[111] 23 Oct. 1863, *The George Eliot Letters*, ed. Haight, iv, 110.
[112] *Letters*, p. 109. Both volumes bear the date 1862.
[113] *Autobiography*, p. 197.

volumes of that much more popular novel. The *Last Chronicle*, of course, was and remained a far more profitable property, as can be seen from Trollope's later negotiations with Smith over their half-profits agreements for the two novels.[114] Yet even the *Last Chronicle of Barset* itself had a rather troubled publishing history. It sold disappointingly when issued in weekly parts—an unusual scheme of Smith's choosing, about which Trollope had earlier expressed his misgivings.[115] For its part, *Phineas Finn* was the first serial in Trollope's unsuccessful *St Pauls Magazine*.[116] Unfortunately it was the only contribution good enough to compete with that journal's mighty rivals. *Phineas Finn* was not vastly popular, although once more the critics were unusually complimentary about it. Trollope himself accounts for its mixed success in terms of its subject-matter, which appealed to a smaller public than his Barsetshire novels could reach:

> It was not a brilliant success,—because men and women not conversant with political matters could not care much for a hero who spent so much of his time either in the House of Commons or in a public office. But the men who would have lived with Phineas Finn read the book, and the women who would have lived with Lady Laura Standish read it also. As this was what I had intended, I was contented.[117]

Orley Farm, Can You Forgive Her? and *The Claverings* also received high praise, but reached a comparatively small public. And all of them appealed to the critics for the same reason: a seriousness in their treatment of human relations which led them to the verge of tragedy.[118]

The case of *Orley Farm* is typical. Looking back in the *Autobiography*, Trollope says, 'Most of those among my friends who talk to me now about my novels, and are competent to form an opinion on the subject, say that this is the best I have written.'[119] One gathers a similar impression from the critics, the most 'literary' of whom praise the book warmly, but give no evidence of any tremendous popularity. To a critic in the *Cornhill*, probably George Henry Lewes, it is 'in some respects the finest of Mr. Anthony Trollope's works' because of 'the noble humanizing pathos of the main story'. R. H.

---

[114] See Trollope's letter to Smith, 10 Feb. 1871, *Letters*, pp. 281–2.

[115] *Autobiography*, p. 274; letter to John Blackwood, 1 Jan. 1867, *Letters*, p. 193.

[116] See *Bibliography*, pp. 237–40.

[117] *Autobiography*, p. 318.

[118] See chapter 2 below, for an account of the critical demand for tragedy. The present chapter deals with the subject only in so far as it bears on Trollope's reputation.

[119] p. 166. Trollope's own favourite was the *Last Chronicle*.

Hutton of the *Spectator* commends it as 'the nearest approach [Trollope] has yet made to the depth and force of tragedy. . . . [T]here is a sensible gathering of the waters as against an obstacle, a temporary deepening of the channel, a straining of the eye into an interior almost beyond the artist's sight'.[120] Yet to the critically feeble William Hepworth Dixon, editor of the *Athenaeum*, *Orley Farm* is by the same token 'not a pleasant book':[121] after all, it is not about Barsetshire, as Dixon predicted it would be in his notice of part one,[122] but 'about law and crime'—'Here is a change!' the bewildered editor exclaims.

For the *Saturday Review* the success of the book depends entirely on the sympathy excited in the reader for the guilty Lady Mason, whom it calls 'one of the best-conceived types of mixed character, neither good nor bad, that modern English fiction has to show'.[123] Similarly Lewes praises the novel as a good example of 'the literature of Character', as opposed to 'the literature of Types' that 'novel-readers' and 'critics . . . of the feebler sort' prefer. He distinguishes in the same way as Trollope between the literary judgment of critics 'competent to form an opinion on the subject', and the demands of the ordinary readers who compose the market.

What is wrong with *Orley Farm* as far as the *Saturday* is concerned, is that Trollope has spoilt the plot for the sake of 'a purpose': to expose the hypocrisy of advocates and the bullying of witnesses:[124]

> [E]ven if he were entirely right as a critic of British institutions, it would be very doubtful if he could possibly be right as a novelist. . . . Mr. Trollope wanted to have a pattern trial illustrating the legal errors he censures. To do this, it was necessary that the guilt of the prisoner should be known to every one . . . The consequence is, that after the middle of the second volume the interest of the book rapidly diminishes, and gets exceedingly faint at the end. The excitement is got over early in order that the trial may bear an instructive character.

This review presents a particularly blatant example of a critic's attention being deflected by non-literary concerns. Although Trollope is interested in a 'pattern trial', his main aim in the novel is the characterization of Lady Mason, and certainly not suspense. The

[120] xxxv, 11 Oct. 1862, 1136–8. The attribution to Hutton is made on stylistic grounds by R. H. Tener, in 'A clue to some R. H. Hutton attributions', *Notes and Queries* (ns) xiv, Oct. 1967, 382–3.

[121] No. 1823, 4 Oct. 1862, 425–6.

[122] No. 1741, 9 Mar. 1861, 319–20.

[123] xiv, 11 Oct. 1862, 444–5.

[124] Similarly the *Home and Foreign Review* praises the scenes at Noningsby, and devotes two full pages to refuting Trollope on the morality of advocacy. ii, Jan. 1863, 291–4.

critic, like many of the *Saturday*'s contributors,[125] is probably a barrister, affronted by a layman's critical temerity. But the deflection is inexcusable in this instance, since Trollope has foreseen just such critical blindness, and made his narrator anticipate the reviewer's objections, by pointing out that it is not his object to create suspense, but to portray character and excite sympathy.[126] In his *Autobiography*, however, Trollope considers the effect slightly misjudged: 'The plot . . . has the fault of declaring itself, and thus coming to an end too early in the book.'[127]

Hutton also notices the anti-sensational nature of the plot,[128] but he attributes it correctly to Trollope's method of characterization, which he sees as largely a matter of character in relation to others, involving also the others' perceptions of the original character, and his awareness in turn of their perceptions. The revelation of Lady Mason's guilt is a brilliant literary stroke, says Hutton, who admires 'the added vividness which her own sense of guilt takes the moment the pressure of constant concealment is removed, and she sees it reflected back from the minds of friends whom she reveres'. Hutton also praises the author's skill with 'the finer professional lines of English character', now shown in his lawyers, as it was before in his clergy: 'The air and tone of a profession once caught, Mr. Trollope appears to possess some artistic Calculus of Variations, which gives him an infinite command over the shades and details of the different specimens.' The critic's admiration embraces the commercial travellers and so on too, whom he hopes Trollope will introduce in later books to delight his public. 'He seems actually to revel in the manipulation of such characters', the *Spectator* remarked months earlier when reviewing volume one of *Orley Farm*:[129] 'Not the slightest detail is omitted . . . At the same time he carefully avoids the extravagance which characterizes the school formed on the model of Mr. Dickens.'

There is a complete split among the critics on the subject of these 'vulgar' characters in *Orley Farm*, and the divergence on this matter does not seem to correlate at all with the critics' other opinions on the novel, or on Trollope in general. George Eliot comments sarcastically on the *Spectator*'s notice of volume one, in a letter of 14 January 1862, in which she expresses her admiration of the novel to date, except for 'Moulder and Co., which by the way, I saw in glancing at a late Spectator, the sapient critic there selects for peculiar com-

---

[125] See M. M. Bevington, *The Saturday Review*, pp. 28–33, and T. H. S. Escott, *Platform, Press, Politics and Play* [1895], p. 185.

[126] Chapter 45; World's Classics, ii, 42–3.

[127] p. 167.

[128] *Spectator* review of *Orley Farm, loc. cit.*   [129] xxxv, 4 Jan. 1862, 5.

mendation. There is no mistake an author can make but there will
be some newspaper critic to pronounce it his finest effort.'[130] The
Saturday and the *Dublin University Magazine* agree with the *Spectator*, but the *National Review* and the *Cornhill*, otherwise quite
divergent in their reading of the novel, unite in condemning the
comic characters.[131] The *Cornhill* finds them 'far from successful . . .
not having the comic gusto which might serve to relieve the more
serious interest of the story'. Yet it adds a scrupulous footnote,
recording that 'an able contemporary [surely the *Spectator*] selects
the Moulders and Kantwise for especial commendation'.

The same review in the *Cornhill* tries to correct a 'wide-spread
prejudice' against the sympathetic portrayal of a criminal character,
using a common mid-Victorian form of argument: 'There can be little
doubt that we should have been fond of this criminal had we known
her in the flesh and blood; why then should the novelist shrink from
representing what is so true to life?' But quoting the narrator's
apology in the last chapter for having asked for sympathy for his
heroine—a passage Hutton also notes as a confession 'that Lady
Mason has grown upon [Trollope] as he wrote, that he has softened
and deepened his own conception as he went on'—the *Cornhill* justly
complains: 'Why did not that very fact of his own awakened sympathy enlighten him as to the sympathy he would awaken in others,
and thus cause him to strike out such a misplaced apology—an
apology which could only be addressed to the very class that would
reject it?' Despite such occasional rebukes, however, *Orley Farm*
is highly praised by the better critics. The story is much the same
for *Can You Forgive Her?*, *The Claverings* and *Phineas Finn*.

Examining the reviewers' opinions in a case like this, reveals a
great deal about the novelist's position at a crucial point in his career.
In this instance, we see that Trollope, the wildly popular middle-class author, also had a numerically smaller following of *literati*.
He seems to have paid little attention to their good opinion, preferring
popularity to a more esoteric success.

In the 'sixties Trollope was regarded in some literary circles as
being very nearly a truly great novelist, but for certain faults which
seemed quite easy to correct. This is the nearest he has ever come
(before his death or since) to a recognized place in the first rank of
English novelists, but we cannot know whether he saw that greatness
was almost within his grasp, and if so, whether he would not or could
not take it. Nothing in his *Autobiography* directly answers these

---

[130] To Sara Sophia Hennell, *The George Eliot Letters*, ed. Haight, iv, 8–9.
[131] *Saturday Review*, *loc. cit.*; *Dublin University Magazine* lxi, Apr. 1863,
437; *National Review* xvi, Jan. 1863, 27–40; and *Cornhill*, *loc. cit.*, respectively.

questions, but an esoteric success was probably less precious to him than popularity. He wrote novels partly to obtain from his social equals the respect he had missed in his boyhood and youth, when he had been 'poor, friendless, and joyless'.[132] It was very important to him when *The Warden* brought him his first social acknowledgement, and, as he writes, 'I could discover that people around me knew that I had written a book'.[133] The craving for social acceptance in club-land may have been a more powerful motive to write than the highest literary praise. Recalling how gratified he felt on being elected to the Garrick Club, he looks back with undisguised bitterness to his early days:

> I have ever had a wish to be liked by those around me,—a wish that during the first half of my life was never gratified. In my school-days no small part of my misery came from the envy with which I regarded the popularity of popular boys. . . . And after-wards, when I was in London as a young man, I had but few friends. . . . It was not till we had settled ourselves at Waltham that I really began to live much with others. The Garrick Club was the first assemblage of men at which I felt myself to be popular.[134]

That was at the age of forty-five or six.

Part of his motivation in writing his political novels was, he tells us, to use them 'for the expression of my political and social convictions',[135] when his loss of the Beverley election in 1868 disappointed his lifelong ambition to sit in the House of Commons. The story is well known. When he was no more than an ordinary Post Office clerk, one of his uncles remarked sarcastically on his presuming to this distinction. The sarcasm still hurt many years later,[136] so that after his defeat at Beverley, he deliberately turned to politics for his fictional subject-matter. 'As I was debarred from expressing my opinions in the House of Commons,' he explains, 'I took this method of declaring myself.'[137] In writing the series of novels which centre on Plantagenet Palliser, he 'had much gratification, and was enabled from time to time to have in this way that fling at the political doings of the day which every man likes to take, if not in one fashion then in another'.[138]

So far as the political novels are concerned, then, he may have deliberately hazarded the enormous following he enjoyed as the author of *The Chronicles of Barsetshire*, in order to secure another kind of social recognition. His last popular triumph was *The Eustace Diamonds*, and apart from this isolated instance, none of his novels

[132] *Autobiography*, p. 132.
[133] *Ibid.*, p. 98.
[134] *Ibid.*, p. 159; see also pp. 157–8.
[135] *Ibid.*, p. 180.
[136] *Ibid.*, p. 290.
[137] *Ibid.*, p. 317.
[138] *Ibid.*, p. 184.

of the 'seventies came near to recapturing his vast public of the 'sixties. On the one hand, to the public at large he remained the author of *The Chronicles of Barsetshire*, whose other novels all fell short of that series. On the other hand, he seems not to have been very concerned with the intellectuals who thought he might ascend the throne left vacant on Thackeray's death in 1863. He never won the distinction granted by one critic to Carlyle, Thackeray, Kingsley and Tennyson, of speaking 'with a forked tongue' to two audiences, 'the thinkers' and 'the million'.[139]

Like many of the reviews of Trollope's work in the mid-nineteenth century, much twentieth-century Trollope criticism has been an effort to establish just where he stands in the ranks of English novelists. No better indicator of his true position as one of the very best of second-rate writers could be found than his equivocal position at the very height of his popularity over a hundred years ago.

The slow decline

Trollope's reputation declined slowly but significantly from the late 'sixties onwards. About this time, he suffered a complicated series of set-backs in the publishing world, involving the failure of one of his publishers, Virtue,[140] while *The Vicar of Bullhampton* had a most troubled publishing history, before it was finally brought out in parts from July 1869 to May 1870. By this time, unfortunately, part issue was outmoded, and could no longer compete with magazine fiction.[141] Moreover, he was crowding his market, and the serialization of *Phineas Finn* in *St Paul's*, and the part issue of *He Knew He Was Right* overlapped from October 1868 to May 1869, and we have already seen in the case of the *Last Chronicle* and *The Claverings* that the market could not at the best of times support two of his long novels simultaneously. Writing of this crucial time around 1870, he says in the *Autobiography*, 'I know now, however, that when the things were good they came out too quick, one upon another, to gain much attention;—and so also, luckily, when they were bad'.[142]

To judge from his declining sales and prices, Trollope was never again, except in the single case of *The Eustace Diamonds* of 1871 to 1873, absolutely in tune with public demand. This was a matter both of changes in his fiction, and of the prevailing literary fashion. Cockshut and Booth dispute the nature of the change in Trollope's fiction from this time on, the former seeing a general darkening of the

[139] 'Reading Raids. No. IX.—Charles Kingsley', *Tait's Edinburgh Magazine* xxii, Oct. 1855, 604–12; p. 605.
[140] See Sadleir, *Commentary*, pp. 298–301, and *Bibliography*, pp. 290–3.
[141] See Sadleir, *Commentary*, pp. 304–7, and *Bibliography*, p. 295.
[142] p. 337.

author's artistic vision, which he attributes to a growing bitterness and disillusion, while Booth (following Sadleir) maintains that the change was deliberately made by Trollope to accommodate his fiction to the fashion of the 'seventies.[134] But the major change was undoubtedly that there were no further novels in the Barsetshire series, on which his popularity was founded. Many critics and readers regarded the series as their ideal of Trollope's fiction, and wished to see it continued *ad infinitum*. A common feeling at the time is expressed by F. N. Broome in *The Times* of 1869:

> [N]ow that Barset, and the Bishop, and the Archdeacon, and all our old friends are done with . . . we find Mr. Trollope still in the same vein, but with a little less vigour, and manifestly writing against time books that are pleasant reading for leisure hours, but are not such imperative claimants on the busiest lives as *Barchester Towers* and *Dr. Thorne* certainly were . . .[144]

The later novels, too, are certainly more cynical, pessimistic or biting, more often than the earlier ones. Yet the difference is not one of subject-matter, but of emphasis. For example, his later interest in abnormal psychology is not entirely new, but he gives it a quite new prominence from *He Knew He Was Right* (1869) onwards.

So far as the reviewers were concerned, there was hardly any new line of attack on Trollope in the 'seventies, in the sense of new objections urged against him, that had not already been anticipated in the 'sixties. Once more it is a question of emphasis. As will be seen in the next chapter, he was frequently accused, even at the height of his popularity, of hasty writing, and superficial mechanical work. Authorial intrusions were castigated as early as *Doctor Thorne*.[145] Sordid realism and the misrepresentation of social institutions, too, were common complaints from the same time onwards.[146] The chief accusation that came into greater prominence in the 'seventies was that of moral irresponsibility, in depicting vice without any 'high and beautiful character'[147] to act as a foil, and in writing about a

---

[143] A. O. J. Cockshut, *Anthony Trollope. A Critical Study*, Collins, 1955, *passim*. B. A. Booth, *Anthony Trollope. Aspects of his life and art*, Indiana University Press, 1958, 'Introduction'.

[144] 26 Aug. 1869, 4.

[145] *Saturday Review* v, 12 June 1858, 618–19.

[146] See, for example, the following *Saturday Review* notices: *Three Clerks*, iv, 5 Dec. 1857, 517–18, for comments on the law; *Doctor Thorne*, v, 12 June 1858, 618–19, for comments on the law, the aristocracy, and love and marriage; *The Bertrams*, vii, 26 Mar. 1859, 368–9, on religion, and morality of advocacy; *Orley Farm*, xiv, 11 Oct. 1862, 444–5, on the morality of advocacy. See also 'Mr. Anthony Trollope and the English clergy', *Contemporary Review* ii, June 1866, 240–62 [Henry Alford—*Wellesley Index*].

[147] *Church Quarterly Review* iv, Apr. 1877, 152–3.

morally bankrupt society without providing an idealized solution to its problems. These topics are dealt with in chapters 3 and 4, but it is difficult to assess their importance in the decline of Trollope's reputation because by far the largest factor in it was a loss of critical interest in him.

From 1870 onwards, with the exception of Hutton, one rarely finds an important critic giving Trollope any serious or sustained attention. A vast number of exceedingly long reviews were still written, but the note of critical condescension that had been there from the beginning, grew, and became more significant as his popularity declined. He was no longer thought of as a next-to-great novelist, but as one who turned out books 'constructed on those well-known lines which secured for him long ago the reputation of a skilful book-builder'.[148] He clearly retained a fairly large public, but mainly as an author of circulating library fiction, and by the end of his life, he was held to be the rival of no greater names than William Black and James Payn.[149]

The compliments he receives in the 'seventies are at best that he is an 'intellectual luxury to which the British public is now so accustomed'[150] that 'there is no novelist who could be less easily spared', despite his variable quality which is due to 'his extraordinary facility of production'.[151] Meanwhile the bantering disrespect of the *Spectator*'s review of *Cousin Henry* in 1879, and its comment the same year that Trollope's novels 'may be laid down and taken up again as readily as a piece of knitting',[152] show what the same paper calls his 'decadence', which it dates from *The Prime Minister*, when 'the grind of the barrel-organ' began to make itself heard.[153]

In 1879 the *Athenaeum* sums up his position by explaining that he is simply out-of-date:

Happy in these days is the writer of fiction who . . . develops new methods and a fresh manner before the world has begun to be sated by what it used to approve. A novelist who has been fairly taken into public favour is not likely to be supplanted by his younger rivals in the affections of his earliest admirers; but, on the other

[148] F. N. Broome's review of *He Knew He was Right*, *The Times*, 26 Aug. 1869, 4.

[149] Review of *Dr. Wortle's School*, *Westminster Review* (ns) lx, Jul. 1881, 283–4, and Julia Wedgwood's review of *Old Man's Love*, *Contemporary Review* xlvi, Jul. 1884, 149–51.

[150] Review of *Ralph the Heir*, *Spectator* xliv, 15 Apr. 1871, 450–2.

[151] 'Contemporary literature—IV: Novelists', *Blackwood's* cxxv, Mar. 1879, 322–44 [A. I. Shand—*Wellesley Index*].

[152] lii, 18 Oct. 1879, 1319–21, and review of *John Caldigate*, lii, 19 Jul. 1879, 916–17.

[153] Review of *John Caldigate*, *loc. cit.*

hand, the art and mannerisms which have pleased one generation are by no means certain to captivate the next. . . . The same strength, and the same weakness distinguish 'John Caldigate' and 'Barchester Towers'. The same characters with which we have so long been familiar reappear in the later story, though under different names. We meet once more with almost the identical scenes, illustrations, and turns of expression, which made Mr. Trollope's first efforts so racy and so successful.[154]

As another reviewer puts it in the *Athenaeum* of 1880, 'Mr. Trollope is not an artist according to the modern school of high art'.[155] Even the *Athenaeum*'s faithful Collyer, who writes seventeen notices of Trollope from 1870 to 1884, soon grows tired, and can no longer take the trouble to task him with his inadequacies, as he had done most eloquently in his review of *Ralph the Heir* in 1871.[156]

Meanwhile a new literary generation was becoming influential, and finding a voice in a new critical journal, the *Academy*. Originally a highly academic monthly, promoting Hegelian learning and university reform, the *Academy* was founded by Charles Appleton in 1869, and edited by him until his early death in 1879. It changed to fortnightly publication in January 1871, and then became a weekly in January 1874, changing its character on the way, and now aiming to replace the *Athenaeum*, and the literary pages of the *Spectator* and the *Saturday*, as the most powerful sources of literary opinion.[157] Although it was financially unstable, Fox Bourne maintains that 'its influence on modern culture is not to be measured by the extent of its circulation; but it failed . . . to achieve the pre-eminence it aimed at'.[158] It pioneered the short, signed review, with a decidedly modern emphasis. Standing for newer literary ideals than the other weeklies, it tended to dismiss Trollope as a fluent, readable irrelevance, for, with reviewers like George Saintsbury and W. E. Henley on its staff, it represented those people who in the 'seventies and 'eighties were offended by Trollope's determined philistinism. The paper was rarely unpleasant to him, however, but just made rather light of his work.

Edith Simcox, for instance, who under her pen-name 'H. Lawrenny' had had a long critique of *He Knew He Was Right* declined by Appleton as unsuitable for the heavy journal the *Academy* then

[154] Review of *John Caldigate*, no. 2694, 14 June 1879, 755 [Sergeant].

[155] Review of *Duke's Children*, no. 2744, 29 May 1880, 694-5 [Cook].

[156] No. 2268, 15 Apr. 1871, 456.

[157] D. Roll-Hansen, *The Academy 1869-1879. Victorian Intellectuals in Revolt*, Copenhagen 1957 (Anglistica 8), p. 11; see also his 'Matthew Arnold and the *Academy*. A Note on English Criticism in the 1870s', *PMLA* lxviii, June 1953, 384-96.

[158] *English Newspapers*, 1887, ii, 316.

was,[159] described *Phineas Redux* as 'Mr. Trollope illustrating . . . the immortal thesis that there are two sides to every question, and that there is so much to be said for each of them that it is really rather hard to tell them apart'.[160] Although George Saintsbury obviously knew Trollope's major novels well, he could find very little to say on such minor works as *Lady Anna* and *Harry Heathcote of Gangoil*.[161] For his part, R. F. Littledale welcomed *The Prime Minister* as a significant advance in realism, but attacked *Is He Popenjoy?* and *An Eye for an Eye* as representing Trollope's most unpleasant vein of fiction—that of *Miss Mackenzie* and *The Eustace Diamonds*.[162] In his obituary article, he asserted that the author's reputation rested entirely on the *Chronicles of Barsetshire*, and concluded that he 'was not exactly a great writer, but few have turned out an equal quantity of work always honest, and generally of good and readable quality'.[163] Meanwhile, W. E. Henley, the champion of George Meredith, could hardly be expected to give more than a flippant *résumé* of such a minor novel as *Kept in the Dark*,[164] and it was left to E. Purcell to administer the *Academy*'s only really vicious blow at Trollope, in saying that 'we . . . are willing to forget utterly what little we remember of his multifarious writings'.[165]

The fiercest attack Trollope ever suffered was at the hands of another Meredith enthusiast, the poet James Thomson, who reviewed the *English Men of Letters* series, including Trollope's *Thackeray*, in the columns of *Cope's Tobacco Plant*, the house journal of a Liverpool tobacco merchant.[166] Thomson asks Trollope ('little t.') how he has the effrontery to associate himself with 'the big T.' (Thackeray), when he himself is 'only a superior postman'. Naturally 'B.V.' is distressed to hear Thackeray called 'lazy', and, having himself been driven to hackwork for *Cope's* in order to scrape a living, he cannot abide Trollope's frequent mention of literary earnings, and his 'favourite tune of "His bags of chink he chunk" '. *Thackeray*, the poet concludes, is 'scribbling' only fit for circulating libraries, and a magazine sketch 'twaddled out' to the requisite length for a volume.

Cope's Tobacco Plant was scarcely an influential place to voice such criticism, but Thomson's attack is part of an increasing revulsion

---

[159] See D. Roll-Hansen, *The Academy*, p. 192.

[160] v, 7 Feb. 1874, 141–3.

[161] v, 2 May 1874, 482, and vi, 12 Dec. 1874, 652.

[162] x, 29 Jul. 1876, 106–7; xiii, 8 June 1878, 505; and xv, 8 Feb. 1879, 117.

[163] xxii, 16 Dec. 1882, 433.

[164] xxii, 25 Mar. 1882, 377–8.

[165] xxiv, 17 Nov. 1883, 328.

[166] ii, Jul. 1880, 504. For the attribution of this article, see W. D. Schaefer's bibliography of Thomson's writings in his *James Thomson: beyond 'The City'*, University of California Press, 1965.

against what was seen as the commercialism of Trollope and some
of his contemporaries. Although there were many reviews of the
Autobiography, and the majority were respectful in their praise
of his industry and achievements, there was a note of protest in
some of them. It is clearly audible in the anonymous article by John
Morley and Mrs Ward in *Macmillan's Magazine*:[167] 'It is evident
that out of this ideal and these methods [of writing] Trollope
extracted as much as could possibly be extracted. Nobody will pretend
that such a system means the highest work.' While they concede
that there is much sense in the book, the reviewers feel that in
places 'the literary ideal is brutalised indeed'. James Payn summed
up the impact of Trollope's *Autobiography* in the *Cornhill* of July
1884: 'He has done his literary reputation as much harm by the
revelation of his method of work as by his material views of its
result. He took almost a savage pleasure in demolishing the theory of
"inspiration," which has caused the world to deny his "genius".'[168]

Critics were increasingly opposed to what Robert Louis Stevenson
in 1881 called the 'penny-wise and virtue-foolish spirit' of regarding
earnings from literature as more important than honour and morality,
honesty and usefulness.[169] Stevenson objected strongly to the terms
in which the recent public debate on the profession of letters had
been carried on, and he spoke of an author whom he liked, but whose
attitude to the question of money he despised. Although the author
is identified elsewhere as James Payn himself,[170] the relevance of
the remarks to Trollope's case as well is inescapable.

All in all, Trollope's stock had fallen very low by this time, and
it was certainly not to him that young writers and their public
looked in these decades for an expression of their literary ideals.

The method of the present chapter has been to extract evidence
from contemporaneous reviews as to the nature of a particular
novelist's success, and his popularity with different sections of the
public, by examining his 'image' with his critics and public. The
establishment of a clearly defined image is seen to be an essential
part of the process whereby the writer rises to popularity, but it is
clear that if a partial view of his work has once become implanted in
the mind of the press and public, it can blind them to his other real

[167] xlix, Nov. 1883, 47–56.
[168] Reprinted in his *Some Literary Recollections*, 2nd edn, 1884, p. 222.
[169] 'The morality of the profession of letters', *Fortnightly Review* (ns) xxix,
Apr. 1881, 513–20; reprinted in his *Essays in the Art of Writing*.
[170] R. L. Stevenson, *Essays in the Art of Writing*, 7th edn, 1919, p. 47, n. 2.

achievements. Meanwhile an author may, like Trollope, appeal in different ways to different sorts of readers simultaneously.

The development of Trollope's public image, and his popularity with different sectors of the reading public, which have been traced, are basic to an understanding of the relation of his work to its age. They are in fact an integral part of his literary biography. But the present investigation of Trollope's particular case has in addition the wider aim of revealing some important aspects of the literary and social context in which all mid-Victorian novelists wrote, and not Trollope alone. This account of his reception underlies the following chapters, which deal with a number of topics central to mid-nine-teenth-century criticism of the novel. From the point of view of Trollope studies, the later chapters in turn add a new dimension to what has so far been a rather perfunctory survey.

2

CRITICAL CONCERNS OF THE 'SIXTIES: TRAGEDY AND IMAGINATION

Omnes omnia bona dicere[1]

During the period of Trollope's greatest popularity, from 1860 to 1869, when half the world was mad over his novels, there were numbers of critics who dissented from the general enthusiasm, and doubted whether his fiction really qualified as art. In fact, they had not as yet settled to their own satisfaction what was the true scope and status of novels, like his, which dealt with contemporary life. He was lauded by many as a fashionable favourite, as a moral preceptor, and as *elegantiae arbiter*, but there were others who found him devoid of passionate intensity, and lacking in imaginative power. He suffered numerous attacks on these scores, notably from the *Saturday Review* and (for a while) the *Westminster*,[2] varying from sneering slights to outright virulence. Meanwhile certain critics stood between the extremes, bestowing qualified but intelligent approval.

---

[1] (Terence, *Andria*, 96–7.) The ironic title of chapter 1 of *Framley Parsonage*, which tells of the high esteem in which the world holds Mark Robarts. The words of the title are taken from a passage in which a father declares (as Trollope renders it) 'that all men began to say all good things to him, and to extol his fortune in that he had a son blessed with so excellent a disposition'.

[2] Apart from a dismissal of *Brown, Jones, and Robinson* as 'unmitigated rubbish' (ns, xxxix, Apr. 1871, 574–5), there seems to be no review of Trollope in the *Westminster* after July 1865, until April 1875, whereafter its notices are all critically insignificant. In the 'sixties the review was on the decline, after its second period of intellectual eminence under George Eliot's editorship, and from 1865 its leading role in radical journalism was largely taken over by the new *Fortnightly*. See G. L. Nesbitt, *Benthamite Reviewing. The First Twelve Years of The Westminster Review 1824–1836*, New York, Oxford University Press, 1934, p. 172. Judging from its reviews of Trollope, the *Westminster* was by the 'sixties no longer championing realism, which had earlier been one of the over-riding concerns of all its contributors. See W. J. Hyde, 'George Eliot and the climate of realism', *PMLA* lxxii, Mar. 1957, 147–64.

Of these, the most influential in their own day and the most interesting to us today, were Eneas Sweetland Dallas of *The Times* and Richard Holt Hutton of the *Spectator*.[3] Unfortunately the former's intelligent notices for *The Times* ceased in 1865, and none of his successors—Dasent, F. N. Broome or Alexander Innes Shand—was a critic of anything like his ability.[4] For his part, Hutton spent much of his effort in analysing exactly what Trollope's shortcomings were—a project which might serve as much to hurt as to enhance an author's reputation with the general public, but which equally could do Trollope's sales no harm in this period of assured popularity. Meanwhile less discriminating approval came only from the pens of such critical nonentities as John Cordy Jeaffreson, Geraldine Jewsbury and William Hepworth Dixon of the *Athenaeum*, or suitably tempered with worldly wisdom, from the indefatigable Mrs Oliphant in the pages of *Blackwood's*.

The commonest grounds for uncritical approval were that he was 'safe',[5] in an age abounding in sensation-novels, which dealt with dangerous topics like infidelity and bigamy.[6] In 1867 Mrs Oliphant found his heroines such a relief after the horrors of Miss Braddon and Miss Broughton[7] (although a few years later she feared Trollope was adopting 'fast' heroines in the persons of Mary Lowther and Nora Rowley[8]). For his part, Jeaffreson thought that the moderation and restraint of *Rachel Ray* should make it a valuable influence in the novel-writing world, because 'it differs from the most memorable specimens of recent realistic art . . . in its entire freedom from scenes

[3] It is exceedingly plausible but not certain that the reviewer of most of Trollope's fiction in the *Spectator* in the 'sixties and early 'seventies was the literary editor, Hutton. There is a consistent train of thought developed throughout and continued through later articles definitely known to be Hutton's (see chapter 5 below). Only the review of *Orley Farm*, however, has been formally attributed to Hutton, by R. H. Tener, 'A clue for some R. H. Hutton attributions', *loc. cit.*; while in his 'More articles by R. H. Hutton', Professor Tener also allows that the notice of *Nina Balatka* is probably (as Trollope asserts) also the editor's. In 1960, Professor Tener, less cautious, attributed eight more of these reviews to Hutton, on 'internal evidence' (see R. H. Tener, 'Richard Holt Hutton's criticism of five nineteenth-century poets: Wordsworth, Tennyson, Browning, Clough, and Arnold; together with a bibliography of his writings on literature', unpublished PhD dissertation, London 1960.

[4] See *Autobiography*, p. 153, for Trollope's confirmation that literary criticism in *The Times* declined after Dallas left.

[5] See, for example, the *Saturday*'s notice of *Lotta Schmidt and Other Stories*, xxiv, 21 Sept. 1867, 381–2, quoted on p. 22 above.

[6] Henry Longueville Mansel stresses the vogue for 'bigamy novels' in his 'Sensation novels', *Quarterly Review* cxiii, Apr. 1863, 481–514, esp. p. 490.

[7] *Blackwood's* cii, Sept. 1867, 275–8.

[8] In *The Vicar of Bullhampton* and *He Knew He Was Right* respectively. *Blackwood's* cvii, May 1870, 647–8.

that either provoke indignation or rouse deeply painful emotions'.[9]
It was thus quite unlike the 'terrible stories of crime and passion'
which came from the pen of Wilkie Collins, who Jeaffreson vainly
hoped to be 'only passing through a phase of mental existence, that
will be followed by the production of far nobler works'.[10] An extreme
but far from unique case of this feeble sort of criticism occurs when
that consistently unintelligent journal, the *London Review*, praises
Framley Parsonage for its 'health and manliness . . . which, to
our thinking,' it adds, with heavy significance, 'is the highest term
of praise to be awarded any work whatever'.[11]

The moral judgments of the better critics can, of course, be much
more meaningful than this. Tacitly assuming that the novelist has a
duty to act as moral tutor and not merely as safe companion, the
Spectator, for example, describes the moral of *The Claverings* as
'one of the healthiest and without soaring very high, one of the
noblest for ordinary men which has been written for many a day . . .
—for men at least— . . . that the mind, the will, can regulate the
affections, as much as any other part of us . . . That is a wholesome
and necessary truth in these days of sentimental novels . . .'[12] The
moral for women is equally sound, says the critic, because of 'the
sincerity' with which Trollope shows 'the true and natural punish-
ment of [Julia's] sin [of selling herself in marriage],—first of all
. . . the disappearance of that true delicacy . . . then, as its external
penalty, the gathering of mean intrigues and meaner intriguers round
her'. Moreover, there are 'fewer unconnected side-pictures than is
usual', and those there are, are 'calculated to heighten the effect
of the principal subject', so that all in all, the *Spectator* concludes,

> *The Claverings* has . . . a higher moral and a more perfect unity
> . . . than any other of Mr. Trollope's previous tales. There is scarcely
> a touch in it which does not contribute to the main effect, both
> artistic and moral, of the story, and not a character introduced . . .
> which does not produce its own unique and specific effect on the
> reader's imagination.

This is high praise indeed. To a mid-Victorian critic the perfect
concurrence of unity, morality and realistic effect is a most rare and
prized quality in a novel. Even the often hostile *Saturday Review*
agrees that the moral of *The Claverings* is 'good and impressive'
because the 'presence of the respectable god of social justice is

[9] *Athenaeum* no. 1877, 17 Oct. 1863, 492–4.
[10] *Novels and Novelists*, ii, 345.
[11] 11 May 1861, *Critical Heritage*, p. 127. While it is possibly good that
weak criticism such as this should be included in the *Critical Heritage* volume,
the *London Review* is surely over-represented with ten examples.
[12] xl, 4 May 1867, 498–9.

perhaps more remarkable than in any previous book from the same hand'.[13] Once again what is praised is moral effect achieved through truth to life.

The borders of tragedy

Even the *Spectator*, however, is not entirely happy with *The Claverings*. It complains that in delineating the feelings of Harry and of his two loves, Trollope 'does not go very deep', and it compares the novel unfavourably in this respect with 'the exquisite picture' of the heroine's emotions in *A Lost Love* by 'Ashford Owen',[14] which it agrees is in other respects a far inferior book. 'Mr. Trollope leaves this deeper element of sentiment in his plot absolutely to the imagination of his readers. He paints for us truly enough how they spoke and acted, but he does not give us much conception of how they felt'. The *Athenaeum* is as squeamish as ever when Geraldine Jewsbury writes, 'There was room in "The Claverings" for deeper studies in human nature; but the book in that case might not have been so pleasant to read.'[15]

What is needed, some reviewers feel, is a novelist who will develop true tragedy in the novel, and thereby ennoble it as a literary form. So they are delighted whenever they see Trollope make an 'approach . . . to the depth and force of tragedy',[16] as in the case of *Orley Farm*, where, as we have seen, the critics praise the 'really powerful and tragic' figure of Lady Mason,[17] this Rebekah in 'modern dress', with whom he 'would fain stir the depths of the human heart and lay bare the secret soul',[18] and whose story provides 'the noble humanising pathos' which gives the novel its value.[19] But the critics feel that in the end Trollope falls short of tragedy, because he does not penetrate his characters deeply enough. Just what was meant by this, and what was involved in the distinction between 'surface' and 'depth' in characterization is examined at length in chapter 5.

Both J. Herbert Stack in the *Fortnightly* and an anonymous critic in the *Spectator*[20] take Trollope to task for not making Lady Glencora leave her husband and actually run away with Burgo Fitzgerald in

[13] xxiii, 18 May 1867, 638-9.
[14] Pseudonym of Anna C. Ogle. Both Hutton and Bagehot praised *A Lost Love* warmly when it appeared in 1855. See Mrs Russell Barrington, *Life of Walter Bagehot*, 1914, pp. 263-4.
[15] No. 2068, 15 June 1867, 783.
[16] Hutton's review of *Orley Farm*, *Spectator* xxxv, 11 Oct. 1862, 1136-8.
[17] *Ibid.*
[18] Dallas in *The Times*, 26 Dec. 1862, 5.
[19] Lewes [?] in the *Cornhill* vi, Nov. 1862, 702-4.
[20] Fortnightly (ns) v, 1 Feb. 1869, 188-98, and Spectator xxxviii, 9 Sept. 1865, 978-9.

Can You Forgive Her? The *Spectator* recognizes what Trollope admits in his *Autobiography*,[21] that Lady Glencora is 'a great favourite of the author's'. Yet, the critic continues, if Trollope

> had had the heart (shall we say the nerve?) to ruin Lady Glencora, he might have given (what is rare with him) a genuinely tragic interest to his story,—but his artistic instinct seems to have an awe of tragedy, the border of which he often brushes, touching it with no little insight and ability, and leaving it again with a sense of relief.

Trollope, the critic surmises, probably planned a tragic ending, but 'shrank back from the picture', as he must have done too in the case of the almost demonic character of George Vavasor. Recognizing that Trollope's greatest ability lies in the social interaction of characters, the reviewer suggests that this skill cannot be used to examine a truly tragic situation:

> Probably Mr. Trollope shrinks less from the imagination of dark thoughts, than from attempting that intensity of *style* required when dark thoughts come to a focus in dark deeds, and there is no room left for the play of those diffuse and piquant levities and elasticities of social life in the picturing of which he so much excels.

J. Herbert Stack makes a similar analysis, but is less prepared to forgive the novelist's shortcomings:

> Lady Glencora Palliser is pretty and true gliding over thin ice with her handsome lover; pretty and true in her candour to her cold spouse; pretty and true with her baby heir to the great dukedom. But suppose she had run away? Is there nothing deep, dark, and deadly in human nature and human sin to be painted vividly so that our souls may be purged by terror, and pity, and stronger thoughts than amusement at unmarried jilts, married flirts, and young mothers?

Even though one may doubt that such a development in a Trollope novel would be truly cathartic, one must agree with Stack that it is potentially present in many of the major novels. But the *Spectator's* rhetoric in speaking of how close Lady Glencora comes to a 'fatal plunge', betrays what would more or less preclude a satisfactory tragedy of adultery in the Victorian period: that is that the woman would be damned immediately by both author and reader for her single act of infidelity, whereas (as Ibsen shows) a tragedy of Victorian society must spring from the conflict between the individual and society. In this case the conflict would be between the woman's desire for freedom, and the social mores, embodied (as Trollope

[21] p. 276.

very brilliantly does embody them in *Can You Forgive Her?*) in her husband, guardians and chaperones. Adultery—the most highly charged subject available for the Victorian novel of domestic life— was also the sin for which a woman could obtain no social forgiveness, and was therefore a subject to be toyed with in the social novel, since it could not be exploited as an area of conflict. As Eneas Sweetland Dallas put it in his *Gay Science* of 1866:

> When women are . . . put forward to lead the action of a plot, they must be urged into a false position. . . . [T]he novelist finds that to make an effect he has to give up his heroine to bigamy, to murder, to child-bearing by stealth in the Tyrol, and to all sorts of adventures which can only signify her fall. . . . [This] leads by a natural process to their appearing in a light which is not good.[22]

Socially very orthodox, the *Saturday Review* commends the way Trollope exploits his 'very accurate knowledge of the natural history of jilts', since jilting is an offence 'especially within the province of a good novelist', and readers do not want descriptions of the feelings of worse offenders.[23] The sympathetic adulteress was not a good proposition for a Victorian novelist in search of a heroine, and without her, this fruitful area of tragedy was inaccessible.

Trollope's success with his readers in *Orley Farm* stems from the fact that he could decently appeal for sympathy for Lady Mason, because her crime of forgery had a maternal motive: to secure for her son the succession to the property. On the other hand, the complication of *He Knew He Was Right* arises from Louis Trevelyan's belief that his wife has been unfaithful, even though she has merely been obstinate in not obeying one of his more unreasonable dictates. It was Trollope's intention to generate tragic feeling by showing how Trevelyan's obsession takes hold of him, and how, by his own agency and urged on by his Iago figure, the private detective Bozzle, he produces an insoluble complication of circumstances, leading to his eventual madness and death. This requires the reader's sympathy for Louis Trevelyan (indeed, with Trollope's multiple viewpoint, it requires sympathy for Mrs Trevelyan as well), and to a modern reader, this part of the novel is extremely powerful. Such, however, was not the author's opinion when he wrote his *Autobiography*:

> I do not know that in any literary effort I ever fell more completely short of my own intention than in this story. It was my purpose to create sympathy for the unfortunate man who, while endeavouring to do his duty to all around him, should be led constantly astray by his unwillingness to submit his own judgement to the opinion

[22] ii, 297.
[23] Review of *Can You Forgive Her?*, xx, 19 Aug. 1865, 240–2.

of others. The man is made unfortunate enough, and the evil which
he does is apparent. So far I did not fail, but the sympathy has not
been created yet. I look upon the story as being nearly altogether
bad.[24]

Perhaps Trollope was influenced by the adverse press the novel
received. F. N. Broome in *The Times* considered *He Knew He Was
Right* to be 'a mere piece of realism' with 'no aesthetic purpose',[25]
while the *Dublin Review* put forward very much the case by which
Trollope later condemned himself:

> [Louis Trevelyan] goes mad, in a subtle tangled, sullen way,
> which demands . . . strength of a different kind from Mr. Trollope's,
> and delicacy other than his adroit *finesse* and circumspection. The
> bareness of truth is a mistake in this case. Mr. Trollope does not
> adorn the man with qualities to inspire interest before his calamity
> overtakes him, and so he fails to evoke compassion after it has
> done so.[26]

As so often, the *Saturday* voices its complaints more violently.[27] It
objects to 'Mr. Trollope's tendency to extreme realism', which is
based upon a 'superstitious adherence to facts which almost excludes
even the selection of the most attractive facts'. At least one character
must be sympathetic if the critic is to find the story 'tolerable',
but in this novel Trollope makes him feel 'a hearty contempt' for
both husband and wife. Although the story could be shown to be
perfectly probable from Divorce Court proceedings, the reviewer
pronounces it 'a great mistake in art to render the people in whose
fate we are supposed to take an interest so intensely contemptible'.
The story is 'simply repulsive' because of the 'pure absence of soul
or intellect' in the couple, while Louis Trevelyan 'becomes so absurd
in his conduct that he has to go mad in order to make his actions
tolerably intelligible; and there are some scenes which are forcibly
described and meant to be pathetic during his final illness. Unluckily
we have learnt to despise him so heartily that we only wish for his
speedy death . . .' In the case of all these journals, any potentially
tragic effect is rejected by the critics because they dislike Louis
Trevelyan, and disapprove of Mrs Trevelyan's recalcitrant behaviour.
As so often, it is the *Spectator*'s criticism which is the most interesting, and even when misjudged, the most perceptive and coherent.
The reviewer of *He Knew He Was Right* judiciously divides praise
and blame.[28] Finding he sympathizes with Louis Trevelyan, the critic

[24] pp. 321–2.   [25] 26 Aug. 1869, 4.
[26] 'The novels of Mr. Anthony Trollope', (ns) xix, Oct. 1872, 393–430;
p. 425.
[27] xxvii, 5 June 1869, 751–3.
[28] xlii, 12 June 1869, 706–8.

praises the tragedy he finds in part of the story, but, because he condemns Mrs Trevelyan's conduct, he must also condemn the morality of the latter part of the novel, where she has more exercise of moral choice. Thus by his interpretation he not only destroys the unity of the strand of the novel which deals with the Trevelyans (the novel's chief fault is its two, almost independent, story lines), but also limits the tragic effect artificially to one of the two protagonists. His case is worth considering at length.

The story of Trevelyan's madness, he says, comes close to tragedy, 'passing beyond the sphere in which [Mr Trollope] usually excels'. This aspect of the book is 'of great power, furnished with a commonplace but very striking moral', especially in the account of 'the influence gained by [Bozzle's] coarse assumptions over his employer's mind'. (This reviewer's account of Bozzle's role in the novel is one of the most sensitive pieces of Trollopian criticism to be found anywhere.) The critic notices too the characteristic Trollopian method and skill in founding 'a tale about a truly tragic jealousy' on no reasonable cause at all. He reserves his disapproval for the second volume, where 'the realistic morality of the tale' breaks down, together with 'the truth and power of the drawing'. 'We are astonished', the critic goes on, 'at the sympathy which the novelist asks for on behalf of Mrs. Trevelyan':

> [W]hen Mr. Trollope tries to lead us into wasting compassion upon her, and yet makes her so unlovely as he does,—so utterly without remorse for conduct which seems to us far worse than her husband's . . . so concentrated in self even in the most solemn moments,— we . . . have a right to say that the art of the story is thereby spoiled.[29]

Mrs Trevelyan, the critic surmises, was probably meant at first 'to be an unlovely character, and gradually became invested with a very false and hollow atmosphere of sentiment as the story grew towards its end'. Apparently the Victorian reader is expected to understand the husband who persecutes his wife, and condemn the wife who resents it. So the author's growing sympathy with his heroine, which the reviewers approved in the case of Lady Mason in *Orley Farm*, is condemned in *He Knew He Was Right* in favour of an attitude of rigid harshness, because of the nature of Emily Trevelyan's offence, in not submitting to her husband. On the other hand, the *Spectator* likes the scenes of the novel which take place in Exeter, and are almost entirely unconnected with the story of the Trevelyans. But

---

[29] To anyone well acquainted with Hutton's prose, the structure of this sentence will suggest his style.

then these Exeter episodes constitute a very undisturbing chronicle of everyday life.

Taking this review of *He Knew He Was Right* as a whole, it is impossible to agree with Richard Stang when he says that it was this novel 'that won Hutton completely over to Trollope' because of its tragic element.[30] Later notices of Trollope in the *Spectator* are no more favourable than those before, and no more interesting than those of *Orley Farm* and the *Small House*, to name but two.

Lack of imagination

The better and more favourable of Trollope's contemporary critics just examined, found various ways of accounting for why he fell short of artistic greatness. All their explanations amount in effect to the diagnosis that he lacked 'imagination', that his subjects were mundane, his treatment of them plain, and that in short he was an 'observer' or 'photographer' rather than an inventive artist. Chapters 3, 4 and 5 are largely devoted to examining the meaning of this judgment in the context of the morality of Trollope's novels, their social acceptability, and his methods of characterization respectively. In addition, the section of chapter 6 which deals with the *Autobiography* contains further comments by Trollope himself on the subject. The present section will show how the criticism of 'lack of imagination' fits in with some theories of the imagination that were formulated during the 1860s.

Many notices in the 'sixties echo the verdict of one of Trollope's very first critics, the reviewer of *The Macdermots of Ballycloran* in the *Spectator* of 1847, who concluded that 'Mr. Trollope fails from want of largeness and imagination'.[31] The *Saturday Review* in 1869 thinks his fiction limited both in subject-matter and treatment, as though it were an easy matter 'to report of men and things as seen through the medium of a colourless imagination'.[32] A few years later it quotes Wordsworth in a more unkind cut still: 'Minds that have nothing to confer find little to perceive.'[33] When the *Saturday* is friendly towards Trollope, it considers it quite a good thing that he should have 'snug and comfortable theories of things, with no transcendental moonshine about them'.[34] But in such a case the reviewer feels compelled to point out the limitations of the subject-matter, and remind one that 'the author is not talking about people with

[30] *The Theory of the Novel in England 1850–1870*, Routledge, 1959, pp. 57–8.
[31] xx, 8 May 1847, 449.
[32] Review of *Phineas Finn*, xxvii, 27 Mar. 1869, 431–2.
[33] Review of *The Prime Minister*, xlii, 14 Oct. 1876, 481–2.
[34] Review of *Can You Forgive Her?*, xx, 19 Aug. 1865, 240–2.

extraordinary depth or fineness of nature'. Such critical equivocation effectively makes any praise of the author depend upon accepting the proposition that he has failed as an artist. This is even true in a friendly notice, like Charles Stewart's review of *Hunting Sketches* in the *Fortnightly*, which sums up this whole complex of attitudes:

> Mr. Trollope has not . . . in any of his writings ventured on high ground . . . and the rare praise may be accorded him of never having attempted flights beyond the strength of his pinions. It would . . . be perhaps a truer description to call his novels photographs than pictures, for though there may be wanting the breadth and vigour of a masterpiece of painting, we have the completeness and minuteness of truth which is only produced by means of the intuitive power of observation.[35]

Most reviewers assume without question that 'imagination' is only required for works of passion and originality, and that Trollopian realism, being apparently deficient in these qualities, cannot therefore be the product of imagination. Once again the better critics like Hutton, Dallas and Lewes, bring the important issues into focus. For example, like many of his lesser contemporaries, Hutton liked to see traces of 'the agony of meditative travail' in a work of literature,[36] and he, too, explained Trollope's method of writing as a matter of observation from without, as opposed to imagination from within. What makes him so much more interesting than, say, Charles Stewart, is that in the course of years of reviewing, he built up a clear picture of how he thought novels were written, and, as an explanation of the paradox of the unimaginative artist, he developed alternative models of the creative process, one for the romantic artist such as Charlotte Brontë, and the other for the realist like Trollope. This aspect of Hutton's work is examined in chapter 5.

The question looked somewhat different to Dallas. Hutton's problem was to account for Trollope's literary success, given that his fiction seemed very ordinary, and his techniques as a writer scarcely noticeable. What status should be granted a novelist who, though supreme in truth, showed few signs of great passion in himself or in his characters? Dallas on the other hand was occupied principally with the workings of the subconscious, or the 'Hidden Soul' as he called it, and it was his work on this subject in *The Gay Science* that made him the best abstract theorist of his day.[37] He could not applaud truth to life as a guiding principle in literature, since to have done so, he thought, would have implied accepting a crude Aristotelian

[35] i, 1 Aug. 1865, 765–7.
[36] Review of *Orley Farm*, *Spectator* xxxv, 11 Oct. 1862, 1136–8.
[37] See A. H. Warren, *English Poetic Theory 1825–1865*, Princeton University Press, 1950, pp. 126–51.

view of art as copying, a doctrine, he complained, that had 'trans-
mitted . . . a sort of hereditary squint' to all criticism since Aristotle's
time.[38] Moreover, he objected to the novel of contemporary life as a
symptom of sentimental individualism, and as part of the unhealthy
curiosity current in the 'age of biography'. 'Our interest in the private
life of our fellow-men', he complained, 'has been developed into a
system . . .'[39] His description of the domestic novel was 'gossip
etherealized, family talk generalized'.[40]

When he reviewed *Orley Farm* for *The Times*, however, he found
himself dealing with a novel which rose above this 'gossipping sense'
of curiosity, and mere fidelity to the appearance of things. Trollope
aimed 'much higher' in this novel, and dealt 'not with mere manners,
but with the heart of humanity'.[41] *Orley Farm* was therefore in
harmony with Dallas's chief aim, which was the pursuit of literature
and criticism as a 'science of human nature', in opposition (among
other things) to the Ruskinian study of nature, which Dallas described as 'all this cant of finding God in the material and not in the
moral world, and of thence lauding the sciences of matter to the
neglect of the science of mind'.[42]

Orley Farm was, of course, somewhat of a special case in the praise
it received from all quarters for its imaginative power, supposedly
unequalled elsewhere in Trollope. Normally when reviewing other
Trollope novels, Dallas left the question of imagination to one side,
and praised the author for his 'vigour',[43] and for providing 'innocent
and rational amusement': 'There is no pretence about him, no sham-
ming, no effort. He is always clever, often amusing, sometimes
even great, or very near being great, but his predominating faculty
is good sense. . . . His style is . . . plain and straightforward, utterly
devoid of clap-trap.'[44] While he was reviewing for *The Times* from
1857 to 1865, Dallas was simultaneously engaged on his principal
work of aesthetics, *The Gay Science*, which was published in 1866.
It is no wonder that his reviews show him working at some of the ideas
later embodied in his book. In particular, even when bestowing the
highest praise on a novelist, he still doubts whether any novelist
qualifies as a truly imaginative artist: that is, he wonders whether

[38] *The Gay Science*, 2 vols, 1866, i, 26.
[39] Compare Dallas's remarks on the public's 'very morbid curiosity', in his
review of *Barchester Towers*, quoted p. 6 above, with this comment from
Gay Science, ii, 285; see also F. X. Roellinger, 'Dallas: a mid-Victorian critic
of individualism', *Philological Quarterly* xx, Oct. 1941, 611–21.
[40] *Gay Science*, ii, 286.
[41] 26 Dec. 1862, 5.
[42] *Gay Science*, i, 48 and 49–50.
[43] Review of *Miss Mackenzie*, *The Times*, 23 Aug. 1865, 12.
[44] 'Anthony Trollope', *The Times*, 23 May 1859, 12.

the description of the imagination which he is working on for *The Gay Science* is applicable in certain individual cases, and especially whether it could be held to embrace a novelist such as Trollope. A brief summary of this aspect of *The Gay Science* will clarify his reviews of Trollope, as well as showing their role in the development of this major book.

Dallas aimed to establish a 'new method of comparative criticism', based on a threefold approach to art. Criticism, he asserted, 'must compare art with art; it must compare art with mind; it must compare art with history; and it must bring together again, and place side by side, the result [*sic*] of these three comparisons'.[45] *The Gay Science* consists largely of his examination of the psychological approach to literature, based on a most unusually explicit theory of the subconscious activity of the mind. Despite his occasional use of pseudo-scientific language, his main impulse is anti-scientific: the desire to dethrone the natural sciences from their current pre-eminence, by establishing 'human' sciences—psychology and criticism—as the worthiest study for mankind. By means of his psychological approach, Dallas attempts to avoid scientific rationalism on the one hand, without falling into Wordsworthian nature worship on the other.[46] Unfortunately, in spite of his fascinating insights into the subconscious, he ultimately fails to bridge the gap between his highly metaphysical psychology and his limited, rhetorical concept of language.[47] Many of his speculations, consequently, hardly bear on the actual practice of criticism at all. Yet he shows himself an acute reader of Trollope, and his difficulties only arise when his judgment leads him into the realm of his as yet uncompleted theory.

His review of *Rachel Ray* in *The Times* for Christmas Day 1863 shows him in exactly this position. He starts with high praise for Trollope, and for the achievement of the best novelists in general: '[Mr. Trollope] is great in judgment. With Mr. Thackeray and George Eliot he stands at the head of the just judges. . . .[T]he knowledge of human nature which they display is of a very high order, and not only ministers to our amusement but raises us in the scale of being.' Then follows the standard formula for mingled praise and blame: 'He never soars very high, nor digs very deep, but he hardly ever disappoints . . .' In this respect, says Dallas, he resembles Defoe, who 'with all his great power was singularly void of imagination'.[48]

[45] *Gay Science*, i, 41–2.

[46] *Ibid.*, i, 48–53; see also R. A. Forsyth, ' "The Onward March of Thought" and the poetic theory of E. S. Dallas', *British Journal of Aesthetics* iii, Oct. 1963, 330–40.

[47] See also 'The language of poesy', in his *Poetics*, 1852, pp. 153 ff.

[48] Most mid-Victorians shared Macaulay's judgment that Defoe's gift was merely 'a knack at making fiction look like truth'; see G. O. Trevelyan,

The critic admits that it 'would be difficult to define what is meant' by this 'commonplace of criticism', because 'nobody has yet been able to define . . . imagination'. And he avoids the problem by supposing that 'on a close analysis' even Defoe might be found to have 'imagination', despite the fact that his chief ability was to 'call up a scene, or describe a series of events with a hard prosaic accuracy, which . . . is supposed to be independent of imagination'. In Trollope's case, Dallas traces the deficiency to the 'rough and ready, downright, prosaic, forceful' narrative style: 'He abjures ornaments, avoids the play of fancy, is purposely plain . . . He may not suggest much; but he is so clear that we do not feel the want of suggestions.'

By the time this ineffectual piece of equivocation has found its way into *The Gay Science*, Dallas has reasoned it out further, and placed it in the context of his whole discussion of the imagination and the subconscious. '[I]magination or fantasy', he says, '. . . is a name given to the automatic action of the mind or any of its faculties —to what may not unfitly be called the Hidden Soul.'[49] He speaks of the 'vast tracts of unconscious, but still active, mind within us', which are 'like the conscious intelligence and yet . . . divided from it by a veil of mystery', while 'between our unconscious and our conscious existence, there is a free and constant but unobserved traffic for ever carried on'.[50] Creative imagination is the working of this traffic: 'When the current of thought flows from within our ken to beyond our ken, it is gone, we forget it, we know not what has become of it. After a time it comes back to us changed and grown, as it were a new thought, and we know not whence it comes.'[51]

Similarly the highest poetic quality in a work of art is that which arouses 'hidden pleasure' in the 'unconsciousness' of the reader, and is

the most wonderful, the most vital, of all elements of art—the element of mystery, that sense of the unseen, that possession of the far-away, that glimmer of infinity, that incommunicable secret, that know-not-what . . . it is the suggestion of this unknown something in art which we are in the habit of signalising as in a peculiar sense poetical.[52]

The unconvincing passage from the review of *Rachel Ray* now fits in, and becomes much more meaningful. Dallas explains his view

---

The Life and Letters of Lord Macaulay, 2 vols, 1876, ii, 455; also John Dennis, *Studies in English Literature*, 1876, p. 105.

[49] *Gay Science*, i, 194.
[50] *Ibid.*, i, 205, 206, 207.
[51] *Ibid.*, i, 207–8.
[52] *Ibid.*, ii, 133 and 134–5.

that 'a man may tell a story well . . . and yet his clear story-telling is not poetry':

> If there be artists who content themselves with adhesion to bare facts, who are never able to transcend fact and to move the imagination, then we must think of them as of Defoe. We take an interest in what Defoe tells us, but it is not the interest excited by art. He sees things clearly and describes them sharply; but the complaint against him is that he has no imagination—that he never touches the hidden sense, which we have been trying to analyze.[53]

To Dallas, then, Trollope fails as an artist because he is too consciously reasonable, and rarely seems to be other than consciously reasonable.

The *Rachel Ray* notice reappears later in *The Gay Science*, where, without naming him, Dallas sums up his view of the status of just such an artist as Trollope: 'I know not who in this generation is better employed than he who—even if he cannot boast of genius, yet with tact and clearness—widens through fiction the range of our sympathies, and teaches us not less to care for the narrow aims of small people than the vast schemes of the great and mighty.[54] This passage has surely sprung from the seasonable exclamation with which the review of *Rachel Ray* ended on Christmas Day 1863: ' Oh, happy art of fiction which can thus adjust the balance of fortune, raising the humble and weak to an equality in our hearts with the proud and the great!'[55] *Rachel Ray* may be morally admirable by Dallas's standards, as well as excellent amusement, but it still does not qualify as imaginative art.[56]

Any discussion of imagination in prose fiction as seen by critics of the 1860s, would be incomplete without a mention of G. H. Lewes, materialist, free-thinker and champion of realism. Although his critical ideas are not expressed at length in reviews of Trollope, they

[53] *Gay Science* i, 331. Dallas's statement on Defoe remains a tautology—but an informative one.

[54] *Ibid.*, ii, 287. Dickens is not intended here, since Dallas is describing the 'domestic novel', of which Trollope is typical. Thackeray was dead by 1866, and is anyway the only novelist expressly conceded 'genius' in *The Gay Science*, ii, 287–8.

[55] A fuller study of Dallas's reviews for *The Times* would show a good deal more of *The Gay Science* as it was developing. His 'Anthony Trollope' (23 May 1859, 12), for example, shows in embryo some of the thoughts about the relation of character to plot which occupy pp. 288–94 of *The Gay Science*, ii.

[56] Dallas distinguishes another 'imagination' (which, however, is not at issue here): '. . . not only the power of imaging or figuring to ourselves the shows of sense, but also that of imagery, the power of bringing these shows into comparison, and using them as types', *Gay Science*, i, 264.

represent an important sector of literary opinion in the period. As editor of the important weekly, the *Leader*, and then of the *Fortnightly Review*, he was an influential figure in the London literary scene, as well as the biographer of Goethe, author of 'the best history of philosophy that the English reader can consult',[57] and one of the leading popularizers of science and psychology of the age. His most extended critical work, apart from his important theatrical criticism, was a series of articles in the *Fortnightly Review* in 1865, entitled *The Principles of Success in Literature*.[58] As a defence of realism the *Principles* can be eloquent, but Lewes constantly contradicts himself, and depends on a specious scientism, with his 'principles' of 'vision', 'sincerity', and so on, and his mechanical 'laws' of style. Moreover, the purpose of the articles is unclear, although, like various other Victorian works of criticism, they suffer from being written partly to guide the aspiring writer.

To Lewes, the 'generic character' of the imagination 'is the power of forming images; it reinstates, in a visible group, those objects which are invisible, either from absence or from imperfection of our senses', while its 'specific character' is 'derived from the powers of selection and recombination'.[59] Materials from the memory store undergo 'a transformation' in the artist's 'soul', whereby all the 'kaleidoscopic fragments are recomposed into images that seem to have a corresponding reality of their own'.[60] The limitations of this mechanistic model are obvious when, in order to defend realists against charges of mere copying, Lewes has to assume that the 'specific character' of the imagination is the basis of all art. Quite contrary to his original statement on the 'generic character', he now asserts that 'artistic power' is displayed in 'the *selection of the characteristic details*', and 'no man imagines what he has not seen or known'.[61] Lewes then goes on to contradict himself yet again by saying that the 'Principle of Vision' (which insists that the artist should 'see' what he depicts), applies also to 'objects that never were seen by the eye, that never could be seen'.[62] When in such an impasse, Lewes appeals to his scheme of 'laws' and 'principles', and (dishonestly in one of his philosophical ability) falls back on an emotive appeal to the reliability

[57] Dallas on Lewes's *Biographical History of Philosophy*, 4 vols, 1845–6, in *Gay Science*, i, 55.

[58] Reprinted as a book, ed. T. S. Knowlson, n.d. [1898]; cited in this edition as *Principles*.

[59] *Principles*, pp. 57 and 58. Cf. Bulwer's 'The normal clairvoyance of the imagination', in his *Miscellaneous Prose Works*, 3 vols, 1868, vol. iii.

[60] *Principles*, pp. 25 and 78.

[61] *Ibid.*, p. 60. Lewes's italics.

[62] *Ibid.*, pp. 76–7.

of science. This is most blatant in the 'Principle of Sincerity', which is the most ludicrously fallacious part of the work.[63]

Despite obvious shortcomings in the theory which ostensibly underlies it, Lewes's *Principles of Success* has important virtues. Most of all, it is significant in putting forward the case for realism as intellectually respectable, imaginative art. Lewes attacks 'false and conventional' realism, and deplores the 'reaction against conventionalism which called itself Idealism, in favour of *detailism* which calls itself Realism'.[64] And he protests that the 'imaginative power' of a work has been 'too frequently estimated according to the extent of *departure* from ordinary experience in the images selected', basing his defence of realism on the 'psychological fact that fairies and demons, remote as they are from experience, are not created by a more vigorous effort of imagination than milkmaids and poachers'.[65] This plea was still necessary in the 'sixties, when many critics and journals persistently failed to recognize the importance of the novel of contemporary life in more than social and economic terms, and when the *Saturday Review* in particular set itself up against many novelists of the day, Trollope among them.

Yet it is significant that in the 'sixties, when there was an almost superstitious belief in the 'advance of mind' on one side, and on the other, a 'dread and dislike of science' (as Lewes put it),[66] the most extended defence of realism should have been based on the most materialistic thinking. To its enemies, therefore, realism remained as firmly as ever associated with the mechanism they deplored.

[63] The 'Principle of Sincerity' contains in germ the illogic which inspires one of the grossest horrors of mid-Victorian criticism, a *Fortnightly Review* article entitled 'Immorality in authorship' (vi, 15 Sept. 1866, 289–300), written by Robert Buchanan, author of the notorious 'Fleshly School' article. It is a small step from Lewes's insistence on 'sincerity' as the basis of 'vision', and true 'vision' as the basis of good art, to the absurdity of Buchanan's argument: 'If . . . morality in literature is dependent on sincerity of vision, and if all immoral writing betrays itself by its insincerity, feebleness, and want of verisimilitude', then (Buchanan argues) it is not necessary to decide what constitutes morality or immorality in art, or even whether a given work is immoral, but (he ends falsetto fortissimo) merely 'to apply the purely literary test', and show that the work 'is not literature'.

[64] *Principles*, pp. 27 and 80 respectively.

[65] *Ibid.*, p. 58. See A. R. Kaminsky, *George Henry Lewes as Literary Critic*, Syracuse (N.Y.) 1968, p. 42.

[66] 'On the dread and dislike of science', *Fortnightly Review* (ns) xxiii, June 1878, pp. 805–15. See also *Spectator* xl, 25 May 1867, 584–5, where Dallas's *Gay Science* is attacked without regard to its anti-scientific tendency, because its title suggests the further encroachment of science on life.

The 'Saturday Review' and mechanical art

Chief among these opponents of realism was the *Saturday Review*. It consistently objected to art it considered to be 'unimaginative', and denounced Trollope's fiction as 'monstrously prosaic'—as showing merely a 'soberness of fancy coupled with a copious variety of detail'.[67] Conscious of their social and intellectual superiority, the university men on the *Saturday* felt a deep scorn for any popular phenomenon, in literature, religion, dress or politics.[68] Hence they looked down on periodical fiction in general. But the chosen enemy was *The Cornhill Magazine*, that 'asylum for lazy or extinct genius'.[69] For a long time there were bad relations between the two journals, and Thackeray was provoked to ask, 'Is the world one great school of little boys, and the *Saturday Review* its great usher?'[70] Although many Victorian commentators, including Fox Bourne and Walter Besant, point out how much the *Saturday* did to raise the standard of journalism in the 'fifties and 'sixties, it was itself 'often more anxious to be smart than to be just'.[71] Examples of what Mark Pattison later called 'the froth and frivolity of its froward youth',[72] are collected in a short polemic work, *The Saturday Review*, by James Grant.[73] Grant successfully convicts the paper of descending to personality, of running spiteful campaigns against various authors, and of carping pettily at grammar. Unfortunately he himself is just as guilty of these faults (but less skilful), and the volume remains readable more for the vituperative quotations from the *Saturday*, than for the author's rather muddled case.

Having already handled *Doctor Thorne* quite roughly in 1858, the *Saturday* proceeds to mount a sustained campaign against Trollope from 1860 onwards, repeatedly accusing him of mechanical and unimaginative work. As part of its broad objection to serial fiction in general, it attacks both *Framley Parsonage* and Thackeray's *Philip*,

[67] Reviews of *Miss Mackenzie*, xix, 4 Mar. 1865, 263–5, and *Phineas Finn*, xxvii, 27 Mar. 1869, 431–2, respectively.

[68] See H. R. Fox Bourne, *English Newspapers*, ii, 314; and T. H. S. Escott, *Platform, Press, Politics and Play*, n.d. [1895], p. 185.

[69] Review of *Framley Parsonage*, *Saturday Review* xi, 4 May 1861, 451–2.

[70] *Roundabout Papers*, no. 14, 'Small-beer chronicle', *Cornhill* iv, Jul. 1861, 123. For other attacks by Thackeray on the 'Superfine Review' see no. 6, 'On screens in dining-rooms', ii, Aug. 1860, 252–6, and no. 8, 'De Juventute', ii, Oct. 1860, 501–12. See also *George Smith: a memoir*, pp. 120–121, and Trollope's *Autobiography*, pp. 369–70.

[71] H. R. Fox Bourne, *English Newspapers*, ii, 314; see also *Autobiography of Sir Walter Besant*, 1902, pp. 92–3.

[72] 'Books and critics', *Fortnightly* (ns) xxii, Nov. 1877, 659–79; p. 663.

[73] Published in 1873, ostensibly as a supplement to his *History of the Newspaper Press*, 1871–2.

and claims that there is something facile and unworthy in 'the plan now so much in vogue' of re-introducing established characters, so that the writer can 'save time by dispensing with . . . fresh draughts upon his own imagination'.[74] This criticism badly misjudges Trollope's ability to sustain a set of characters over many years, and develop them by submitting them to a great variety of fictional situations. But the accusation that he wrote more than was good for his reputation, because 'in so much there could not but be considerable inequality',[75] sticks harder. There is indeed a great deal of repetition of characters and situations, and the modern reader may well join the *Westminster* in asking why Trollope did not 'care enough for his well-earned reputation to refrain from striking off more copies of an idea than the plate will bear'.[76] The important fact for the present discussion is not merely that Trollope was attacked, but the critics' use of mechanical imagery of manufacture and commerce, in connection with an 'unimaginative' writer. Take, for example, the *Saturday*'s critique of *Rachel Ray*: 'There is a brisk market for descriptions of the inner life of young women, and Mr. Trollope is the chief agent in supplying the market. . . . Mr. Trollope . . . has taught himself to turn out a brick that does almost without straw, and is a very good saleable brick of its kind.'[77] This sort of language, and words like 'photograph',[78] 'kaleidoscope',[79] 'stereotype'[80] and 'Manchester

[74] Review of *Framley Parsonage*, xi, 4 May 1861, 451–2. Compare its review of *Philip*, 23 Aug. 1862, repr. in *Thackeray: the Critical Heritage*, pp. 310–11. See also reviews of *Framley Parsonage* in *Westminster* lxxvi, Jul. 1861, 282–4, and *Dublin University Magazine* lix, Apr. 1862, 405–6, for further comments on the 'merciless introduction of old friends'. Meanwhile the *Spectator* takes the opposite view, that Trollope's new characters are never as effective as those carried over from previous novels, because of his gradual, progressive method of characterization. See, for example, its review of *Miss Mackenzie*, xxxviii, 4 Mar. 1865, 244–5, and chapter 5 below.

[75] F. R. Oliphant and M. Oliphant, *The Victorian Age of English Literature*, 2 vols. 1892, ii, 181.

[76] Review of *Can You Forgive Her?* (volume one), (ns) xxviii, Jul. 1865, 284–5.

[77] xvi, 24 Oct. 1863, 554–5.

[78] For examples of this favourite Victorian critical term see: review of *Ralph the Heir*, *Athenaeum* no. 2268, 15 Apr. 1871, 456 [Collyer], and of *Eustace Diamonds*, no. 2348, 26 Oct. 1872, 527–8 [Collyer]; review of *Hunting Sketches*, *Fortnightly Review* i, 1 Aug. 1865, 765–7, Charles Stewart (sgd); review of *Orley Farm*, *National Review* xvi, Jan. 1863, 26–40, p. 32; reviews in the *Reader* of *Rachel Ray*, the *Small House* and *Miss Mackenzie*; review of the *Small House*, *Westminster* (ns) xxvi, Jul. 1864, 251–2. See also J. H. Friswell, *Modern Men of Letters Honestly Criticised*, 1870, p. 137.

[79] e.g. Review of *Orley Farm*, *Spectator* xxxv, 11 Oct. 1862, 1136–8 [Hutton].

[80] e.g. Review of *Belton Estate*, *Saturday Review* xxi, 3 Feb. 1866, 140–142.

goods',[81] appear again and again in descriptions of realism. To make matters worse, Trollope constantly used the comparison of author to cobbler, in order to stress the importance of diligent labour in his work.[82] The critics took up the idea with glee, and frequently announced that he was no more than a literary journeyman, some-times even advising him not to try higher flights, but to stick to his last as a portrayer of mundane subjects.[83] The result of his hasty, mechanical work, says the *Saturday*'s critic of *Framley Parsonage*, is superficiality. The whole of his fiction resembles Millais's illustration 'Was it not a lie?' in volume one of that novel: 'The subject of the plate is Lucy Robarts' crinoline, and the reader's eye following the folds of the crinoline, will come at last upon Lucy Robarts' face and shoulders, which have retired into a corner of the picture, in conces-sion to the social claims of muslin and lace.' With its faultless instinct for hurtful remarks, the *Saturday* has chosen to exemplify Trollope by the one illustration by Millais he thoroughly disliked, because it overemphasized the absurdities of fashion. ' I can hardly tell you', he wrote to George Smith on 23 May 1860, 'what my feeling is about the illustration . . . It would be much better to omit it altogether . . . The picture is simply ludicrous, & will be thought by most people to have been made so intentionally.'[84]

Typical of the 'Saturday Reviler's' dual attack on Trollope's subject-matter and style, is its review of *The Belton Estate*,[85] with the usual underlying assumption that Trollopian realism is easy and unimaginative—the facile result of hasty writing. *The Belton Estate* is not one of Trollope's best novels, of course, and other reviewers were disappointed in it too. The *Saturday*'s remarks, however, apply to his work as a whole, and appear in less concentrated form in many of its other notices. Trollope, says the reviewer, is like an artist who year after year submits to the Royal Academy a painting of a donkey

---

[81] Review of *Framley Parsonage*, *Westminster* (ns) xx, Jul. 1861, 282–4; review of *Tales of All Countries* (2nd series), *National Review* xvi, Apr. 1863, 522–5.

[82] The comparison occurs many times, particularly in *Autobiography*, pp. 120–1; *Letters*, pp. 57 and 191. See also H. E. Scudder, *James Russell Lowell*, 2 vols, 1901, ii, 82–3, for Lowell's account of Trollope's use of the comparison in conversation.

[83] *British Quarterly Review* on *Castle Richmond*, xxxii, Jul. 1860, 233–4; *Dublin Review*, 'The novels of Mr. Anthony Trollope', (ns) xix, Oct. 1872, 393–430. See also review of *Castle Richmond*, *Saturday Review* ix, 19 May 1860, 643–4.

[84] *Letters*, pp. 59–60. Later in another letter to Smith on 21 July, he drops his complaint: 'I will now consent to forget the flounced dress. I saw the *very pattern of the dress* some time after the picture came out.' *Letters*, p. 64 (Trollope's italics).

[85] *Saturday Review* xxi, 3 Feb. 1866, 140–2.

between two bundles of hay. He has published no fewer than three novels in the past twelve months, all concerning someone who is hesitating between two loves, and the only difference between them is that the 'expression of the donkey's eye may vary a little'. Of course, the critic continues, no greater variety and inventiveness can be expected from a novelist who publishes so often:

> Such fertility is not in nature. Only why should the novelist 'do' his three novels a year? Of course, if Mr. Trollope only looks upon his art as manufacture, there can be no reason why he should not take as just a pride in turning so many novels out of his brain in the twelvemonth as a machine-maker takes in turning so many loco-motives or looms out of his shed. . . . Unfortunately . . . [h]e loses all freshness and interest and vivacity, and grows at each repetition heavier and more mechanical.

His style naturally suffers under this repetition, and '[i]n the present instance, it would be less truly described as limpid than as limp'. Yet this is of no consequence, for Trollope's aim is so low that his humble means suffice him. Clara Amedroz, the heroine, is intended to be 'exceedingly commonplace', and the whole book displays 'a realism that is sordid and pitiful', consisting of 'the careful portraiture of the meanest and most sordid set of human traits'. It is not to be excused on the plea 'that such things are, and that therefore they are the fit subjects of art'. Only the low status of prose fiction as an art, says the reviewer, prevents people from seeing 'the grossness of [this] fallacy'. The last two pages of *The Belton Estate*, with Will and Clara retiring to bed after entertaining Captain Aylmer and his new wife, are beyond the critic's endurance: 'The heroine protesting that her old lover's wife is plain and over forty and has a horrid red nose, and the hero meanwhile turning his gigantic back and snoring—there we leave them. O sublime picture! This is what a crude half-considered notion of realism comes to.'

It is in this context that Lewes's apology for realism must be read, and a passage from his regular editor's column in the *Fortnightly* a few months later, forcefully challenges the *Saturday*'s position:

> The realistic form of art is a legitimate form. When the subject is high, realism is the highest possible form of art; and when the subject is commonplace, realism gives it a warrant. But the only excuse for the artist keeping us amid details of commonplace is that thereby the commonplace is raised into art; and it can only be so raised by truthful presentation.[86]

The attacks on realism can be seen as part of the general fear that materialism was engulfing the whole of man's spiritual and physical life. Therefore the debate about the value of tragedy in the novel, and

[86] 'Causeries', iv, 15 Apr. 1866, 635–8; p. 637.

about whether a novelist can be called an imaginative artist, was of great concern in the mid-nineteenth century, the age of the novel. The purpose of the present chapter has been to examine this situation, by seeing how one particular novelist fared in this debate, and thereby also to place the work of Anthony Trollope in its critical and historical context.[87]

[87] For a fuller consideration of the moral and social dilemmas facing the mid-Victorian realist, see chapters 3 and 4 below.

3

THE MORALITY OF
FICTION AND THE
DEPICTION OF VICE

Charges of moral irresponsibility

Trollope came under frequent critical attack from his contemporaries
for his immorality, or at least for a supposed moral irresponsibility in
the choice and treatment of his subject-matter. Not that he ever gained
George Meredith's reputation (expressed by the *Spectator* in 1866),
of having 'a rather low ethical tone'.[1] Some of Trollope's novels were
regarded as morally quite unexceptionable—such as the Barsetshire
novels, or *Rachel Ray*—while others, such as *The Claverings*, were
positively lauded for their healthy and noble moral lessons.[2] Yet
when he brought out *Is he Popenjoy?*, the *Spectator* found it 'un-
wholesome in tone', and the critic thought 'it would not be well that
a popular and justly popular novelist like Mr. Trollope should trade
on his reputation, and write inferior tales, without some critical
protest'.[3] And critical protests the *Spectator* certainly voiced, when
it felt them to be necessary. *The Eustace Diamonds* it had already
condemned as utterly repulsive, in a passage of invective which
itemizes two of the chief moral fundamentals of mid-Victorian criticism—the need for moral 'proportion', and a preference for 'grand'
evil:

> . . . the defect of the novel is its want of anything like moral
> contrasts, its horrors in the way of sordidness and coarseness with-
> out any adequate foils, the feeling it gives one that the meannesses,
> basenesses, and moral vulgarities of life, overshadow the heavens
> and shut out the sun. It is a depressing story, in which all that is
> coarse and base is painted with lavish power, but where evil itself
> is not on a grand scale, and where the few good characters are so
> insignificant that you almost resent the author's expectation that
> you shall sorrow in their sorrows and rejoice in their joys.[4]

[1] xxxix, 3 Feb. 1866, 136.   [2] See pp. 39–40 above.
[3] li, 5 Oct. 1878, 1243–4.   [4] xlv, 26 Oct. 1872, 1365–6.

'There is something a little too suffocating for Art in this picture', the reviewer complains, and the *Spectator*'s notices of a number of the following novels continue the stream of violent language, with its lavish wasteland imagery of fog, marsh and disease. *The Way We Live Now*, says Meredith Townsend, is like a sewage-farm, for in it Trollope 'has surrounded his characters with an atmosphere of sordid baseness which prevents enjoyment like an effluvium', and his 'occasional clevernesses no more make the book pleasant than a few gas-lamps serve to make a London fog endurable'.[5] Townsend also finds *The Prime Minister* 'tainted' with its author's 'disposition to attribute to the majority of mankind an inherent vulgarity of thought'. The reviewer of *Is He Popenjoy?* longs to see 'the blue sky over all'[6] and to breathe 'the sweet breezes of heaven',[7] while the critic of *An Eye for an Eye* finds that book like a breath of the Atlantic after the 'sands and marshes and all kinds of muddy fen-countries', the 'stifling atmosphere of a London alley', the 'nightmare' and the 'moral malaria' that have characterized some of Trollope's recent books.[8]

These books are not only considered repellent, but dangerous too, even though the diseased quality the reviewers find in them is not the result of falsification: for as Townsend acknowledges, Trollope is hardly ever inaccurate.[9] Indeed they are rendered dangerous by this very realism—the fact that, as the *Athenaeum* supposes, Trollope 'disclaims any moral purpose beyond the photographic delineation of human meanness'. Hence a danger of his teaching by example, by 'inducing the reader to suppose that the leading personages are intended to be at all typical of excellence'.[10] There can be no better illustration than this of the fact that a reader's reactions to a work are as much determined by his expectations and the conventions in which he has been raised, as by the author's express intentions, or the work itself. Right at the beginning of his career, Trollope rejected the heroic in his novels, and this rejection involved him in an unending struggle against such conditioning in his readers.

Occasionally a critic will take a different view, and regard the persuasiveness of realism as salutary, when properly used. To the *Saturday Review*, Trollope's story 'The Spotted Dog' 'exemplifies the

[5] *Spectator* xlviii, 26 June 1875, 825–6.
[6] *Spectator* xlix, 22 Jul. 1876, 922–3.
[7] li, 5 Oct. 1878, 1243–4.
[8] *Spectator* lii, 15 Feb. 1879, 210–11. As one of many examples, compare Robert Bell's review of *Vanity Fair*, *Fraser's Magazine* xxxviii, Sept. 1848, 320–33, with its comments on 'this pestiferous region . . . this stifling malaria': *Thackeray: the Critical Heritage*, p. 65.
[9] *Spectator* review of *The Way We Live Now*.
[10] Review of *Eustace Diamonds*, no. 2348, 26 Oct, 1872, 527–8 [Collyer].

legitimate use of a good realistic description' in the presentation of 'the tragedy of common life', because Trollope's 'resolute adherence to plain matter of fact brings out the tragic element with unusual felicity . . . The directness and verisimilitude of his manner, and the absence of any attempt at fine writing, enable him to be far more really pathetic than the professed dealers in this kind of sentiment.'[11] Besides, says the *Saturday* elsewhere, plain statement of an 'obnoxious thing' reaches many people 'whom anything like acrimony repels',[12] even though a good and unmistakable moral may turn out to have been 'taught at some cost to the reader's finer sensibilities'.[13] Meredith Townsend still finds *The Way We Live Now* immoral as well as repulsive, although he concedes Trollope's skill: 'for Mr. Trollope intended us to hate the greedy race he portrays, and we do hate them . . .'[14]

As we have already seen, the dominant opinion is that when excessive realism is not simply boring (as the *Spectator* finds it in *The Belton Estate*), it is truly repulsive, as the *Saturday* considers it in the same novel,[15] and most critics attribute Trollope's detailed interest in 'unsuitable' subject-matter to a failure of imagination on his part. The *Saturday* supposes that Trollope introduces Lady Desmond's love for her daughter's suitor into *Castle Richmond* because he is

desperately sick of inventing a new exquisitely attractive girl every year, and devising a distinct piece of lovemaking for her. It is intelligible enough that under such pressure the mind should be compelled to turn to monstrosities but such expedients are unpleasant to the reader and cannot be justified by any principle of artistic propriety.[16]

The Prime Minister, the same paper claims, displays the author's 'want of imagination' and failure of 'independent invention'.[17]

At the same time, as Stang and Graham point out at length,[18] and as is further illustrated here in chapter 4, Trollope and his contemporaries all advocated 'truth to life' as one of the highest qualities

---

[11] Review of *Editor's Tales*, xxx, 13 Aug. 1870, 211–12.

[12] Review of *Miss Mackenzie*, xix, 4 Mar. 1865, 263–5.

[13] Review of *Eustace Diamonds*, *Saturday Review* xxxiv, 16 Nov. 1872, 637–8.

[14] Review in the *Spectator*.

[15] *Spectator* xxxix, 27 Jan. 1866, 103, and *Saturday Review* xxi, 3 Feb. 1866, 140–2. See pp. 55–6 above.

[16] ix, 19 May 1860, 643–4.

[17] xlii, 14 Oct. 1876, 481–2.

[18] Stang, R., *The Theory of the Novel in England 1850–1870*, chatper 4; K. Graham, *English Criticism of the Novel 1865–1900*, Oxford University Press, 1965, chapter 2.

fiction could achieve, and the *Saturday Review* went so far as to talk of the writer's 'contract' with his reader to create and maintain the illusion of reality in his novel.[19] Two of the critics' fundamental demands—for perfect morality and for perfect truth to life—thus naturally contradict each other on many occasions, especially when the subject-matter is ethically dubious to the mid-Victorian mind.

But the moral qualities which Trollope's contemporaries found in a work of fiction did not depend upon the subject-matter alone, but on the way it was arranged and presented as well.[20] The present chapter will explore some of the devices Trollope's critics advocated as an escape from the dilemma of the recognized need to portray vice in fiction.

The depiction of vice

'Vice, for vice is necessary to be shown, should always disgust', wrote Dr Johnson in a *Rambler* essay on modern fiction.[21] Trollope's contemporaries were equally convinced of the writer's duty to make vice repellent, and quite often attacked Trollope for failing to distinguish clearly enough between his good and bad characters. From the terms in which they frame their objections, they can be seen to stand in the same position as Samuel Johnson on the question of moral teaching in the novel, and how it should be effected. A closer examination of this *Rambler* essay demonstrates the continuity of the tradition of thought involved.

Johnson's underlying assumption—like that of Trollope and his contemporaries—is that fiction is the imitation of human nature, by the presentation of individual characters. He begins by defining the fiction he is speaking about, and differentiating it from 'heroick romance':

> The works of fiction, with which the present generation seems more particularly delighted, are such as exhibit life in its true state, diversified only by accidents that daily happen in the world, and influenced by passions and qualities which are really to be found in conversing with mankind. . . . Its province is to bring about natural events by easy means, and to keep up curiosity without

[19] v, 12 June 1858, 618–19.

[20] In *The Theory of the Novel*, Professor Stang deals in detail with the problem of 'the cheek of the young person', in his fifth chapter, so that the subject of straightforward prudery is largely ignored here. Professor Stang implies that certain subjects were universally objectionable to most critics, but this is not borne out by a study of Trollope's reviewers, who are more concerned with treatment than subject. Hence the value of using Trollope as a touchstone of opinion, since he was less obviously objectionable than, say, Meredith, and the attacks on him are therefore less direct.

[21] No. 4, 31 Mar. 1750; quoted from 11th edition, 1789, i, 18–24.

the help of wonder. . . . [I]t requires . . . that experience which
. . . must arise from general converse and accurate observation of
the living world.

This realism Johnson prefers to the 'wild strain of imagination' and
the 'incredibilities' of romance, but he points out the dangers to
which it exposes the writer by way of criticism from the 'common
reader', who knows 'the original' of the picture, as well as did the
shoemaker who censured the slipper of the Venus of Appelles.

Having first put forward his demand for realism, which in one
form or another runs through most of his criticism, Johnson goes on
to a second of his essential principles—that of moral purpose—it
being the intention of *Rambler* no. 4 to reconcile these two demands
in the case of modern prose fiction. But the tension between the two
ideals remains, and it is one of the central difficulties in his criticism
as a whole.[22] His moral demands are extreme in this particular essay,
because—like mid-Victorian critics of the novel—he considers the
literature he is discussing as 'written chiefly to the young, the ignorant,
and the idle, to whom they serve as lectures on conduct, and introduc-
tions into life'. (One is inevitably reminded by this last clause, on the
education of the young, of chapter 12 of Trollope's *Autobiography*,
'On novels and the art of writing them', where he maintains that it
is from novels that the young learn grace, propriety, honour and
manliness.)[23]

'In the romances formerly written', says Johnson, 'every transac-
tion and sentiment was so remote from what passes among men, that
the reader was in very little danger of making application to himself'.
So the morality of such literature was a matter of small importance.
These romances could teach neither virtue nor vice. But the newer
fiction can do either, since the attention of the reader is inevitably
attracted by 'an adventurer . . . levelled with the rest of the world'.
Fiction must therefore not only avoid corrupting the reader, but make
positive use of the power it has of instilling 'the knowledge of vice and
virtue' more compellingly than can be done by 'the solemnities of
professed morality'.[24] And this is to be done through the judicious
selection of subject-matter, as Johnson explains in an argument which
reappears a hundred times in the writings of Trollope's contemporaries:

> The chief advantage which these fictions have over real life is,
> that their authors are at liberty, though not to invent, yet to select

[22] See R. Wellek, *A History of Modern Criticism*, Cape, 1955, i, 82.
[23] This aspect of Trollope's thinking on the novel is summarized by
B. A. Booth in his 'Trollope on the novel', in *Essays Critical and Historical
Dedicated to Lily B. Campbell*, University of California Press, 1950.
[24] Compare for example *Autobiography*, pp. 220–1.

objects, and to cull from the mass of mankind, those individuals
upon which the attention ought most to be employed. . . . It is justly
considered as the greatest excellency of art, to imitate nature; but
it is necessary to distinguish those parts of nature, which are most
proper for imitation: the greater care is still required in representing life, which is so often discoloured by passion, or deformed by
wickedness. If the world be promiscuously described, I cannot see
of what use it can be to read the account: or why it may not be as
safe to turn the eye immediately upon mankind as upon a mirrour
which shews all that presents itself without discrimination.

It is therefore no sufficient vindication of a character, that it is
drawn as it appears, for many characters ought never to be drawn;
nor of a narrative, that the train of events is agreeable to observation and experience . . . The purpose of these writings is surely . . .
to initiate youth by mock encounters in the art of necessary defence,
and to encrease prudence without impairing virtue.

Johnson's argument unfortunately leads him to praise the quality
of moral insipidity in fiction, as critics in the same dilemma were still
to do a century later. It also causes Johnson to disapprove of the
sympathetic portrayal of what the *Saturday Review* was to call 'types
of mixed character, neither good nor bad',[25] such as Lady Mason,
who was one of many Trollope felt himself compelled to defend in
authorial apologies in different novels throughout his career. 'Many
writers,' Johnson says, 'for the sake of following nature, so mingle
good and bad qualities in their principal personages . . . that we lose
the abhorrence of their faults, because they do not hinder our pleasure,
or, perhaps, regard them with some kindness for being united with so
much merit.'

There is clearly a very close parallel in detail between these
judgments of Johnson's, and the corresponding pronouncements of
Trollope's contemporaries. Both the eighteenth- and the nineteenth-
century arguments involve themselves in the same conflict between
their fundamental demands of fidelity to nature and of morality, and
both try to extricate themselves from this uncomfortable position
by positing the correct selection of subject-matter as the guiding
principle. So it comes about that the rather uncertain dividing line
between moral and immoral realism is intended to cut 'selected' and
arranged pictures of reality off from something the critics assumed
to be possible—that promiscuous mirroring of the world, to which
Johnson so vehemently objected.

The complaints of the critics about Trollope's moral irresponsibility
in not selecting his fictional material properly, are heard throughout
his career from the *Macdermots* onwards. But the failing is felt to be
most vicious in the cases of *He Knew He Was Right*, *The Eustace*

[25] Review of *Orley Farm*, xiv, 11 Oct. 1862, 444–5.

Diamonds, The Way We Live Now, The Prime Minister and *Is He Popenjoy?* As we have seen, the *Saturday* finds *He Knew He Was Right* perfectly accurate as regards its subject-matter, but thinks its 'extreme realism' overdone, because of Trollope's supposed failure to select his characters and events at all.[26] The *Spectator* puts the case for selection in its attack on *Is He Popenjoy?*: 'In order to produce a true picture, men and women with low worldly aims or vicious propensities must be represented, to some extent as they are, but the artist has the choice of his materials; . . . he can invigorate us instead of depressing us by his representation of life.' For its part the *British Quarterly Review* claims that *He Knew He Was Right* is unpleasant 'to pure-minded readers', because it typifies the 'morbid infatuation of modern novelists for plots and stories turning upon conjugal infidelity', so that it is to be hoped that Trollope may 'be preserved from the fascination of French romance '.[27]

What the *Spectator* praises in explicit preference to the horrors of *The Way We Live Now*, is the 'simple and great' fictional action of *An Eye for an Eye*, in which 'the guilt, the grief, and the crime all have their roots in the natural instincts of man'. But of course *An Eye for an Eye*, although a story of seduction, murder and insanity, was an Irish peasant novel, and as such was automatically distanced somewhat from a London reviewer. The writer was allowed greater freedom in presenting 'mastering passion'[28] or coarse humour, than he was in a middle- or upper-class English context, where in any case, as Hutton points out, education taught people to conceal their passions, so that the novelist was compelled to portray his characters' feelings indirectly.[29]

Much, of course, could be done with dubious material by tactful treatment. The *Spectator*, reviewing *Cousin Henry* in 1879,[30] regards Trollope as distinctly dated by this time, but points out that he has generally dealt with the most sensational subject-matter in such a way that it has lost its alarming character, and—to this consciously modern critic, at least—much of its interest too, owing to the calmness and perfect control with which the author relates it:

> There may be . . . as many murders, forgeries, abductions, found-
> lings, missing wills, in Mr. Trollope's novels as in any others;

[26] See p. 43 above.
[27] Reviews of *He Knew He Was Right*, 1, Jul. 1869, 263–4; and *Last Chronicle* and *Lotta Schmidt and Other Stories*, xlvi, Oct. 1867, 557–60, resp. The *British Quarterly Review* was 'the organ of the Nonconformists', aimed especially at Congregationalists and Baptists; see F. R. Oliphant and M. Oliphant, *The Victorian Age of English Literature*, ii, 302.
[28] *Spectator* review of *An Eye for an Eye*.
[29] See 'Trollope as a society-novelist', in chapter 5 below.
[30] lii, 18 Oct. 1879, 1319–21.

but they are not told about in a manner to alarm us, we accept them quite philosophically . . . Not only does he never offend the modesty of nature,—he encourages her to be prudish . . . His touch is eminently civilising; everything, from the episodes to the sentences, moves without hitch or creak . . .

As the *Saturday Review* puts it, 'there is no depth of vulgarity . . . that may not be overcome by a refined and searching perception of the most significant truth'.[31] And the *Saturday* can even consider that Trollope's treatment of the delicate subject of bigamy in *John Caldigate* has been successful in producing a fine work of art, while still feeling 'how little wholesome are the subject and its treatment for the classes who constitute the body of novel readers', especially since there is no poetic justice at the end.[32] Some subjects, on the other hand, are so unpleasant that certain critics believe that no amount of delicacy in their handling can make them fit to read about. Of Lady Desmond in *Castle Richmond*, for example, Geraldine Jewsbury says that 'not even the very gentlemanlike tone and manner in which the author speaks of her . . . can avail to mitigate the contempt and indignation she inspires'.[33]

Moral proportion

It was more or less universally agreed among Trollope's reviewers that there should be a distribution of virtues and vices in any novel —that the evil which must necessarily be shown should at least be counterbalanced by goodness. There were various ways in which this could be achieved, of which the most obvious was to make some characters the representatives of virtue and others of vice, since, as the *Saturday* explains when objecting to the universal sordidness of the persons in *The Way We Live Now*, evil should be 'balanced by its contraries. Benevolence, frankness, simplicity, uprightness should have their representatives, or how are our compassion and indignation to be aroused?'[34] Meredith Townsend in the *Spectator* agrees that *every* character except Roger Carbury is utterly mercenary: 'There is no relief, no pleasantness, the subordinate characters even being disagreeable'. Conversely, if the persons in a novel should be predominantly good, it is considered advisable to have objectionable people as well, as 'a foil'.[35] But the critics' complaints are usually of the lack of anything 'to relieve the dead-level sordidness of the story', when there is no foil to such a character as Lady Eustace.[36]

[31] Review of *Prime Minister*.   [32] xlviii, 16 Aug. 1879, 216–17.
[33] *Athenaeum* no. 1699, 19 May 1860, 681.
[34] xl, 17 Jul. 1875, 88–9.
[35] *Saturday Review* notice of *Miss Mackenzie*.
[36] See Meredith Townsend's review of *Eustace Diamonds* in the *Spectator*.

The critics do not protest in this manner simply because they cannot find a character in a given novel pleasant enough to be an 'acquaintance'—although Townsend and others do complain on this score[37]—or respectable enough to excite 'a pleasurable interest'.[38] Rather, the reviewers are anxious lest the author—and consequently the reader—should lose all sense of what the characters' moral failings mean, especially since Trollope is admitted to lack George Eliot's power of 'moral discrimination'.[39] *The Way We Live Now*, for example, fails in Victorian eyes as satire, because it 'loses all force by its indiscriminate onslaught'.[40] The average critic, in short, wants something to maintain his faith in human nature, and 'a good fiction should offer us some point of stability, something for us to trust'.[41]

It is Richard Holt Hutton who gives the most coherent and deliberate account of this critical need for moral stability. He goes further than his contemporaries, and proposes that the artistic essence of literature is a moral quality. Hence for him moral proportion is not only an ethical imperative but also a fundamental precondition for literature. The basis of his argument is the unity he (like Carlyle) would see between theology and literature.[42] Regarding literature as an essentially moral activity, he saw that it must display both the positives and negatives of human existence, so as to show the connection between mankind and God. The best books, he said, were those which revealed man's 'awestruck recognition of the heavens above and the hell beneath him'.[43] The idea to which G. H. Lewes among others subscribed, that an artist was greater 'for entirely ignoring all moral partialities', was one Hutton constantly attacked. He saw it as not only mistaken, but vicious too, since it could be used to excuse what he regarded as irreligion in literature. He went further, and denied that it was possible to imitate character at all—the basis of literature for him—without marking the moral characteristics of the persons depicted, since portraiture was impossible without what

[37] e.g. his review of *The Way We Live Now* in the *Spectator*.

[38] *Spectator* review of *Is He Popenjoy?*

[39] Meredith Townsend on the *Eustace Diamonds*.

[40] Review in the *Saturday*. For an account of the difficulties facing a satirist in the period, see C. C. Loomis, 'Thackeray and the plight of the Victorian satirist', *English Studies* xlix, Feb. 1968, 1–19.

[41] Review of *The Bertrams*, *Bentley's Quarterly Review* i, 1859, 456–462.

[42] See A. K. Stevens, 'Richard Holt Hutton: Theologian and Critic', unpublished PhD thesis, University of Michigan, 1949, pp. 181–5. Compare Carlyle's 'Characteristics' (1831): 'Literature is but a branch of Religion, and always participates in its character: however, in our time, it is the only branch that still shows any greenness . . .', *Collected Works of Thomas Carlyle*, 16 vols, 1864, iv, 18.

[43] 'The various uses of books', *Spectator* lix, 16 Jan. 1886, 77–8.

he called 'moral perspective'.[44] Without 'light' and 'shadows' in the set of persons in a work, the characters would inevitably suffer from a want of 'outline', a shortcoming the *Spectator* notices in at least two of Trollope's heroines, Alice Vavasor and Miss Mackenzie.[45] For Hutton, then, 'moral proportion' is imperative,[46] for without it moral characterization fails, and thus even truth to nature (that is human nature) is threatened. So the expression 'the realistic morality of the tale' has a definite meaning in Hutton's terms,[47] indicating the presence of 'moral graduation' in a work. 'Outline', runs Hutton's most quoted dictum, 'is a result of comparison,—moral outline of moral comparison. You cannot compare without an implied standard'.[48] And it is this standard that must somehow be embodied in the work of art.

The key issue is therefore that good qualities should be portrayed somewhere, or indicated somehow, and that no work of art should be based entirely on moral negatives—a view Hutton shared with his colleague Townsend, and with most of his other contemporaries. After all, the *Spectator* conceded that Trollope inspired hatred in the reader for the characters of *The Way We Live Now*, and 'contempt' for those of *Is He Popenjoy?*: 'No doubt this is a feeling which a novelist may call forth legitimately enough', says the reviewer of the latter. But the demand for moral 'relief' still stands, together with a preference for stories in which 'human nature performs its part with credit'.[49]

[44] 'Goethe and his influence', *Essays Theological and Literary*, 2 vols, 1871, ii, 45.
[45] Reviews of *Can You Forgive Her?* and *Miss Mackenzie*, respectively, xxxviii, 9 Sept. 1865, 978-9, and 4 Mar. 1865, 244-5.
[46] 'Goethe and his influence', p. 46.
[47] *Spectator* review of *He Knew He Was Right*, xlii, 12 June 1869, 706-8. See p. 44 above.
[48] 'Goethe and his influence', p. 47. Compare George Brimley's comments in his review of *Esmond*, on Thackeray's 'moral antithesis of actual and ideal . . . which reflects so well the contradictory consciousness of man as a being, with senses and passions and limited knowledge, yet with a conscience and a reason speaking to him of eternal laws and a moral order of the universe. . . . He could not have painted Vanity Fair as he has, unless Eden had been shining brightly in his inner eyes.'—*Spectator* xxv, 6 Nov. 1852, 1066-7; reprinted in his *Essays by the late George Brimley*, *M.A.*, ed. W. G. Clark, 1860. See also p. 102n of Septimus Berdmore's 'Thackeray', in his *A Scratch Team of Essays*, 1883, repr. from *Westminster* of 1864; and (even) G. H. Lewes, on moral contrasts in art—*Thackeray: the Critical Heritage*, p. 46.
It is curious to see T. H. S. Escott rather absurdly applying a similar maxim to explain the need for characters of various social classes in a novel, on the grounds that 'without contrast there can be no artistic effect'— 'Political novels', *Frazer's Magazine* (ns) ix, Apr. 1874, 520-36, p. 521.
[49] Review of *Lady Anna*, *Saturday Review* xxxvii, 9 May 1874, 598-9.

Hutton's position on the depiction of evil in fiction is expressed in his article 'The Hard Church Novel' in the *National Review* of July 1856,[50] where, obeying the perpetual tendency of his mind, he bases his argument in his theological beliefs, and his presumption that literature should present 'living images . . . in relation to the one life in which they were made', so as to draw men 'with full insight into *man*'. From this religious assumption he deduces the principles shared by nearly all his contemporaries, and condemns literature in which 'human evil is pictured without the consciousness that it is also human *degradation*', or where there is no moral or religious significance given to an artist's 'insight into what man *is*, and *men might be*'.[51] Hutton's theological explanation is very personal, but since he was systematizing what was already the practice and prejudice of his age, his account of the artist's conventional ways out of the dilemma of having to portray vice, remains enlightening.[52]

What he insists, then, is that the artist portray vice in such a way as to give the reader confidence in a 'moral standard of character', while aspiring at the same time to the high aim of relating human character to the eternal image of God.[53] The first way in which Hutton proposes that these things be effected is by contrasts between different characters in a work of literature, to produce the necessary 'moral perspective' and 'contrasts', as the means of achieving 'moral outline' by 'moral comparison'. He goes, however, far beyond those critics who merely demand characters to sympathize with, as the representatives of virtue, in order that their 'compassion and indignation' may be aroused: for behind these less well formulated criticisms—and perhaps behind Hutton's too, but more deeply hidden—there lies the critic's fear of being persuaded to identify with a character of which he cannot approve morally; so that he must be given a 'good' person to involve himself in, in order to avoid 'the possibility of contamination' from such characters as are not 'what gentlemen and Christians should be'.[54] Hutton, for his part, proposes that the artist who presents characters singly—one by one—can never produce fully

[50] iii, 127–46, repr. as part of his 'The Hard Church' in *Essays Theological and Literary*—see R. H. Tener, 'R. H. Hutton's *Essays Theological and Literary*: a Bibliographical Note', *Notes and Queries* ccv, 1960, 185–7.

[51] Hutton's italics.

[52] At least one reviewer of Hutton's *Essays*, however, objects to his 'inclination to regard literary phenomena as the results of theological opinions', but concedes that even when wrong, 'his careful statement of the results of much thought not only enables us to appreciate an antagonistic view, but also helps us to clear up our own opinions . . .' (a remark which remains true today)—*Athenaeum* no. 2276, 10 June, 713–15 [Jackson].

[53] 'The Hard Church Novel'; see also 'Goethe and his influence', pp. 45–8.

[54] Review of *Orley Farm, National Review* xvi, Jan. 1863, 27–40.

satisfactory literature, because he should be working on groups of persons instead. Only thus can the writer attain to a 'delineation of men drawn from full insight into *man*'; while in this way he can hopefully manage to counter 'the tendency of literature without theology to lose all trace of unity, and break up into numberless accidental forms of discoloured humanity'.[55]

Although he constantly regretted Trollope's apparent inability to penetrate to the depths of human nature, Hutton could not feel, ideally, that any individual character should be presented with only scant reference outside, however 'deep' the portrayal. Consequently, while noting Trollope's weaknesses, he naturally applauded the author's insights into interpersonal psychology, and his use of, as it were, an interpersonal method of characterization. Goethe, on the other hand, despite his deep insight into individual character, 'had no moral graduation for his groups,—no natural admirations which gave a unity to the whole and determined the line of the shadows', because of 'the microscopic nature of his insight, which only travelled very slowly over a large surface of life', missing the significance of macrophenomena in its attention to minutiae. Just as it was the constant compulsion of Hutton's mind to attempt to unify all thought into one theologically based system, so was it his horror to see any lack of unity in thought or art at all, such that the presentation of 'truth' should 'break up', become 'discontinuous' or 'inorganic',[56] or 'grope' and become 'dissolved', and so lack the 'grace of form';[57] and his desire for 'grouping' is one consequence of this holistic set of mind.

The presentation of fictional people in sets, as opposed to piecemeal characterization, could also be the means of operating poetic justice without resort to that 'inartistic divinity', the *deus ex machina*. The 'respectable god of social justice' could do his work instead,[58] and the writer's moral assessment of his characters could be shown by the way he made them regard and treat each other with varying degrees of approval and disapproval, according to their positions on the scale of virtue. But of course, these procedures would be impossible to an artist suffering from the moral myopia Hutton diagnoses in the case of Goethe.

Dr Johnson, too, connects interpersonal attitudes within a work, and the operation of poetic justice without theotechny, into a whole scheme of purposeful allocation of virtues and vices. One of Shakespeare's

[55] 'The Hard Church Novel'.
[56] *Ibid.*
[57] 'Goethe and his influence', p. 47.
[58] Both quotations from the *Saturday*'s notice of *The Claverings*, xxiii, 18 May 1867, 638–9.

failings, he says in his *Preface to Shakespeare*, is that he 'makes no just distribution of good or evil, nor is always careful to shew in the virtuous a disapprobation of the wicked; he carries his persons indifferently through right and wrong . . . and leaves their examples to operate by chance'.[59]

Hutton, however, is subtler than this, since he recognizes another means of moral proportioning. In some of Goethe's work, for example, where in his opinion moral oppositions or distinctions among persons are lacking, what is required is 'some dim picture in the minds of Werther, Meister, Tasso, and Faust of what they *would* be,—what it is possible would lift them out of the imbecility of their purposeless career'; and if this were supplied, other foils might be unnecessary. Hutton's view of Shakespeare therefore conflicts with Johnson's. 'Shakespeare', he says, 'frequently gives no foil to the character whose weakness he is delineating; but he always gives it some clear vision of the nobleness and the strength above it. Hamlet knows what he could do and dare not. Lady Macbeth knows what she should do, and will not. Antony knows what he would do, and cannot.'[60] Hutton's chief weakness in the foregoing argument was his fundamental assumption that the system of religion and morality to which he subscribed was universally valid. Indeed, as we shall see, his best-known criticism was part of a lifelong effort to protect his values from erosion in society by agnostic materialism.

To Hutton, the artistic consequences of moral failure are grave. If an author does not display his 'moral predilections' in his 'conception' of character, the 'picture becomes feeble, watery, wavering',[61] as in the case of such a 'misty' character as Trollope's Alice Vavasor, whose nature is 'morbid' because of its lack of moral definition.[62] (A 'morbid nature', Hutton explains elsewhere, is one so occupied in self as not to understand the connection between its own human suffering and that of Christ, or of martyrdom.)[63] So what is needed is a point of moral reference within the character, in the form of conscience, instinct, or internal conflict, or some incontrovertible virtue.

'The Eustace Diamonds'

The grounds of the *Spectator*'s attack on *The Eustace Diamonds* are now fully explained by Hutton's analysis. If the article is not his (and the violence of its language anticipates Townsend's notice of *The*

---

[59] *Johnson on Shakespeare*, ed. W. Raleigh, 1908, Oxford University Press (repr. 1949), p. 21.
[60] 'Goethe and his influence', p. 48.
[61] *Ibid.*
[62] *Spectator* review of *Can You Forgive Her?*
[63] Intro. to J. Hinton, *The Mystery of Pain*, 1911 edn, pp. xxv–xxvi.

Way We Live Now, and is less reminiscent of the reviews of Trollope known to be Hutton's), it fits into his whole scheme of thought. It also illuminates from the moral side his demand for characterization in 'depth', examined in chapter 5.

Comparing Lizzie Eustace and Becky Sharp, much to the disadvantage of the former, the *Spectator* says:

> Lady Eustace, though she is never guilty of murder, as Becky Sharp certainly is, is a much meaner and more contemptible creature than Becky. She is far less enterprising, far more cowardly, equally selfish, less capable of a disinterested regard such as Becky certainly feels at the end of *Vanity Fair* for Amelia, and more wholly false, more utterly incapable of discriminating between truth and falsehood in herself. . . . Lizzie Eustace is too utterly false to understand where falsehood begins,—when she is using it deliberately as a means, and when she is toying with it out of mere inability to be true. She is a liar by nature, not by policy.

Hence the critic comes to the curious conclusion that voluntary wickedness is to be preferred to involuntary wickedness, on the grounds that it implies at least a consciousness of some standard of goodness. (His preference is surely to be understood as pertaining to the realm of art, and not life.)

> There is [says the reviewer] something, in its way, grand about Becky's evil. She is wicked and cruel by free choice. Lizzie Eustace is wicked by the law of a mean, and cunning, and greedy nature, with no power in it to do otherwise. Indeed, throughout the long story of her craft and meanness, we do not remember a single occasion on which Mr. Trollope suggests that there was even a glimpse on her part of a better and a worse, or the faintest possible struggle to choose the former. Yet with a will so lost in temptation as hers, one wants, at least for the purposes of Art, the consciousness of evil and the struggle against it, however faint, to relieve the oppressive sordidness of the story.

While the least intelligent mid-Victorian critics prefer 'pure' embodiments of virtues and vices, we find the *Spectator* advocating 'mixed characters' for the sake of a kind of Protestant morality in literature, whereby salvation should be able to come from within. Trollope usually broadly agrees with the Hutton view, on the grounds that 'mixed characters' are true to life, and so serve to point a moral better than 'simple, single' characters, as he calls the others in *The Eustace Diamonds*.[64] 'The true picture of life as it is', he says in this connection, '. . . would show men what they are, and how they might rise, not, indeed, to perfection, but one step first, and then another

[64] *Eustace Diamonds*, 1950 (The Oxford Trollope), i, 163.

on the ladder.'[65] This apology for his unheroic hero, Frank Greystock, displays Trollope's perpetual concern with dilemmas of social morality, so often expressed—as in this case—by his characters' internal debates on their own conduct.

On the other hand, he explicitly states that Lizzie is *intended* to be a single character,[66] and throughout *The Eustace Diamonds* he derives much of his interest and a great deal of his humour from her lack of self-awareness and the consequent contradictions in her behaviour. What the *Spectator* is objecting to is in fact central to Trollope's whole method in the book. For example, her conduct towards Frank is determined by the fact that she is 'heartless', but 'probably thought that an over-amount of heart was the malady under which she specially suffered'.[67] Similarly, after learning some eight or nine lines from near the beginning of 'Queen Mab', she really believes she has read and absorbed the whole work, 'and when, in after days, she spoke of it as a thing of beauty that she had made her own by long study, she actually did not know that she was lying'.[68] The modern reader would not dream of sacrificing the psychological interest of this self-deceit, nor its humorous consequences, for the sake of any moral teaching, however perfect; and cannot see, either, why the narrator's constant revelation of Lizzie's worthlessness should not suffice to protect even the Victorian young lady from emulating her.

Lizzie, then, is intentionally a 'superficial' character, lacking in self-knowledge and sense of identity—unlike Lucy Morris who, although a 'most unselfish little creature', nevertheless 'had a well-formed idea of her own identity'.[69] Thus the *Spectator* is attacking the very foundation of the novel by saying that 'a writer with more of a taste for *inward* portraiture of character than Mr. Trollope, would have found some means to relieve the ignoble tone of the picture by something better than beauty and wealth'. As is frequent in the reviews of this period, the critic reacts to certain indisputably important qualities in the novel, but puts a questionable construction on them, because of his need to judge them morally. This is clearly a case in which Trollope's fiction was written in fundamental opposition to the proclaimed standards of at least one important section of opinion of the age, and not even the explanations of his method that we have found embedded in the novel could reconcile the *Spectator* to it. Hutton's scheme of thought was largely self-consistent on the question of literary morality, but it could not accommodate a *Eustace Diamonds* at all. To him, all fiction had to partake to some extent

---

[65] *Eustace Diamonds*, 1950 (The Oxford Trollope), i, 230; see also ii, 329–30.
[66] i, 163.   [67] i, 241.   [68] i, 198.   [69] i, 24.

of the qualities of theodicy, and, if not explicitly 'justify the ways of God to men', at least it should set evil in a large enough religious context to *suggest* a vindication of the divine attributes of goodness and justice.

Grandeur and idealization

Running right through mid-Victorian criticism (including the *Spectator* review of *The Eustace Diamonds*) there is a vein of thought which unwittingly contradicts the main tenets of Hutton's literary morality—that is an approval of grandeur in literary villains, and a desire that evil, when presented, should be on a really large scale. This Byronic streak in criticism is part of a general love of 'grandeur' and amplitude in art, and belongs to the same set of artistic standards as the demand for 'elevation' and 'idealization'. It is the other side of the same coin as the concern with perfect chivalry, for example, and was one expression of the fear lest the now dominant literary form—prose fiction based on modern life—should be unable to satisfy society's spiritual needs, because of its dependence on 'truth to life'.[70] The idea of the grand villain—surely a Romantic legacy—offered an escape from what otherwise appeared a serious failing of distinction in literature, and a consequent decline into cultural nonentity.

The admiration for grand evil-doers is frequently expressed, although the rationalization of the taste can be exceedingly unconvincing. 'Great villains', says the *Saturday Review* credibly enough, when disapproving of Cousin Henry, 'have always and necessarily, some qualities which are admirable in their own nature, though not in their application of them'.[71] But the same paper is less convincing when it becomes more circumstantial, as it does in its discussion of the character of Melmotte in *The Way We Live Now*:

> His hero is a swindler, and by his audacity and the magnitude of his operations, rises almost into respectability out of the base level of meaner worthlessness . . . His is a life of fraud demanding such constant vigilance, such habits of self-control, such foresight and preparation, such self-reliance and courage, that it is almost great. It is impossible not to sympathize in a degree with a struggle so manfully maintained; not to appreciate the power implied in bearing singly the weight of a terrible secret, the strength of endurance that dispenses with help, whatever the extremity, asks no counsel,

[70] In his *British Novelists and their Styles*, Masson feared that the novel was suffering 'a serious contraction of its capabilities', and being converted into a mere 'love and marriage story' (p. 294). He quotes Baron Bunsen's wish for an epic in novel form, 'a new Iliad or Odyssey' (pp. 2-3 and 6-7).

[71] xlviii, 25 Oct. 1879, 515-16. In *Rambler* no. 4, Johnson specially disapproves of such characters, as making vice alluring.

and can live alone. The dramatist or the novelist finds in the per-
version of strong qualities material worthy of his genius.

This over-solicitous apology shows the critic to acquiesce in the social
system the novel is attacking. He is prepared to accept a Melmotte
figure as respectable, just as, Trollope is complaining, society is.
Inevitably the reader retains the idea that this critic has confirmed
the important message of the novel—that the 'virtues' of speculative
capitalism are basically immoral. Irrelevantly the *Saturday* now
continues its statement on Melmotte by asserting that 'a character
of this sort should be balanced by its contraries'—a view which has
no necessary connection with the admiration previously expressed,
and has the air of a standard arbitrarily imposed in order to bring
the criticism into line with a sterner morality.

In the *Spectator*'s review of *The Eustace Diamonds*, just as great an
effort of rationalization can be seen in the critic's apology for Becky
Sharp:

> It is hardly possible not to feel it on the cards even to the last
> that her character might under certain circumstances assert its
> power, and break through that labyrinth of intrigues in the con-
> struction of which it has delighted. . . . There is something, in its
> way, grand about Becky's evil.

> [T]here is at least a sufficiently pure embodiment of iniquity to
> satisfy the artistic instinct. . . . If you can create a man or woman
> *above* conscience, the picture has, at least, a grandeur of its own.

In contrast, Lizzie is 'without a capacity even for any hatred rising
above the level of spite'. The main fault in the novel, the reviewer
concludes, is total sordidness, because even 'evil itself is not on a
grand scale'.[72]

The critical demand for a basis of moral security within a work of
art undoubtedly stems from anxiety about change in all areas of life,
and specially the fear that civilization might be undermined by both
philosophical and social materialism. Coupled with this demand, the
apparently contradictory acceptance of great, Byronic villainy, suggests a dread of lapsing into fruitless greyness—into the wasteland,
from which even the depiction of evil could save them, if on a grand

---

[72] Compare the opinion of Wynton, a character in G. H. Lewes's early
novel, *Ranthorpe* (1847, written 1842). Wynton is explaining to Ranthorpe
why an 'unprincipled woman' is despicable: 'A demon, in our conception
the incarnation of malignity, is not so odious as the incarnation of egotism.
Malignity is respectable in comparison: there is force and energy in it . . .
and a power which extorts sympathy from us. . . . Satan is grand, terrible,
sublime; Iago is utterly despicable. Moloch is loveable in comparison with
Blifil' (p. 97).

enough scale.[73] The *Spectator*'s imagery of marsh, sewage-farm, fog and disease[74] exemplifies what alarmed the critics most, as opposed to the fresh air and blue heavens of the literature which, Frederick Greenwood said, the paper championed, and which was characterized by the 'sanity, sweetness, order, honesty of perfect health'.[75] The constant inclination of Hutton's mind, as we have seen, was to fight against all sorts of formlessness, dissolution and disintegration. In fact his efforts to embrace all thought in one theological system, represent a striving after unity, in the face of advancing scientific agnosticism.[76] Not that the polymath Hutton was alarmed at the increase in scientific knowledge as such, for he was rather a man of science himself, Professor of Mathematics at Bedford College, a founder member of the Metaphysical Society (the aim of which was to bridge the gap between religion and science),[77] and a writer who delighted to use scientific and mathematical imagery in his articles. Nevertheless he distrusted the developments taking place around him, and expressed his disquiet in a poem entitled 'The Roseg at Midnight', in which the glacier is seen as a relentlessly advancing blight, reducing life in its path to desert, and exemplifying

> . . . such dreams of fevered brain
> As wise men conjure now from sky and sod,—
> That Love shrinks back from Law's advancing reign,—
> That the Ice-sea of science threatens God.[78]

In an age obsessed with such fears, the Broad Church *Contemporary*

[73] Curtis Dahl, in his 'The Victorian wasteland', in *Victorian Literature*, ed. Austin Wright, N.Y., Oxford University Press (Galaxy Books), 1961, shows the wasteland in Victorian poetry often to have stood for spiritual desolation and uncertainty, through which strength of individual character could carry the search after truth. It is always the place of ignorance, sterility and doubt.

[74] p. 59 above. This imagery, and its contrary imagery of fresh air and health, is common to all mid-Victorian critics.

[75] Quoted by J. Hogben (anon), *Richard Holt Hutton of the Spectator*, Edinburgh 1899, p. 59.

[76] G. C. LeRoy, in his 'Richard Holt Hutton' (*PMLA* lvi, Sept. 1941, 809–40), shows Hutton in his role of opponent of materialism, who was trying to demonstrate how religious values could be maintained in the face of scientific progress; see in particular p. 811. Although it was Huxley who coined the terms 'agnostic' and 'agnosticism', it was apparently Hutton who first popularized them in a sub-leader entitled 'Pope Huxley', in the *Spectator* xliii, 29 Jan. 1870, 135–6. See R. H. Tener, 'Hutton and "Agnostic" ', *Notes and Queries* ccix, Nov. 1964, 429–31.

[77] See A. W. Brown, *The Metaphyisical Society. Victorian minds in crisis. 1869–1880*, New York, Columbia University Press, 1947; especially pp. 167–230, for the influence of the Society on journalism.

[78] *Holiday Rambles in Ordinary Places. By a Wife with her Husband*, 1877 [by R. H. Hutton]; repr. from *Spectator*, 1867–76.

Review (itself drawing many of its contributors from the Meta-physical Society)[79] welcomed the primacy of theology in Hutton's mind. It saw his all-embracing system of thought, and his conviction of 'the divine life . . . as the true centre of human life', as supremely important, because 'the balance of parties in Christendom has gradu-ally changed during the last few generations—the Church losing, and "Free Thought" gaining; so that by far the large proportion of intellectual activity now stands outside of Christianity in all the most civilized countries of Europe'.[80]

On the social plane the fear of breakdown or fragmentation remained intense throughout the period, and was common to thinkers of all creeds and parties. Harman Grisewood, surveying the analyses put forward by the many eminent contributors to *Ideas and Beliefs of the Victorians*,[81] summarizes the 'negative aspect' of Victorian social thinking as 'the weakening ties on the individual in his rela-tions with others (e.g. family, neighbours and employers) and the growing inadequacy of Victorian ideas to cope with major problems'. John Morley, for example, denounces England as that 'community where political forms . . . are mainly hollow shams disguising the coarse supremacy of wealth, where religion is mainly official and political, and is ever ready to dissever itself alike from the spirit of justice, the spirit of charity, and the spirit of truth . . .'[82] Ruskin, in an infernal vision, warns against 'a society in which every soul would be as the syllable of a stammerer instead of the word of a speaker, in which every man would walk as in a frightful dream, seeing spectres of himself, in everlasting multiplication, gliding help-lessly around him in speechless darkness'.[83]

This—like Morley's description of England—is the sort of vision Trollope projects in *The Way We Live Now*, that strange, impersonal desert, peopled by lifeless automata, wholly given over to money-making: a world such as that described by Ruskin again, in *The Crown of Wild Olive*—his vivid language contrasting strangely with Trollope's almost total lack of imagery—as 'that great foul city of London there,—rattling, growling, smoking, stinking,—a ghastly heap of fermenting brickwork, pouring out poison at every pore', where everybody is engaged in the grasping 'play' of making money,

[79] See Brown, *The Metaphysical Society*, chapter 9.

[80] Review of *Essays Theological and Literary*, xvi, Mar. 1871, 634–50, S[ophia] D. Collet (sgd). See also the anonymous review of the 2nd edition, xxix, Feb. 1877, 528–31.

[81] Harman Grisewood, ed., New York, Dutton, 1966.

[82] *Critical Miscellanies*, 1923, pp. 74–5; quoted by J. H. Buckley in his 'Victorianism', in *Victorian Literature*, ed. Wright, p. 6.

[83] *The Elements of Drawing*, Letter II § 133, in *Works*, ed. E. T. Cook and A. Wedderburn, 1903–12, xv, 117 (1st published 1857).

and yet more money.[84] (It is worth arguing that Trollope's vision was never taken as seriously as it deserved because his language lacked the pyrotechnic effects of a Ruskin or a Carlyle, or of a Dickens.)

In his exceedingly interesting article 'From Miss Austen to Mr. Trollope', Hutton remarked on the social stresses that were distorting human beings even in the comparatively calm world of Barsetshire,[85] while as early as 1859 *Bentley's Quarterly Review* had perceived in Trollope the theme of Victorian man become the victim of impersonal social forces:

> The individual's struggle with society is his theme, the characteristics which secure success and failure his study; and he prefers to draw man the creature of circumstances, led by temporary aims, rather than in that attitude of defying and controlling them, which constitutes the hero. Probably he would argue that it is thus human nature has shown itself to him, and that every course of action is moulded by events; but neverthless, a good fiction should offer us some point of stability, something for us to trust.[86]

This critique explains an apparent contradiction in Trollope's reception. If he was writing about a subject of such concern to the socially preoccupied among his contemporaries, it would seem strange that he should not have been acknowledged by any of them. One answer is undoubtedly that his image as the author of the Barsetshire Chronicles prevented the more advanced thinkers of the day from taking him seriously as a social critic. Yet another reason is that his readers did not find any moral, religious or philosophical 'point of stability' in his work. '[L]iterature', wrote John Morley in the tirade quoted above, 'does not as a rule permit itself to discuss serious subjects frankly and worthily',[87] and Collyer in his review of *Ralph the Heir*,[88] attacked Trollope for shortcomings in this direction, protesting that the public already knew

> that materialism in philosophy, religion, and politics has choked amongst the wealthy few the more spiritual values . . . that even

---

[84] Lecture I § 24. *Works*, xviii, 406 (1st published 1866). **In his reviews of** *Sesame and the Lilies* and *The Crown of Wild Olive*, it must be remembered, Trollope praised Ruskin as a stylist, and as the art critic who had taught a whole age to see. But he dismissed him as a 'prophet' or 'preacher', on the grounds that his words did not 'contain that innate, conspicuous wisdom which alone can make such preachings efficacious'—*Fortnightly Review* i, 15 Jul. 1865, 633–5, and v, 15 Jun. 1866, 381–4, respectively.

[85] *Spectator* lv, 16 Dec. 1882, 1609–11. In its review of *Can You Forgive Her?* vol. i, the *Westminster* praises Trollope's 'just appreciation of the manifold variety of influences which are brought to bear upon each unit in our closely-packed modern existence . . .'—(ns) xxviii, Jul. 1865, 284–5.

[86] Review of *The Bertrams, loc cit.*   [87] Quoted by Buckley, *op cit.*, p. 6.

[88] *Athenaeum* no. 2268, 15 Apr. 1871, 456.

> the aspirations of the struggling masses . . . are sordid and ignorant,
> based on a superficial estimate of true happiness and real dignity,
> and aiming at the dethronement not the consummation of humanity;

but he expressed grave doubts whether

> minute photographs of the existing state of things, unrelieved by
> imagination, unsanctified by the presence of any higher models,
> inanimate, prosaic, and petty, are likely to do any thing for the
> realization of the ugly features of our civilization, in the sense of
> inspiring any one to turn to more exalted aims in life and conduct.

Collyer wants some 'positive desiderata' to be 'more than hinted at',
and calls for a novelist who would build as well as pull to pieces,
'one who, in this age of criticism, would put some constructive poetic
energy into our literature'.

So Trollope's 'dead-level' realism (as his contemporaries judged
it), together with his apparently neutral style, led to his reviewers'
demands for 'idealization', for a novel that 'would do something for
us besides giving us these accurate likenesses of the common run
of those whom we see or know'.[89] There is a kind of prophetic side
to mid-Victorian criticism—or rather, a critical demand for a prophetic
genre of fiction—that no amount of effort in the Trollopian mode could
satisfy. Trollope remained a novelist who, though he could touch
accurately enough on the anxieties of his age, could not achieve true
greatness in its estimation, because it was outside his chosen scope
to propose remedies for the ills he diagnosed. He was descriptive while
his critics sought for prescription, and self-restrained as a social com-
mentator when they longed for a prophetic cry.

[89] Review of *Rachel Ray*, *Saturday Review* xvi, 24 Oct. 1863, 554–5.

4

MORAL AND SOCIAL ACCEPTABILITY

The critical tight-rope

The Victorian novelist had to tread a tight-rope of moral and social acceptability. On the one hand he risked offending against very strict but often imprecisely formulated canons of behaviour; on the other hand he might be overcautious, and fall into dullness and consequent popular failure. At the summit of his popularity Trollope successfully performed this feat of balance, having risen in public and critical esteem by hitting on the exact blend of raciness and propriety in *Barchester Towers* and *Framley Parsonage*. His, re-marked the *Saturday Review* in 1867, is the literature of 'the moral and respectable middle-class mind', and combines interest with moral unexceptionableness to the satisfaction of readers of all ages. 'The most careful mother need not make a pioneer excursion among Mr. Trollope's pages in quest of naughtiness forbidden to her daughters; and yet few young people, save of the very fast pattern, will call those pages slow . . .'[1]

The *Saturday* lays down a formula for success in writing about two important Victorian subjects—women and the Church. In it we recognize the same mixture of titillation and innocence which in *Miss Mackenzie* thrills the female Stumfoldians in their fashionable clergyman in Littlebath, when he refers familiarly to the saints as 'Peter' and 'Paul', and suggests that even he himself may have the failings universally attributed to humanity. 'In dealing with women and with the Church', says the *Saturday*,

> . . . a little wickedness and a little cynicism are expected of the novelist, but both must be duly watered with veneration and senti-ment. If the infusion is too strong, he loses caste; if it is too weak,

[1] Review of *Lotta Schmidt and Other Stories*, xxiv, 21 Sept. 1867, 381–2 see p. 22 above).

he loses readers. The proprieties must be observed, *ruat coelum*: and yet the most rigid sticklers for them do so love a little naughtiness. It is a great triumph to be able to gratify their tastes without incurring their displeasure; and that triumph has certainly been won by Mr. Trollope.[2]

As Trollope himself says in *Barchester Towers*, 'When we become dull we offend your intellect; and we must become dull or we should offend your taste.'[3]

The *Saturday* is professedly talking about the necessary conditions for popularity with ordinary novel-readers, and not for the esteem of critics; but it frequently applies similar dual standards itself, and presents the novelist with an almost insoluble dilemma. The tight-rope of propriety is nowhere more clearly seen than in the *Saturday*'s notice of *Tales of All Countries* (2nd series); and nowhere is Trollope more highly praised for his skill in treading it. In the story 'A Ride across Palestine', a young lady named Julia dresses herself as a man, calls herself Mr Smith, and rides across Palestine in the company of a gentleman who does not know the truth of her sex. The critic commends Trollope's handling of the scene in which her identity is revealed when they have reached their destination, and her companion (the narrator) has to admit that he is married: 'To let Julia's disappointment be seen, and yet to make her perfectly proper—to give the impression that she is sorry her days of being Mr. Smith are over, and yet that she has not involved herself too deeply—is a task which few artists could fulfil as Mr. Trollope has fulfilled it.'[4] Trollope manages to play on the area of embarrassment without transgressing the strictest morality: but it is essentially a subject of potential impropriety, and thus a suitable area for titillation. 'A Ride across Palestine' is not a great short story, of course, but Trollope certainly handles the unveiling scene very cleverly, with adequate psychological insight, and without striving after any artistically improper effect. To the modern reader he is so little daring that it is sometimes difficult to appreciate wherein his 'little wickedness' lay to his contemporaries. Indeed it must be that relations between the sexes were such a highly charged matter that any slightly free touching upon them was automatically shocking, humorous, or inordinately impressive.

One hypersensitive critic in the *British Quarterly Review*, for example, protests at the subject of *He Knew He Was Right*, because

---

[2] xxvii, 27 Mar. 1869, 431–2: review of *Phineas Finn*.

[3] Chapter 51, World's Classics, p. 488.

[4] xv, 28 Feb. 1863, 276–8. In general, this and other critics are not very enthusiastic about Trollope's short tales. Perhaps none but *An Editor's Tales* are worth preserving, and those mainly for their subject.

although no marital infidelity actually happens, the reader is distressed to feel he has been on a course parallel to real sin.[5] Two years
earlier, Mrs Oliphant praises Trollope for keeping to the safe regions.
His gentlemen, she explains, are like those 'we' know: 'There may
be unpleasant talk at their clubs . . . but they don't . . . bring it into
their intercourse with their friends. . . . On this level we miss the
primitive passions, but we get all those infinite shades of character
which make society in fact, as well as society in a book, amusing and
interesting.'[6] Any critic is bound to prefer his fiction on the bland
side if, like Mrs Oliphant, he takes society 'in fact, as well as . . . in a
book' to be the same thing.

Trollope himself warns against going too close to the edge:

> The regions of absolute vice are foul and odious. . . . But there
> are outskirts on these regions in which sweet-smelling flowers seem
> to grow and grass to be green. It is in these border-lands that the
> danger lies. The novelist may not be dull. If he commit that fault,
> he can do neither harm nor good. He must please; and the flowers
> and the soft grass in those neutral territories sometimes seem to
> give too easy an opportunity of pleasing![7]

Religion had exactly the same possibilities, as Mr Stumfold of
Littlebath so well knew, and in dealing with it Trollope cannot be
charged with taking unfair advantage of his subject-matter. He is
pursuing verisimilitude, not working for a false response from his
readers analogous to that produced by much sentimental writing. As
far as the moderately High Church *Saturday Review* is concerned, he
balances perfectly between the impossibly dull and the inadmissibly
improper, for 'though he has been quietly laughing at the parson for
any number of years, he has never yet laughed at him in a manner
unworthy of the most exemplary church-goer'.[8] Right from the time

---

[5] l, Jul. 1869, 263–4.

[6] Review of *Last Chronicle* and *The Claverings* in 'Novels', *Blackwood's*
cii, Sept. 1867, 257–80, pp. 276–7.

[7] 'Novel-reading' (review of the collected works of Dickens and of
Thackeray), *Nineteenth Century* vi, Jan. 1879, 24–43, p. 40; much of this
article reappears in the *Autobiography*.

[8] Review of *Phineas Finn*. On the other hand, both the Nonconformist
British Quarterly Review and the Catholic *Dublin Review* take his picture
of the Church of England more seriously, and use it to point their own predict-
able morals: 'Did . . . any representative of the Liberation Society, any
extreme political Dissenter, any tract issuing from a Winchester press, ever
succeed in exhibiting the vulnerable points of our National Establishment, or
the miserable weakness of the clerical order, as an order, so successfully as
Mr. Trollope has done?'—Review of *Last Chronicle* and *Lotta Schmidt and
Other Stories, British Quarterly Review* xlvi, Oct. 1867, 557–60.
'If the [Barsetshire] series of novels had been cunningly prepared by an

of *Barchester Towers* his success in this direction was acknowledged by the *Saturday* as 'wonderfully great', in his reconciliation of liveliness and reality, without vulgarity, or profanity. And yet there is something in the portrayal of churchmen as ordinary men, with ordinary human failings, that provokes the paper to remark on it with unusual pleasure: 'The theologians, unlike most theologians in novels, are thoroughly human, and retain the mixed nature of ordinary men; and, what is more, they are described impartially.'[9]

While sexual matters were the subject of strict social conventions, reflected in the novel, Trollope's venial and delightful offence in the case of the clergy was more directly literary. If clergymen in fiction were usually governed by the literary conventions set out in this quotation, Trollope must have caused his public of the late 1850s and early 1860s a mild delight by breaking through these set lines, and giving his churchmen 'the mixed nature of ordinary men'.

Trollope's whole reception by the *Saturday* in the sixties illustrates the critical tight-rope yet again. As we have seen,[10] the paper's treatment of him in these years was dominated by a hatred of 'realism', which to its contributors indicated an 'unimaginative' writer, and an appallingly mechanistic theory of art. We have examined this attitude in relation to the theories of imagination held by some important critics of the novel in the decade, but obviously the attack on 'realism' was strongly motivated by social prejudice as well. The gentlemen of the 'Superfine Review' refused to be drawn into enthusiasm for *Framley Parsonage*, because they believed it to be intellectually beneath them, as it appealed too much to the mass of readers. And in the same decade, they condemned Trollope's less popular books, like *Miss Mackenzie* and *The Belton Estate*, because

---

enemy, as a device to illustrate the hopeless division, the untenable pretensions, the utter departure of Protestantism from the principle of unity, the abandonment of the supernatural in authority, and the spiritual in object . . . it could not have been better adapted to its purpose.'—'The Novels of Mr. Anthony Trollope', *Dublin Review* (ns) xix, Oct. 1872, 393–430, p. 417. This critic is so hot on clerical celibacy that he goes on to display Griselda Grantly as 'illustrative of the perfection to which the education of a clergyman's daughter in the ways of this world may be brought' (p. 424). See also 'Mr. Trollope's Last Irish Novel' (*Phineas Finn*), *Dublin Review* (ns) xiii, Oct. 1869, 361–77, p. 364.

Meanwhile the Establishment itself was not altogether happy. In 1866 Henry Alford, Dean of Canterbury and editor of the *Contemporary Review*, bitterly attacked *Clerical Sketches*, accusing Trollope of being 'evidently more at home among phenomena of unbelief, than among those of undoubting faith and obedience'.—'Mr. Anthony Trollope and the English Clergy', *Contemporary Review* ii, June 1866, 240–62, p. 261.

[9] Both quotations from the review of *Barchester Towers*, iii, 30 May 1857, 503–4.   [10] pp. 53–6 above.

in them he applied his usual method of careful, everyday realism to the wrong areas of human activity—money concerns in the former, and Clara Belton's bedtime conversation in the latter, and concerned himself with the 'careful portraiture of the meanest and most sordid set of human traits'.[11] From the *Saturday*'s point of view, Trollope frequently errs into either dullness or sordidness, and critics often fail to distinguish between when they are bored and when they are shocked. The *Saturday's* attack on *The Belton Estate* is a case in point, and shows that the distinction is problematical, since dullness and sordidness share a common damning feature—that in either case the subject-matter is not 'idealized'.

Two key words in the *Saturday*'s critical battery are 'realism',[12] which is almost invariably a term of abuse, and frequently applied to socially unacceptable subject-matter; and 'commonplace', which refers to characters so recognizable from everyday life that the sophisticated reader can take no intelligent interest in them. Clara Amedroz in *The Belton Estate* is, and is meant to be, 'exceedingly common-place', and 'is never meant to stand out of her class, or be a "creation," any more than a young lady in one of Mr. Frith's paintings is meant to be a creation'. On the other hand, by depicting characters from too far down the social scale (that is tradespeople), and doing it sympathetically (as in *Miss Mackenzie*) and not humorously, Trollope falls into the error of 'realism that is sordid and pitiful', treating the problems of an insolvent oilcloth business, for example, as a matter of some consequence,[13] while the anxieties of a lodging-house keeper are to him 'neither mean nor amusing, but genuine sorrows' such as an artist might legitimately describe.[14] When he treats tradespeople humorously, however, he escapes censure. Referring to the Tappitts, the family of brewers in *Rachel Ray*, the *Saturday* critic points out the delicate control Trollope must have over his material in order to meet with critical approval: '[A] novelist who can paint vulgarity of this sort while he manages to inspire a constant conviction that he himself is not in the least vulgar, can do what few people could do'.[15]

Money troubles afflicting the more respectable characters are equally faultily treated in the *Saturday*'s view, 'and this not from the comic, but from the serious point of view': 'A bailiff in a house represents to Mr. Trollope nothing either funny or sordid, but a grave

[11] Notice of *Belton Estate*, *Saturday Review* xxi, 3 Feb. 1866, 140–2.

[12] The discrimination of a few of the uses of 'realism' in the period is discussed in Appendix I, below.

[13] *Saturday*'s notice of *Belton Estate*, referring to *Miss Mackenzie*.

[14] Review of *Miss Mackenzie*, *Saturday Review* xix, 4 Mar. 1865, 263–5.

[15] xvi, 24 Oct. 1863, 554–5.

human care . . .'[16] So the fault he commits lies in his straightforward
approach to some of the realities of life—in this case the financial facts
of life—which would either not appear at all in an 'idealized' picture,
or would be rendered tolerable by humorous handling. After all, the
Saturday's reviewer of *Miss Mackenzie* says he has no objection to
Mr Skimpole or Mr Micawber, because the unpleasantness is distanced
and transformed by Dickens's laughing imagination.

A. S. Kinnear (later to become 1st Baron Kinnear, a judge, and
the leading expert on Scottish feudal land tenure) has similar social
preferences. In an article in the *North British Review* of 1864,
he attacks Trollope for being 'content to copy, with dull veracity'
obnoxious persons like Mr Moulder in *Orley Farm*. 'He must idealize
and exaggerate', the young advocate complains, 'if he would not
shock instead of amusing us.' After all, Mrs Gamp is 'probably quite
as repulsive a figure . . . But the hand of a master has seized upon
every ludicrous point in her character; idealized every feature . . .'[17]
'That such things are, and that the saddest lessons are to be read from
them . . .', says Kinnear of *The Macdermots of Ballycloran*, 'are no
sufficient reason for describing them in a novel': 'All the agonies of
the Macdermots, it is true, are trifling compared with the tremendous
woes which we are not unwilling to contemplate in tragic poetry.
But these are the woes that spring from the high passions of great
natures. Unmixed pain in a novel of to-day is merely intolerable.'[18]

As we have seen in chapter 1, Trollope's popularity was attributed
largely to his truth to life; and not his popularity alone, but his
claim to the serious attention of critics too was based on similar
qualities: on his reasonable, good sense in producing 'mixed characters',[19] and on being a 'man of the world',[20] as well as 'great in the
physiognomy of all practical pursuits'.[21] He was essentially the author

[16] It had after all occurred to Trollope's family in his youth; review of *Miss
Mackenzie*.
[17] (ns) i, May 1864, 369–401, p. 390. This embryo Dean of the Edinburgh
Faculty of Advocates predictably goes on to defend the law and lawyers from
Trollope's attacks.
[18] p. 39. Kinnear periodically relapses into the by then old-fashioned
notion that novels are entirely for light reading: 'We wish to be amused, and
not disquieted in mind' (p. 394).
[19] Review of *Orley Farm*, *Saturday Review* xiv, 11 Oct. 1862, 444–5.
[20] Review of *Sir Harry Hotspur of Humblethwaite*, *Spectator* xliii, 26 Nov.
1870, 1415.
[21] Review of *Hunting Sketches*, *Spectator* xxxviii, 27 May 1865, 587–8.
But see Bulwer Lytton: 'Knowledge of the world, as a man of the world
comprehends it, does in itself belong rather to the prose than to the poetry
of life.' It is antagonistic to poetic effort, by which Lytton means the elevation
and alchemic transformation of the 'material elements of earth'.—'Knowledge
of the World', in his *Miscellaneous Prose Works*, 3 vols, 1868, pp. 410–94, p. 428.

of the everyday things of the world. Yet the same concern with the ordinary things of life, and the same everyday perceptiveness could be damning in the critics' eyes when he applied them wrongly, and took a serious, non-humorous interest in the class of tradesmen, for example—what the *Saturday* called 'the state of semi-civilization, the border-land of social decencies'.[22] Or again, 'the patient reproduction of the outward realities of life' could be seen as the mere recital of 'insignificant facts', in which 'a certain class of minds' might share the author's 'naïve delight', but which was clearly ignoble to the discerning reader. At best only 'a negative triumph' of journalistic proficiency could be open to him.[23]

He was, then, caught dangerously between various conflicting demands: the literary requirement of truth to life, in which he totally acquiesced, even if he differed with his critics about its application; the moral and social imperative of respectability; and the readers' demand for interest and stimulation. Because he advocated and prac-tised an extreme form of realism, relying so much on the perfection of his illusion, he more than any other novelist condemned himself to a very limited range of material which would pass his sensitive critics. And his frequent comments about the novel in his novels must be seen as part of his never-ending struggle to extend the social and psychological range of the subjects to which he might permissibly apply his type of realism. It is because he found the perfect formula in the clerical society of Barsetshire—safe yet racy, pricking the pomposity of individuals without threatening the institution, and showing a calmly secluded life in tension with the forces of change of the metropolis—that these novels were so successful and so accept-able. The *Saturday Review*'s description of the world of *Barchester Towers* makes this clear,[24] as does R. H. Hutton's interesting article 'From Miss Austen to Mr. Trollope', in the *Spectator* of 16 December 1882.[25] Meanwhile it is necessary to remember the violence with which some of the other novels were met.

The apotheosis of Colonel Newcome

This examination of some of the objections to Trollopian realism shows how mid-Victorian critics frequently confused social and literary criticism.[26] Such a comment as the *Saturday*'s on Trollope's relish at watching 'animals at their feed' when he depicts the family

[22] Review of *Ralph the Heir*, Saturday Review xxxi, 29 Apr. 1871, 537–8.
[23] Review of *Prime Minister*, Saturday Review xlii, 14 Oct. 1876, 481–2.
[24] See p. 5 above.   [25] lv, 1609–11.
[26] It is not common for a critic to state the distinction, as the *Dublin Review* does, when it declares itself 'rather impressed by his realism, than attracted by the realities'—'The Novels of Mr. Anthony Trollope'.

life of a breeches-maker, shows a breathtaking degree of class antagon-
ism at work; and surely concern for the novelist's own gentility is
expressed in the comment that Neefit's 'racy turn of phrase . . . comes
almost too naturally and readily to the author's needs'; for in *Ralph
the Heir* the critic fears that Trollope, once a gentleman in all he
wrote, has sacrified the standards of the class into which he was born,
in order to pander to the vulgar among his readers:

> The worst of personifying vulgarity, and giving it a prominent part,
> is that you are obliged to make it so very vulgar that the decorum
> of art runs a chance of being infringed. All novel-readers are not
> refined, and some of them are probably vulgar under any canon
> of manners that was ever established. Yet all must see and be at
> once amused and outraged by Mr. Neefit, and feel his lengths
> absolutely beyond their reach.[27]

The apotheosis of the social and moral prejudices of the moment
into timeless rules of 'art' is a recurrent feature of these articles on
Trollope. It is illustrated once more in the *Saturday*'s objection that
each 'vulgar' character in *Miss Mackenzie* and *The Belton Estate* was
'drawn . . . without so much as a hair of the creature's head idealized';[28] or the *Spectator*'s that the atmosphere of moral meanness
in the *Eustace Diamonds*, although plausible, is 'too suffocating for
Art'.[29] 'Literature', the *Saturday Review* explains, 'demands something of reserve', and prohibits the freedom of speech to which we
are accustomed in real life, because the failure of morals or manners
that hasty words display should not be preserved for later perusal[30]
—an interesting blurring of the distinction between reality and
fiction!

It is no wonder that faced with this sort of incomprehension,
Trollope should frequently pause in his novels to apologize for his
choice of characters or his moral concerns; and no wonder either
that later critics who do not share his contemporaries' exacting standards, should have found these apologies unnecessary and artistically
offensive.

It is just these social prejudices that the *Saturday Review* treats as
the immutable laws of 'art', that Thackeray gently satirizes in *The*

---

[27] Compare James Hannay's theory that Dickens was the victim of his
'middle-class' origins and readership, with 'faults belonging to a too zealous
and narrow worship of modern social ideas, and a too great neglect of established, classical, and ancient literature'—see his *Course of English Literature*,
1866, p. 321. The socially fastidious Hannay, well born, but a Grub Street
casualty, eventually drank himself to death as British Consul in Barcelona.
[28] Review of *Belton Esttae*.
[29] xlv, 26 Oct. 1872, 1365–6.
[30] Review of *Is He Popenjoy?*, xlv, 1 June 1878, 695–6.

Newcomes, showing them to be laughable and quaint even by the standards of the 1830s, when the action takes place. Yet essentially the same judgments recur throughout the 'sixties and 'seventies. 'Do you suppose', asks Colonel Newcome, with reference to Fielding's novels,

> that I want to know what my kitmutgars and cansomahs are doing? I am as little proud as any man in the world: but there must be a distinction, sir; and as it is my lot and Clive's to be a gentleman, I won't sit in the kitchen and boose in the servants' hall. As for that Tom Jones . . . I wouldn't sit down in the same room with such a fellow, sir. If he came in at the door, I would say, 'How dare you . . . to sully with your presence an apartment where my young friend and I are conversing together?' . . . If Mr. Fielding was a gentleman by birth, he ought to have known better; and so much the worse for him that he did not.[31]

Three of the Colonel's judgments are paralleled in the *Saturday*. First, the need to maintain a distance between different social levels can be seen in the disgust at some of Trollope's 'low' characters, especially in the 'mingled loathing and despair' that the characters in *Brown, Jones and Robinson* excite.[32] Secondly, the good Colonel's refusal to have social intercourse with Tom Jones corresponds closely to the *Saturday*'s distaste at being 'introduced' to unpleasant people in *Miss Mackenzie*,[33] and the reviewer's embarrassment at overhearing the free language in *Is He Popenjoy?*[34] Thirdly, we find the common belief that an author who is a gentleman should not fall into such errors as Trollope commits when he writes of the Neefits with 'gusto'.[35] Although Thackeray was satirizing an old-fashioned attitude in Colonel Newcombe's literary opinions, it was still to be met with in the influential critics of the *Saturday Review*, two decades after *The Newcomes* had appeared in 1854-5.

[31] *The Works of William Makepeace Thackeray*, 26 vols, 1888, v, 46-7.

[32] Review of *Miss Mackenzie*.

[33] The *National Review* objects to Signora Neroni in *Barchester Towers* on the same grounds: 'It is a pity that such a person should have been allowed to force herself on the reader's acquaintance, or on the eminently respectable society of the cathedral city.'—'Mr. Trollope's Novels', vii, Oct. 1858, 425. Trollope himself (his critical articulation lagging behind his practice) sometimes uses similar standards, as for example when writing of *Vanity Fair* he says, 'As we desire to love Amelia Sedley, we wish that the people around her were less vulgar or less selfish.'—*Thackeray*, p. 98.

[34] Charles Dickens junior was also sensitive to the language of *Is He Popenjoy?*, and when it appeared in *All the Year Round* suppressed or altered many passages, especially a number dealing with Mary's pregnancy and breast-feeding. See 'Victorian editors and Victorian delicacy', *Notes and Queries* clxxxvii, 2 Dec. 1944, 251-3, signed 'T.C.D.'

[35] Review of *Ralph the Heir*.

All the objections mentioned above have concerned the impropriety of the pictures of the world that Trollope produces, not their accuracy. The *Saturday* constantly tries to refute the basic principles of Trollopian realism, but does not seek to deny the 'truth' of his representation of the world, pointing instead to 'these photographs of what is meanest in life, without beauty or grace, without idea, without the faintest shade of significance', in order to prove the 'grossness' of the realistic 'fallacy' of portraying things as they are.[36] As the *British Quarterly Review* puts it: 'Like all Mr. Trollope's writings, [*He Knew He Was Right*] is uncompromisingly realistic—the flaws of his heroes and heroines are remorselessly exhibited. It is no justification of this pre-Raphaelitism that it is true to life. A work of art should not be true to life, but should idealize—that it may elevate it.'[37]

In all the cases where such judgments occur, it is not so much the critics' intellectual faculties as their social susceptibilities that have been offended. The principles of Victorian literary propriety have been defied. It is possible to regard these principles as a sub-set of the whole system of social and moral values of the age, but it is also important to recognize the purely literary defences which could be called on, and to see the role played by certain literary conventions in the defence of propriety. Besides the apotheosis of Colonel Newcome, the critics had another bulwark against distasteful realism. A number of their traditions of novel-writing, especially those of 'low' characters, and of secondary, humorous characters, were used to protect the *convenances*.

Principal and secondary characters

In his attack on Dickens in *The Warden*, Trollope shows himself to be aware of a system of decorum which specifies what can and what cannot be allowed in characters of different types, and he draws an important distinction between what is expected from a 'good' lower-class character and a 'secondary' one:

> [Mr. Sentiment's] good poor people are so very good; and his hard rich people so very hard; and the genuinely honest so very honest. Namby-pamby in these days is not thrown away if it be introduced in the proper quarters. Divine peeresses are no longer interesting, though possessed of every virtue; but a pattern peasant or an immaculate manufacturing hero may talk as much twaddle as one of Mrs. Ratcliffe's [*sic*] heroines, and still be listened to. . . . If his

[36] Review of *Belton Estate*.

[37] Review of *He Knew He Was Right*. As Calverley said in his parody of Tupper, '. . . if thou canst not realize the Ideal, thou shalt at least idealize the Real'—*A Century of Parody and Imitation*, ed. W. Jerrold and R. Leonard, 1913, p. 301.

heroes and heroines walk upon stilts, as heroes and heroines, I fear, ever must, their attendant satellites are as natural as though one met them in the street . . .[38]

Conventionally, that is, there is a correct way of 'idealizing' the principal characters, while the secondary ones are the proper objects for 'realistic' treatment.

Trollope, as is well known, rejected the conventional 'heroic' hero along with all mystery, suspense and romance, maintaining in frequent narrative asides that 'heroes and heroines, as so called, are not commonly met with in our daily walks of life'.[39] His fellow-novelist, Mrs Oliphant, persisted in misunderstanding his attitude, and found the mess Harry Clavering makes of his love-life 'humiliating, and . . . against the very character of a hero', who might be forgiven 'a tragic mistake which ruins or compromises him fatally'.[40] Trollope often preferred to expend his energies on maturer protagonists, such as Dr Thorne and Lady Mason—an interest he explains in *The Three Clerks* when he says of Mrs Woodward crying, that 'when one has reached the age of forty, the traces of such tears are not easily effaced from a woman's face', although at her daughter's age 'tears are the easiest resource in time of grief'.[41] But this was not his only rebellion against the conventions. The implication of various critical comments over the years is that he sometimes also abandoned the convention of 'second-rate characters', as he calls them in *The Warden*,[42] and put forward as protagonists, characters who would normally have been relegated to a secondary status. The *Home and Foreign Review*, for example, thought it 'a bold effort' to have a 'principal heroine' who was a criminal, like Lady Mason in *Orley Farm*, and praised Trollope for succeeding where he dared.[43]

With his very first novel, as we saw, one critic was in doubt as to how to respond to his characters: 'The family of Macdermots are essentially peasants, raised above the class, not in education or circumstances, but only by prejudice and accident. [§] The matter of the story should excite an interest which we cannot feel for the characters, either as gentry or peasants, because they belong to neither.'[44] This critic is totally confused because the novel has denied

[38] Chapter 15, World's Classics 1961, p. 192.
[39] *Three Clerks* chapter 47, World's Classics 1952, p. 544. See also *Doctor Thorne* chapter 1, World's Classics 1956, p. 7, and *Ralph the Heir* chapter 57, World's Classics 1939, ii, 337-9; and B. A. Booth's 'Trollope on the Novel', *op. cit.*
[40] Review of *Claverings* and *Last Chronicle*, *Blackwood's* cii, Sept. 1867, 275-8.   [41] Chapter 37, World's Classics p. 444.
[42] Chapter 15, World's Classics p. 192.
[43] Review of *Orley Farm*, ii, Jan. 1863, 291-4.
[44] *Spectator* xx, 8 May 1847, 449.

him the conventional reactions corresponding to a normal system of characterization which he understands.

Worse still, the breaking of these conventions can lead in the eyes of the *Saturday Review* to the very worst and most hateful 'realism', when less attractive types of people who would normally be 'second-rate characters' are brought into prominence, as happened in *Brown, Jones, and Robinson* and *Miss Mackenzie*:

> Of course it is necessary to have a foil in the shape of artful, stuck-up, selfish, or vulgar people, but these have commonly been kept judiciously in the background, and only interest us incidentally on account of the vexation they inflict on their pleasanter friends. A dreadful story, [*Brown, Jones, and Robinson*] it is true, was ascribed to Mr. Trollope, in which the chief characters, motives, and incidents were so odiously vulgar and stupid that the staunchest champions of realism were forced to give up in disgust.[45]

And something similar happens in *Miss Mackenzie*, the critic says. Even *The Times* and the *Dublin University Magazine*, who praise Trollope for making his unlikely subject interesting in *Miss Mackenzie*, recognize in their very judgment that he is doing something unconventional.[46]

Before proceeding further, it is necessary to examine a quartet of words which occur in the passage from the *Saturday* just quoted: 'artful', 'stuck-up', 'selfish' and 'vulgar', which cover both social status and moral nature. 'Vulgar' in particular is a most usefully vague term of abuse in the hands of, say, the *Saturday*, or Meredith Townsend, because it can be applied to anything which offends the social or moral susceptibilities of the critic. It can be applied almost automatically to any lifelike and prominent working-class or lower middle-class character, or at the other extreme to an aristocrat who fails in the exercise of perfect gentility. Townsend, for example, uses it of the Duke of Omnium for turning Major Pountney out of Gatherum Castle: 'an insult to the reader's social sense',[47] he objects. 'The thing could not have occurred.' The word, in fact, was used

---

[45] Review of *Miss Mackenzie*. Compare Dickens's letter to Percy Fitzgerald on 27 July, 1864, about the latter's story 'Miss Manuel': '. . . Captain Fermor wants relief. It is a disagreeable character, as you mean it to be, and I should be afraid to do so much with him, if the case were mine, without taking the taste of him, here and there, out of the reader's mouth. It is remarkable that if you do not administer a disagreeable character carefully, the public have a decided tendency to think the *story* is disagreeable, and not merely the fictitious person.'—*The Letters of Charles Dickens*, ed. M. Dickens and G. Hogarth, 3 vols, 1880–82, ii, 217.

[46] *The Times*, 23 Aug. 1865, 12, and *D.U.M.* lxv, May 1865, 576, respectively.

[47] Review of *Prime Minister*, *Spectator* xlix, 22 Jul. 1876, 922–3. The whole of this notice is about 'vulgarity' and 'snobbishness' in high and low places.

to refer to anything which offended the critics' social over-sensitivity.

The fault of the 'vulgar' characters in *Brown, Jones, and Robinson* and *Miss Mackenzie* (who can more reasonably be called 'of the people' than the Duke of Omnium) is that they are seriously concerned with money and social status. In Townsend's eyes, this is the fault even of the Pallisers in *The Prime Minister*, and of the mass of people in *The Eustace Diamonds*, too, to whom Trollope attributes 'an inherent vulgarity of thought'. The same strenuous critic finds Ferdinand Lopez 'simply intolerable, not because he is criminal . . . but because he is such a "cad" . . . a "snob" of the lowest type, who excites no feeling but loathing of the most contemptuous and irritated kind'.[48] On these social questions the critics often become so agitated that they lose all control over their rhetoric in their passion. The period was one obsessed wtih money and social position, when wealth was acquired and lost at a great rate, and social mobility was unprecedentedly high; yet the age also created the myths of the flawless gentleman and of the perfectly virtuous workman. The rage of the critics with an author who dared to show up these official myths as so much sham, knew no bounds.

The convention of secondary characters was intended safely to encapsulate such threatening material, and it is interesting to observe how Trollope treated the convention, and how his critics reacted. The *National Review*'s description of *Orley Farm* shows the role of the convention in preserving the reader from too intimate a contact with anything unpleasant or threatening:

> The Bohemians that now and then flit across the stage are the tamest imaginable, and are only just sufficiently Bohemian to be picturesque without violating propriety. There are occasional villains, of course, but they only belong to an outer world, with which the audience has so little in common that it can afford to treat their crimes as a matter of mere curiosity. The low Jewish attorney, the brass-browed Old Bailey practitioner, Mr. Moulder in his drunken moods, Dockwrath in his revengeful spite—are none of them models of what gentlemen and Christians should be; but they are never brought sufficiently near to display the full proportions of their guilt, or to suggest the possibility of contamination.[49]

The three main weeklies, even the hypersensitive *Saturday*, all approve of Mr Moulder and Mr Kantwise (the iron-furniture salesman), presumably on the same grounds, although Lewes in the *Cornhill* finds them insufficiently humorous to provide adequate light relief.[50] So *Orley Farm* may be accounted one of Trollope's critical successes

---

[48] *Ibid.* [49] xvi, Jan. 1863, 27–40.

[50] vi, Nov. 1862, 702–4. In its review, the *Home and Foreign Review* says, 'The funny people are there but not the fun.'

from this point of view, because he subordinates the 'vulgarity' in the story by embodying it entirely in 'second-rate characters', who are kept at a little distance from the reader, by humour or otherwise, to avoid the risk of social 'contamination'.

The case of *The Vicar of Bullhampton* shows that Trollope knew how to obey the rules when he thought it necessary:

> *The Vicar of Bullhampton* was written chiefly with the object of exciting not only pity but sympathy for a fallen woman, and of raising feelings of forgiveness for such in the minds of other women. I could not venture to make this female the heroine of my story. To have made her a heroine at all would have been directly opposed to my purpose. It was necessary therefore that she should be a second-rate personage of the tale;—but it was with reference to her life that the tale was written, and the hero and the heroine with their belongings are all subordinate.[51]

In the preface that he wrote to the novel 'in defiance of an old-established principle' of his, he explains that he did not want to make the life of a prostitute glamorous, as he should have had to do had he made her his heroine.[52] So she had to be a subsidiary character, to stop 'our sisters and our daughters' identifying with her too closely. Pity and sympathize they might, for there was a conventional mode in which this could be done. (In another context the *Saturday Review* writes of 'the kind of pity . . . we [have] for a fallen woman' in a novel.[53]) And Trollope succeeded in getting this past the moral watch-dogs. *The Times*, the *Saturday* and the *Athenaeum* were not at all perturbed about the rehabilitation of Carry Brattle as a fictional subject, although Collyer of the *Athenaeum* seriously doubted, as a point of fact, whether a 'fallen woman' could be reformed at all.[54] George Dasent in *The Times* proclaimed that 'the general safeness of the story will make Bullhampton Vicarage welcome in all well-regulated families', although it would add nothing to Trollope's reputation. For its part the *Saturday* gives a perfect illustration of the rules of decorum in being able to accept Carry Brattle as a

[51] *Autobiography*, pp. 329–30.
[52] *Ibid.*, pp. 330, 331–2.
[53] Review of *Can You Forgive Her?*, xx, 19 Aug. 1865, 240–2.
[54] *The Times*, 3 June 1870, 4; *Saturday* xxix, 14 May 1870, 646–7; *Athenaeum* no. 2218, 30 Apr. 1870, 574 [Collyer].
Collyer protests against 'any confusion between the selfish fears of those who are harsh to their "unfortunate" relations, and an honest pride of race, which is not too common, and which, in the absence of a wider Christianity, does much to maintain the purity of English families'. He objects to the concern of most philanthropists, including the eponymous Vicar, with 'raising and comforting the fallen', while ignoring 'the keener pangs endured by those whose life's struggle it is to stand upright'.

secondary character, but objecting violently to the 'immodesty', 'violence' and 'savagery' of the so-called genteel people.

A severe case of a rupture of the conventions is to be seen in *Ralph the Heir*, which the *Saturday* condemns so vehemently for its vulgar preoccupation with tradespeople. The *Spectator*, on the other hand, commends the novel for just this same social interest, but bases its compliment on the identical perception that Trollope is doing something out-of-the-ordinary in bringing readers into contact with such fictional people. The critic makes it clear that he too regards this contact as equivalent to real-life acquaintance, or in fact as even better, since the social barriers which would keep the reader and Mr Neefit apart in real life are overcome in Trollope's fiction. Readers gain experience from such a novel that they could not gain elsewhere, he says, even by 'their own personal contact with the prototypes, if prototypes there be'. One knows one's friends less thoroughly than one knows the Underwoods and the Newtons, and with such a one as Mr Neefit, the breeches-maker, one could normally have no intimacy at all.[55]

Many of the 'low' characters in *Orley Farm*, which are so acceptable to the critics, are explicitly conceived by the critics to be conventional 'comic' characters. The *Saturday*, for example, calls them Trollope's material for his 'comic writing', assuming, as all critics seem to, that a novelist naturally divides his novel into serious and comic parts, with a clear distinction between the two. The only problem is to choose where to draw the line. The system of decorum as it affects Trollope's comedy is clearly stated by the *Westminster Review* in its notice of volume one of *Can You Forgive Her?*: 'As he deals simply and solely with human nature as it appears in its most conventional aspects (he rarely attempts children or rustics), he is naturally driven to vulgar people for his comedy, and very richly comical are Mrs. Greenhow and her lovers . . .'[56] As we have already seen, the *Saturday* takes exception to the blurring of the division between the serious and the comic in *Miss Mackenzie*, when, instead of creating a Skimpole or a Micawber, Trollope treats money troubles 'not from the comic, but from the serious point of view'. In this case, the breach of the normal expectations is perceived, just as the following of convention is accepted in the mocking of the sanctimonious clergyman in the person of Mr Prong in *Rachel Ray*. The *Athenaeum*, the *Saturday* and the *Spectator* all take Mr Prong in their stride, although Norman Macleod, the Presbyterian editor of *Good Words*, for which *Rachel Ray* was destined, did object, and the novel was never serialized. Trollope is disingenuous in suggesting that 'some dancing in one of the

[55] *Spectator* xliv, 15 Apr. 1871, 450–2.
[56] (ns) xxviii, Jul. 1865, 284–5.

early chapters' was the reason for Macleod's rejection.[57] Which
religious conventions in novel-writing are subscribed to is clearly a
sectarian matter.

In the *Saturday*'s notice of *The Way We Live Now*[58] there occurs
the most interesting case of all, where the expectation that a 'low'
character will be humorous prevents the critic seeing what Trollope
is really doing, by protecting him from the need to look at the un-
palatable social truth the author is presenting. The case is that of
Ruby Ruggles, the poor country girl whom Sir Felix Carbury sets
out systematically to seduce. Instead of seeing that Trollope is condemning Felix Carbury for his total lack of human life—for his
zombie-like existence, as Steven Marcus calls it[59]—the reviewer complains that Ruby, 'the heroine of humble life, about whom gathers
the comic interest of the story', is as unlikeable as the rest of the
women, and hence the 'comic' element fails. The critic does not
consider her as a victim, as the modern reader must. This plainly
inadequate response is paralleled in Meredith Townsend's review
in the *Spectator*: 'Mrs Pipkin, an old woman who watches over a
pretty servant-girl whom Sir Felix feebly wishes to seduce, and who
is *intended to be comic*, is made *unintentionally* as disagreeable as the
rest . . .'[60] This part of the book is not meant to be comic relief.
Trollope is showing how mercenary and heartless attitudes permeated
the whole of society and all its activities. The fact that this part of
The Way We Live Now can be so misrepresented by assuming that
this kind of 'low' character should not be taken seriously, illustrates
the barriers that conventional expectations could erect—in this case
in defence of the Victorian myth of propriety against a realistic portrayal of a world in which gentlemen frequently did seduce and
'ruin' young servant-girls.[61]

A conventional ending

Another common convention of the Victorian novel that can be seen
in the breach and the observance in Trollope's novels, is the convention of the happy ending which involves a marriage ostensibly in

[57] See *Autobiography*, pp. 186–7.

[58] xl, 17 Jul. 1875, 88–9.

[59] *The Other Victorians*, Weidenfeld & Nicolson, 1966, p. 140.

[60] xlviii, 26 June 1875, 825–6: my italics.

[61] Elsewhere the *Saturday* on one occasion accepts one of Trollope's revela-
tions (it was often not averse itself to discussing 'the social evil' quite openly),
and praises Burgo Fitzgerald in *Can You Forgive Her?*, 'a really worthless
fellow . . . a man so bad . . . as deliberately to plan the carrying off of his
neighbour's wife, and the sort of man too whom most of us are familiar
with . . .' Burgo is another (more sympathetic) of Trollope's characters who
leads a life immediately recognizable from Marcus's *The Other Victorians*.

defiance of social pressures, but made acceptable by some revelation or *deus ex machina*.[62] Three obvious examples of the use of this formula stand out in Trollope's novels: Mary Thorne and Frank Gresham in *Doctor Thorne*, Daniel Thwaite with Lady Anna in the novel of that name, and George Roden and Lady Frances Trafford in *Marion Fay*.

In the first of these Trollope overcomes all the financial difficulties for the couple by manipulation of the plot, which his brother had in fact drawn up for him. But, while he makes sure that there shall be no objection possible to the bride on the score of her upbringing, he does not attempt to solve the problem posed by her illegitimacy in any terms within the conventions of the sentimental novel or drama, preferring to allow the matter to sink out of sight, so that no realistic solution need be offered either. In any case, Mary Thorne's is the only case of the three where it is the bride who is at the social disadvantage—an important consideration in the working out of a story, since a man could elevate his wife to his own rank, while a woman could not raise her husband, but must fall herself. In *Lady Anna* there is comparatively little compromise with convention—except that of *amor vincit omnia*—and the marriage of the earl's daughter and the journeyman tailor remains at the last in defiance of a large part of the fictional society, although one must bear in mind the verdict of the character of the Solicitor-General in the novel, who says that Daniel 'is an educated man, with culture much higher than is generally found in the state of life which he has till lately filled', who will be in Parliament in five years, and be made Sir Daniel in ten.[63] But although Trollope's tailor is a superior tailor, the social conflicts are not at all glossed over, but are in fact the subject of the novel. *Marion Fay*, on the other hand, represents an almost total capitulation to the standards of popular or of sentimental circulating library fiction.[64] There are two courtships across class barriers. Lord Hampstead's pursuit of the consumptive Quaker girl from Holloway is frustrated by her opportune and touching death (a death quite free from unpleasant symptoms, in the true sentimental manner), while the Post Office clerk who succeeds in winning the young nobleman's sister, very fortunately—and most unexpectedly—turns out to be an Italian duke after all.

[62] In *Popular Fiction 100 Years Ago* (Cohen, 1957), Margaret Dalziel says, 'People who marry for love are traditionally poor, yet almost always the stories contrive a comfortable existence for them, pretending that the conflict between love and prudential considerations is not a real one' (p. 119).

[63] *World's Classics* 1944, chapter 41, p. 437, and chapter 42, p. 441.

[64] Margaret Dalziel points out that popular fiction tended to ignore class difference as a source of conflict in marriage, and denied 'the possibility of a conflict between love and the laws of society'; *op. cit.*, pp. 119–20.

The critics' response to these three books is correspondingly various. Discussing the moral tone of the first of them, the *Spectator* critic[65] points out that Mary Thorne is not a representative example of an illegitimate child, because of the extraordinarily normal conditions of her upbringing, and while he would rather in a way the author had made her turn out to be legitimate after all, he has to acknowledge that Trollope 'has too sensible a logic to proceed in this wise', in order merely 'formally' to satisfy objectors: 'Mr. Trollope proceeds less conventionally; but he is quite as exceptionable though in a less obviously formal and fallacious way, inspiring interest by a heroine with a favourable training that could but rarely happen'. The author 'appears to attach too little weight to the moral of example'. The *Saturday*,[66] on its part, objects to the improbability of Mary's inheritance, by which Trollope contrives things so that 'the desert blossoms as the rose' for the young lovers. The reviewer would like to see more truth to life in novelists' depiction of love in general, so that the dangers and drawbacks of love matches were shown up as well as the delights, and so that young people's unreasoning optimism was not flattered as it is by such improbabilities as Mary's sudden accession of wealth. The *Saturday* is here attacking a current novel convention because it sees marriage for love alone as a social evil which a novelist should not encourage, since young people are too ready to marry without thought in any case. It returns to the subject in several reviews of Trollope. Thus this severe judge for once—uncharacteristically—appears to advocate greater realism, as a form of healthy didacticism, pointing a moral for the benefit of the over-hasty young reader. What is under attack is a sentimental convention that the *Saturday* finds offensive to its commonsense. Incidentally, to follow the reviewer's advice of showing 'the man-traps, the spring-guns, and the prosecution of trespassers' in the 'wood' of love (the reviewer's language is heavy with sexual imagery), would require a supreme feat of equilibration if the novel were not to fall foul of his exacting moral standards. The most important factor in these comments on *Doctor Thorne*, however, is that both the *Spectator* and the *Saturday Review* acknowledge a direct opposition between the conventional happy ending and consistent truth to life, although they differ in their opinions as to whether Trollope fulfils the conditions of 'truth' and 'art'.[67]

---

[65] xxxi, 29 May 1858, 577–8.   [66] v, 12 June 1858, 618–19.

[67] 'Truth' and 'art' in this context, although used vaguely, correspond roughly to Aristotelian 'possibility' and 'probability' respectively. The critics, in demanding both 'truth' and 'art', are looking for a probable (or internally consistent) series of events chosen from out of the realm of the historically possible.

This particular sort of happy ending is seen in its pure form in the last of these novels, *Marion Fay*. Here plausibility is entirely sacrificed to the reader's desire to have his cake and eat it. Having identified with the young lovers in their adversity, the reader is both gratified to find that he has bestowed his sympathy on a young man whose nobility deserves it, and is also able to glory in the triumph of the young man's superior rank after the *deus ex machina* has done its work. Again we find the ending acknowledged as improbable—not 'artistic' is the way the *Spectator* critic, Miss Lock, phrases it—though she adds the proviso that most readers will probably prefer it as it stands.[68] She clearly— and with justice, I should consider—recognizes the novel as belonging to the genre of sentimental library fiction, when she commends the unusual 'sweetness' of the pathetic scenes of Marion's death.

Such an ending as this obviously prevents any social shock to the reader, whose romantic instinct has been excited while his sense of what is socially fitting is not affronted. Yet this way of avoiding the snares of realism—of shirking the responsibility to resolve the real social conflicts and oppositions raised in the body of the novel—is rightly condemned by Trollope's contemporaries as inartistic. It might also be called immoral, despite, or because of, its purpose, which is to avoid offence to Victorian social susceptibilities. The *Saturday*, however—always a champion of commonsense against sentiment[69]— rejects the conventional happy ending as part of its wholesale attack on pernicious sentimentality and sensation.

This is not to say that it is necessarily happy with a realistic ending—quite the contrary, for it comes out strongly in condemnation of the ending of *Lady Anna*.[70] The terms of the attack in its review clearly reveal the social function of the sort of ending which merely plasters over the cracks in the world of the novel. It is fair to say in passing that no ending added to *Lady Anna* could have made it acceptable to the *Saturday*, because the convention demands that the novelist should prepare the hero from the very start for the revelation that is awaiting him. Oliver Twist's remarkably standard English is an example of such a convention at work. But Daniel Thwaite is altogether anathema to the *Saturday*—the satyr to Felix Holt's Hyperion, the critic says—because Trollope works his purpose of this marriage through from beginning to end. The reviewer is appalled by the impudent presumption and lack of respect for rank, that Daniel Thwaite and his father display throughout, and feels so strongly

[68] lv, 19 Aug. 1882, 1088–9.
[69] See, for example, 'Sentimental writing', *Saturday Review* x, 25 Aug. 1860, 235–6.
[70] xxxvii, 9 May 1874, 598–9.

about the outcome of the story that he reveals it to his readers, lest they too be 'betrayed into reading' the novel, and suffer a like shock to their 'susceptibilities'. The subject is so appalling that it is bound to alienate much of Trollope's public, who will not like to contemplate 'such disruptions of social order as this', which can only be thought up by 'a man . . . embittered by some violent present exasperation', for it would, the reviewer says, be beyond 'Radicals in the abstract' to devise such horrors. It is the subject that is so very offensive, for once again the critic acknowledges the need for consistency in handling the story, pointing out that 'Mr. Trollope knows his art too well' to falsify his picture of the tailor in order to make him an acceptable husband for an earl's daughter, despite his social background. Having chosen his subject, Trollope has again run into trouble with the critics because of his consistent handling of it.

It is now commonly accepted that rather than working from a basis of plot, the logic of certain novels begins from the assumption that some particularly interesting event has occurred or situation arisen. Sadleir, Cockshut and Booth all recognize this in the case of books like *Mr. Scarborough's Family*, *The Fixed Period*, and *Dr. Wortle's School*, and all show the connection between Trollope's approach and the workings of Elizabethan and Jacobean drama. *Lady Anna* is clearly another case in point, the underlying question being what would happen if the daughter of an earl did decide to marry a tailor, and how it would come about. According to the *Dublin Review*, in fact, an anecdote was circulating at the time, that *Lady Anna* was 'written as the result of a bet Trollope had made with a friend, to the effect that he would write a novel in which an Earl's daughter should marry a tailor, while he would force his readers to sympathize with her for so doing'.[71] One need not believe the *Dublin Review*, of course, but Trollope does work from such a starting point, and he works without compromising with convention. As he says in the *Autobiography*: 'The horror which was expressed to me at the evil thing I had done, in giving the girl to the tailor, was the strongest testimony I could receive of the merits of the story.'[72] In fact the novel, as such, is by no means great, and from the point of view of the present discussion it is important because the basic assumption is disruptive of the social order, and Trollope has carried his idea through to the end, in marked contrast to *Marion Fay*, where he does not face the problem, but withdraws behind a more or less dishonest novel-writing convention, which even his less discriminating contemporaries view as deficient in 'art'.

[71] 'The novels of Anthony Trollope' (3rd ser.) ix, Apr. 1883, 314–34, p. 331.
[72] p. 347.

The happy ending which consists in a revelation of noble birth or an unexpected inheritance obviously has a large portion of wish-fulfilment in it. From the point of view of its function of protecting the reader from socially unpleasant facts, it may be put side-by-side with the convention of secondary characters, although the two conventions have quite different artistic statuses. The former is a worn cliché, while the latter is one of the main tools of the social novelist— a ready-made system for portraying reality, and almost building it up from prefabricated sections.[73] Yet, as I have shown, it can also come to be treated as a means of avoiding a significant portrayal of social reality.

Trollope's contemporaries could recognize far more quickly than we can how far he was following and how far rejecting these conventions which were the stock-in-trade of the novelists of the period: and it is therefore valuable to know how they read him, in order both to examine the conventions, and to find out what it was that Trollope was trying to do when he worked so tirelessly in the cause of his uncompromising realism.

[73] Bagehot partly saw that story elements and recognized character types were used in this way. Reviewing Thackeray's *Philip* in the *Spectator* (9 Aug. 1862), he enumerated them from that novel, and said, 'They are the best part of the recognized stock in hand of narrative artists. If a writer could accomplish nothing with this capital apparatus, it is not likely that he will accomplish much with any other. He has as good a chance with the machinery as he is ever likely to have with any.' Yet, he concluded, *Philip* was a failure 'as far as "plot" is concerned'. *Collected Works*, ed. N. St John-Stevas (Economist, 1965–), ii, 314. Bagehot is interesting in his initial perception, but his intentionalist judgment is quite fallacious.

5

RICHARD HOLT HUTTON
AND TROLLOPE'S
CHARACTERIZATION

In Trollope's opinion, Richard Holt Hutton of the *Spectator* was 'of all the critics of my work . . . the most observant, and generally the most eulogistic'.[1] Yet Hutton's criticism of Trollope has been largely ignored, except by Richard Stang, whose *Theory of the Novel in England*, however, gives a rather distorted impression of the critic's work by concentrating on the aspect of it Professor Stang calls 'the search for tragedy', and which is discussed here in chapter 2.[2] Bradford A. Booth, in his *Anthony Trollope*, is briefly complimentary about one of the regular *Spectator* reviews—that on *The Small House at Allington*—but not much more.[3] Students of Hutton show little interest in his criticism of Trollope either, preferring to tread more fashionable paths, even when they range as low down the literary scale as Charles Reade and Wilkie Collins.[4] So, between the Trollopians and the Hutton scholars, this important criticism goes largely neglected. Yet it is intrinsically very interesting, since Trollope sets Hutton a serious and fascinating complex of problems. We shall examine the way in which the critic deals with these prob-

[1] *Autobiography*, p. 205.
[2] pp. 40–5 above.
[3] 'One of the most thoughtful and most understanding brief critiques of Trollope that I know' (p. 238). Indeed two pages in Professor Booth's book turn out on examination to be closely based on this article.
[4] There is no mention of the Trollope articles in any of the following: R. A. Colby, ' "How It Strikes a Contemporary": The *Spectator* as Critic', *Nineteenth Century Fiction* xi, Dec. 1956, 182–206; A. K. Stevens, 'Richard Holt Hutton', PhD thesis, Univ. of Michigan, 1949; G. Thomas, 'Richard Holt Hutton', PhD thesis, Univ. of Illinois, 1949; while R. H. Tener, the greatest Hutton expert, wrote his thesis on Hutton's criticism of poetry (London 1960). R. Helling, the chronicler of Trollopian criticism through an entire century, can do no more than mention Hutton's name: *A Century of Trollope Criticism*, Helsinki 1956.

lems, because they involve some central Victorian assumptions about the nature of fictional characters, and the nature of artistic creation itself.

Naturally it cannot be assumed that all the best notices of Trollope's fiction are Hutton's, but there is at least such a continuity in them in thought and style that they can reasonably be treated together; and so much similarity with those articles known to be his, that it is profitable to examine them all in the context of his whole output. According to William Watson—who had good reason to appreciate the editor's generosity in championing him as a new writer, and who dedicated his *Lachrymæ Musarum* to Hutton and his colleague Townsend—Hutton *was* the *Spectator*.[5] so that Robert Colby can speak of the 'homogeneity, which makes it possible to consider the *Spectator* of this period as a kind of collective critic',[6] citing Hugh Walker as evidence: '[Hutton] is not to be measured by the work, important as it is, which bears his own name. He is also the head of what may be called a school. Consciously or unconsciously, he has influenced the majority of the numerous writers who must have collaborated in the weekly literary articles of the *Spectator*.'[7] It is thus possible to treat the anonymous criticism of Trollope in the *Spectator* under Hutton's literary editorship from 1861 onwards as a more or less coherent whole, merely pointing out such inconsistencies as are met with on the way.

Not all writers mention Hutton with respect. Virginia Woolf, for example, complains that his voice is 'a plague of locusts—the voice of a man stumbling drowsily among loose words, clutching aimlessly at vague ideas'.[8] George Saintsbury, although not blind to some of the editor's virtues, condemns him for his 'distaste of pure criticism', since Hutton, in his opinion, always wrote articles in which the literary interest was 'allayed and sweetened by sentimental, or political, or

---

[5] *Excursions in Literary Criticism*, 1893, p. 113.

[6] ' "How It Strikes a Contemporary" . . .', p. 183. A. J. Church, in his *Memories of Men and Books*, 1908, p. 214, claims that contemporary readers often could not tell when one of the editors took over the other's functions, so uniform was the style of the paper. This is true of Trollope himself, in his misattribution of the review of *The Prime Minister* to Hutton; see my 'The *Spectator*'s attack on Trollope's *Prime Minister*: a mistaken attribution', *Notes and Queries* (ns) xv, Nov. 1968, 420–1.

[7] 'Living Critics—IV. Mr. R. H. Hutton', *Bookman* ix, Jan. 1896, 120.

[8] *The Common Reader* (1st series), Hogarth Press [1925], repr. 1951, p. 269. James Thomson, as a modernist, an atheist, and a Meredithian, was a natural contemporary enemy. See his attack on the *Spectator* in 'The Swinburne controversy' in Bradlaugh's *National Reformer* of 23 Dec. 1866, reprinted in Thomson's *Satires and Profanities*, 1884, pp. 99–104. Thomson, however, was very fair in his treatment of Hutton's *Sir Walter Scott* in the English Men of Letters series, in *Cope's Tobacco Plant* ii, Sept. 1879, 384.

religious, or philosophical, or anthropological, or pantopragmatic adulteration'.[9] He goes on: 'Mr. Hutton's criticism was, it is believed, by far the most popular of his day; the very respectable newspaper which he directed was once eulogised as "telling you what you *ought to read*, you know"—a phrase which might have awakened in a new Wordsworth thoughts too deep for tears or even laughter.' Saintsbury entitles his next paragraph on Hutton 'His evasions of literary criticism', and claims in accusation that 'if Literature as literature, makes any advance to him, he leaves his garment in her hands and flees for his life'.[10] Saintsbury, of course, was deliberately trying to discredit the previous generation, but even so those essays of Hutton's which he knew best—that is those republished in volumes of collected essays—cannot be defended from his attack. Indeed in his recent book *The Rise and Fall of the Man of Letters*, John Gross makes a similar accurate but partial judgment on the basis of the same material.[11] Yet most of the reviews of Trollope's novels are of a quite different character from the collected pieces, and cannot be dismissed on the grounds of 'pantopragmatic adulteration' or moral prescription, from which, indeed, they are remarkably free. At the time of writing his *History of English Criticism*, from which these comments come, Saintsbury would probably not have considered Trollope a fit subject for serious and sustained attention, for he 'never met more than one competent critic (a personal friend, by the way, of the author of "The Warden")' who thought that Trollope had 'genius', and remembers 'very well the difficulties under which I found myself when I had to criticise more than one' of his novels, not wishing to speak ill of a writer who had once given him pleasure. It seems reasonable to infer from this that Saintsbury's whole evaluation of Trollope at this time, before he recanted, was coloured by the memory of having to review two of the author's less important novels, *Lady Anna* and *Harry Heathcote of Gangoil*, for the *Academy*.[12] It would therefore be unfair to point out that Hutton was a far more perceptive critic of Trollope than Saintsbury was in his early and middle life.

The material dealt with in the present chapter at first sight gives a markedly different impression from that examined with regard to the morality of fiction in chapter 3. There is, however, a common underlying scheme of thought. There we noted how Hutton's literary

[9] *A History of English Criticism*, Blackwood 1962, p. 496 (first publ. 1900–1904).

[10] *Ibid.*, p. 497.

[11] Weidenfeld & Nicolson, 1969, pp. 82–3.

[12] *Corrected Impressions* 1895, pp. 172–3. We have already seen that Appleton, the editor of the *Academy*, rejected an article on *He Knew He Was Right* by Edith Simcox, as unsuitable for an intellectual periodical. See Diderik Roll-Hansen, *The Academy*, p. 192, and pp. 33–4 above.

criticism was one aspect of his all-embracing theology, but most
of his consequent moral and religious concerns are curiously absent
from the majority of his Trollope criticism. In particular his belief
that 'theology and literature—the study of God and the study of
Man—need to go hand in hand',[13] hardly shows up clearly except in
his obituary article, where he regrets that Trollope does not portray
the positive influence of religion over men's minds.[14] He mentions the
deficiency in an article intended to sum up the author's whole life's
work, but naturally hardly comments on it elsewhere: for his is a
method of criticism that works by sympathetic immersion or 'satura-
tion' in the work in question,[15] so that he normally concentrates his
analysis on what he finds in the work, and not what is missing. There
is something in Trollope's work that brings out the best in Hutton
as a practising critic. He does not feel obliged to parade his philosophical and theological concerns in his approach to Trollope, because
nothing in Trollope calls them forth.

Instead, given his particular habits and flexibility of mind, Hutton
cannot resist tracing the connections between Trollope's novels and
contemporary society, and the changes the society has undergone
during Trollope's writing life. Although the social aspect is not
allowed to swamp the artistic, Hutton remains, as Glyn Thomas puts
it, 'dedicated . . . to the purpose of making clear to his reading public
the various aspects of the age in which they lived'.[16] But the absence
of subjects for theological debate in Trollope's novels turns his
attention to their purely literary aspects, and he exercises his intellect
principally on the problem of why they give such an effective picture
of people in society, given an apparent superficiality in the author's
grasp of human nature.

Superficiality and depth

A novel was regarded by mid-Victorian critics as the imitation of
human character. A *Spectator* article, 'Literary impressionists', holds
that the highest imaginative achievement open to the writer consists
in 'coherent conceptions of the true power of either intellectual or
moral character'.[17] Hutton, who required the connection between man
and god to be made manifest, asserted that 'if you are to delineate
man at all, you must delineate him with his human nature, and

---

[13] 'The Hard Church Novel', *National Review* iii, Jul. 1856, 127–46, p. 131.
[14] lv, 9 Dec. 1882, 1573–4.
[15] K. Stevens, 'Richard Holt Hutton', p. 213.
[16] *Ibid.*, p. 344. That these were too often religious aspects is regrettable;
but it is the value of the reviews of Trollope that scarcely anything in
Trollope's novels incited the critic to theological outbursts.
[17] lix, 19 June 1886, 810; quoted by Colby, *op. cit.*, p. 204.

therefore you can never really omit from any worthy picture that conscience which is its crown'.[18] Judging this picture of the conscience, and the conception of a character's 'true power of either intellectual or moral character' to be largely missing in Trollope's people, he consequently complained of the author's 'superficiality'.

The charge of superficiality is the commonest to have been levelled at Trollope. Voiced a thousand times during his lifetime, it has stuck, to be reiterated in every generation by, among others, Henry James, David Cecil and Bradford A. Booth.[19] Although the criticism is usually vague, its purpose is to exclude Trollope firmly from the ranks of true greatness, because of a supposed lack of intenseness and imagination, as Professor Booth's comments demonstrate:

> It is not often that Trollope looks deeply into man's heart and attempts to study the basic, primary emotions. He renders the surface of living with admirable fidelity to observed experience, and he is therefore one of our cherished social historians. But his shallow dredging of felt experience does not lay bare much of what is inexpressible. He must therefore be forever excluded from the company of first-rate creative artists.

David Cecil sees the shortcoming as a neglect of 'the spiritual and animal aspects of human nature'. Trollope, he says, lacked the 'prevailing intensity' of a Brontë, and his 'imagination was never fired to discover [the] guiding principle' of character, 'to penetrate beneath its surface' like George Eliot.

Hutton's case is more interesting than that of most other writers who have made the distinction between 'surface' and 'depth' in Trollope. Hutton constantly questions its validity, and in the process reveals a set of ideas which (in loose terms) constitute a mid-Victorian theory of literary composition. Moreover, this theory elaborates the division we observed in chapter 2 between so-called 'imaginative' and 'mechanical' artists, and develops it into a distinction between expressive and representational art.

Hutton's obituary article, with the exception of his specifically religious preoccupation, shows the same concerns as Professor Booth's:

> For a writer who dealt, and who always professed to deal, chiefly with the surface of society, Mr. Trollope has been singularly sincere, never seeking to hide from us that there are deeper places of human

---

[18] Quoted by Stevens, *op. cit.*, p. 396, from Hutton's *Literary Essays*.

[19] Henry James, 'Anthony Trollope', repr. in his *The House of Fiction*, ed. L. Edel, Mercury Books, 1962, p. 90; David Cecil, *Early Victorian Novelists*, Collins 1964, pp. 189 and 199; and Booth, *Anthony Trollope*, p. 82. The question of 'superficial' characterization is not dead but still reappears today.

nature into which he does not venture . . . He paints only a part of human life, but he paints that part precisely as he sees it, extenuating nothing, but letting us know that he does not profess to see all, and does not try to divine by imaginative power what he cannot see.

In this article, as in Professor Booth's book, the opposition that is posited is between society and the surface of life on the one hand, and human nature and depth on the other; and Hutton, like David Cecil, attributes the lack of 'depth' to a failure of imaginative power.[20] In the same article, Hutton elaborates his charges. 'It is not often that [Trollope] takes us into the world of solitary feeling at all,' he says, while the reader learns hardly anything from him about 'the power of the positive influence of their religion over men'. Despite these shortcomings in the genre of Trollopian fiction, Hutton is highly complimentary of its successes within the limits of its form, although at its best it must necessarily belong to a lower order of literature than that which probes deeper into the universals of human character and the divine aspects of existence. Trollope's name, Hutton predicts, rather bravely for 1882, 'will live in our literature, and though it will certainly not represent the higher regions of imaginative life, it will picture the society of our day with a fidelity with which society has never been pictured before in the history of the world'.[21]

Hutton's discussion of how such great success is possible within these limits, depends upon his idea of the inner and outer parts of human personality, which he explains in his essay on Wordsworth in *Essays Theological and Literary*,[22] where he twice makes a division of the personality into inward and outward aspects. Talking of what he calls 'the imperfect unity between Wordsworth's spirit and sense', he refers to 'the inward' aspect as showing itself in meditation, and 'the outward' in the poet's sensuous relationship with the natural world.[23] The 'inward' domain of the spirit corresponds to what he sometimes calls the 'essence' of character,[24] and to 'the world of solitary feeling' he finds missing in Trollope's characterization. The

[20] 'Surface of life', 'human nature', 'depth' and 'imaginary power' are to be understood to be the terms of the writers quoted. Any definition of them turns out to be circular. But although therefore the statements of these writers are tautologies, they are informative metaphorical tautologies.

[21] For 'soul' or 'depth' versus 'society' or 'surface', see also (as two among a thousand examples) Dallas's review of *Orley Farm* in *The Times*, 26 Dec. 1862, 5, and George Barnett Smith's article on the Brontës in the *Cornhill* xxviii, Jul. 1873, 54–71.

[22] 'Wordsworth and his genius', ii, 101–46.   [23] pp. 127–8.

[24] See his essay on Browning in *Essays Theological and Literary*, 2 vols, 1871 (quoted hereafter as '*Essays*'), ii, 190–247, p. 206; and review of *Tales of All Countries* (series 1), *Spectator* xxxv, 18 Jan. 1862, 80.

other important statement of Hutton's psychological assumptions makes a division into common human nature and individual characteristics: 'There are two selfs [*sic*] in every man—the private and the universal;—the source of personal crochets, and the humanity that is our bond with our fellow-men, and gives us our influence over them.'[25] Hutton's complaint about Trollope is that he works at the level of personal idiosyncrasy alone, and never penetrates to universal human nature. The critic states his ideal in an essay on George Eliot:

> ... what we care chiefly to know of men and women, is not so much their special tastes, bias, gifts, humours, or even the exact proportions in which these are combined,—as the general depth and mass of the human nature that is in them,—the breadth and the power of their life,—its comprehensiveness of grasp, its tenacity of instinct, its capacity for love, its need of trust. A thousand skilful outlines of character based on mere individualities of taste and talent and temper, are not near as moving to us as one vivid picture of a massive nature, stirred to the very depths of its commonplace instinct and commonplace faith.[26]

Reviewing *Can You Forgive Her?* the *Spectator* complains that Alice Vavasor's character is left 'indistinct', because Trollope has not studied how to describe 'what critics call "subjective" feeling', and therefore fails to show the reader her motives.[27] Again, in the review of *The Small House at Allington* the critic objects that 'Mr. Trollope's intellectual grasp of character . . . goes . . . only now and then much below the surface . . .',[28] while a full-length exposition of the nature of the socially visible part of character appears in the notice of the first series of *Tales of All Countries*:

> 'Mr. Trollope throws off slight tales of a certain tenuity of fibre with so much special capacity for the task, that we are sometimes

[25] p. 135. Hutton may not have subscribed to any systematic psychology—the Hutton scholars do not help us here. For his inner–outer distinction in criticism, see his essay on Dickens in *Criticisms on Contemporary Thought and Thinkers*, 2 vols, 1894, i, 89–90, where he talks of deep penetration of character as sinking a 'shaft . . . beneath the characterising stratum of some particular type of manners' to reach 'a general knowledge of the passions and heart and intellect of man'—something in which, he says, Dickens notably fails.

[26] 'The Novels of George Eliot', *Essays*, ii, 294–367, p. 304; repr. from *National Review* of 1860, with many alterations and additions—see R. H. Tener, 'Hutton's *Essays Theological and Literary*: a bibliographical note', *Notes and Queries* ccv, May 1960, 185–7. In this passage, a pseudo-exact scientific rhetoric invades Hutton's language. It is characteristic of the age that an opponent of materialism should have treated abstract qualities as analogous to measurable physical properties, and hereby have undermined his argument by turning it from metaphor into fallacy.

[27] xxxviii 9 Sept. 1865, 978–9.   [28] xxxvii, 9 Apr. 1864, 421–2.

astonished how he can beat out gold plate already so fine into the dimensions of his frequently long tales. . . . His long tales scarcely go at all deeper into the *substance* of human nature than his briefest; they are far more finished, more elaborate, more carefully polished and shaped; but all of them have more of acute observation than of deep imagination. Even Mr. Sowerby, in 'Framley Parsonage' . . . is a superficial picture, most thoughtfully and carefully coloured, with no trait of life left out; but without that broad common humanity about him which very inferior *artists* —like Mr. Charles Reade, for example—manage to give. Mr. Trollope catches the mere flying surface of life more exactly, and with less sense of its inadequacy, than any of his many and great rivals. As a painter of the transient impress which the outward circumstances—social position, profession, and the like—leave on a man, there is no one who is his equal. As a painter of the inward forces of a man's own character, there are very few among his more eminent rivals who are not greatly his superiors.

While 'inward portraiture' works from the imagination, and embodies the universals in human passion and emotion, superficial portraiture deals only with the contours left by the moulding forces of the environment, which it grasps by observation from without. Trollope himself takes human character to be malleable in youth, when it becomes moulded by the world, as in the case of Charley Tudor in *The Three Clerks*, who 'took at once the full impression of the stamp to which he was subjected'.[29] Thus Trollope allows a far more radical role to environmental forces than Hutton does—unless, that is, the latter's 'impress' of 'outward forces' is 'transient' only in teleological terms. Trollope's people often have an awareness of themselves almost exclusively in terms of their interactions with those around them. This arguably makes them specifically modern people, and perhaps Trollope was examining an altogether new phenomenon. However that may be, as far as Hutton was concerned, Trollope's method of characterization left a sense of 'intellectual thinness', because he was not fulfilling the essential requirement of the highest type of literature—'the study of man' as Hutton saw it.

Finding that so negative a statement does not do justice to Trollope's characterization, Hutton suggests how by a method of multiple exposure the author manages to convey something of universal human nature, although the critic seems unsure as to whether the result is not achieved almost by happy chance:

So many forms of men and women, and so few men and women, are at times oppressive, but then the variety of lights under which they are regarded, the multitude of circumstances amidst which we

[29] Chapter 2, World's Classics 1907, repr. 1959, p. 17.

are enabled to catch their aspect and their demeanour, does help to *suggest* deeper conceptions of the character at last. Photograph a man in fifty circumstances of his life, and though you won't get the real man even from that number of copies of him, you will at last reach some defined *impression* as to the essence of his character ; and so in his longer tales Mr. Trollope has managed to convey to us indirectly, never directly, some knowledge of the stuff of which his men and women are really made.[30]

Length is of the essence of Trollope's fiction, because 'all his favourite characters are . . . capable of being drawn out, like the joints of a telescope, to almost any conceivable length',[31] and must be extended in this way, because it is only 'when the picture is developed, as life develops a character, in a long series of terms, that we understand its full fidelity to nature'.[32] The reviewer lists the 'attitudes' in which the reader is shown Adolphus Crosbie through the *Small House* and the *Last Chronicle*, concluding that the later views modify the earlier impressions, so that it is not until he is seen 'finally, in the attitude in which he is at last seen by Lily as a fat and mediaeval widower, with all the brightness gone out of him, that we fully realise the force and completeness of the picture'.[33] At one point the *Spectator* embodies this idea of multiple views of a character in a long and elegant image, such as Hutton delighted in using:

> Mr. Trollope's power is not concentrated, but extensive and gradual in its approaches. The skill with which he gives us view after view of his different characters, each looking, at first, as if it were only the old view over again, but proving before long to have a something added, which gives you a sense of a completer know-ledge of the character, reminds us of nothing so much as the zigzags of a road terraced up a steep hill-side from which you are constantly getting the same view of a valley repeated again and again, but each time with some novelty of aspect and additional command of its relation to other neighbouring valleys, in conse-quence of the added height.[34]

Nevertheless Trollope's characters are 'neither less distinct nor better known' than our everyday social acquaintances, and the author's mind is more like a kaleidoscope forming new patterns for each novel from the same materials, than a truly creative faculty.[35]

[30] *Spectator* review of *Tales of All Countries* (1st series).
[31] Review of *Tales of All Countries* (2nd series), *Spectator* xxxvi, 7 Mar. 1863, suppl. to no. 1810, 20–1.
[32] Review of *Editor's Tales*, *Spectator* xliii, 8 Oct. 1870, 1203.
[33] *Ibid*.
[34] Review of *Lotta Schmidt and Other Stories*, xl, 21 Sept. 1867, 1062–3.
[35] Hutton on *Orley Farm*, *Spectator* xxxv, 11 Oct. 1862, 1136–8.

Trollope as society-novelist: imagination versus observation

The distinction between 'inward' and 'outward' portraiture is based on certain assumptions as to authors' materials and methods of work, that Hutton sets out in his famous article on George Eliot in *Essays Theological and Literary*. He discusses the 'school of society-novelists' —that is Jane Austen, Mrs Gaskell, Trollope and Thackeray—who, he says, by virtue of their chosen genre, achieve only superficial portraiture:

> What one remarks about the works of those who have studied any particular society as a whole far more deeply than they have studied the individual characters in it, is that their creations all stand on one level, are delineated, with great accuracy, down to the same not very considerable depth, and no further; that all, in short, are bas-reliefs cut out on the same surface.[36]

Despite the almost infinite social variety of these authors, 'all of them disappoint us in not giving more insight into those deeper roots of character which lie beneath the social surface'. The 'society-novelists' necessarily have 'mobile sympathies' and the 'faculty of readily realising . . . the workings of other minds', but these very abilities are 'to some extent inconsistent with that imaginative intensity and tenacity which is needful for the deeper insight into human character'. The 'deeper elements of human life' would be displayed if the characters' minds were 'exhibited in any direct contact with the ultimate realities of life', or 'seen grasping at the truth by which they seek to live, [or] struggling with a single deadly temptation'—that is, if they were seen in Hutton's religious terms, 'in relation to the one life in which they were made'.[37] Although these novelists 'sometimes probe the motives of their leading characters', at a 'very small depth below the surface the analysis fails to detect any certain results'.

Behind this passage lies the assumption that these authors create a kind of social reality, which is then susceptible to examination in the same way as the actual world, and Hutton goes on implicitly to identify the world of their novels with the actual world, characterizing their work as having the effect (he does not say the purpose) of supporting the ideals of Victorian society: 'The artist's graver just scratches off the wax in a few given directions till the personal bias of [the character's] taste and bearing is sufficiently revealed, while the pervading principle of the society in which the artist lives is strictly preserved.'[38]

[36] *Essays*, ii, 294.   [37] 'The Hard Church Novel'.
[38] p. 297. Compare Bagehot's comment that Thackeray's region was the 'subsoil of life—not the very surface, but just the next layer, which one little painful scratch will bring up'—*Works*, ed. St John-Stevas, ii, 316.

As a contrast to this literature of social acquiescence,[39] Hutton cites the disruptive art of Charlotte Brontë, who, he says, begins her creation of character with a full-grown notion of the passions and emotions involved, and then must try, sometimes successfully, sometimes unsuccessfully, to clothe these 'deeper elements' in a social exterior, for which, thanks to the singular circumstances of her life, she has little everyday experience to guide her. Here the 'essence of character' precedes action and determines it. With Trollope it is the reverse: the conception is social, and if the essence is to be seen, it is glimpsed through the action. The Brontë method is one of 'directness of drawing', demanding a firm grasp of the whole essence, but tending to produce characters 'less lifelike' than those of the 'society-novelists', and not permitting the author easily to suggest anything beyond what is actually portrayed; whereas 'the indirectness, the allusiveness, the educated reticence' of the 'drawing-room novelists' is the secret of their charm, and of their art itself. Hence, says Hutton, the qualities of passion and intensity belong to the one school, while the possibilities of humour and 'irony' belong to the other.

In his later article on *Orley Farm* in the *Spectator*, Hutton again compares Trollope and Charlotte Brontë, showing how evidence of romantic creative struggle and intensity can be found in the expressive novelist, but is missing from the work of an observer like Trollope:

> Mr. Trollope's imagination is not one that ever seems, to the critic's observation, at least, to brood long over visions that task its full power. ... There is nothing, apparently, of the agony of meditative travail about his mind. We know how Miss Brontë used to brood for months before she could satisfy herself about the life of her imaginative offspring, when all at once the mist drew up before her mind and she saw how to strike out a great scene or reach a new passion. No true critic, we think, who read Miss Brontë's novels, could have failed to gather this impression long before it was confirmed from her own pen. No one would gather it . . . from Mr. Trollope's tales. There is an easy, sliding manner about Mr. Trollope's imaginative delineations that, at least, disguises, if it does not disprove, the birth-throes which ushered them into the world of art.

Because he holds a Coleridgean idea of the artist's creativity as a repetition of the divine act of creation,[40] Hutton naturally regards Charlotte Brontë as far greater than Trollope, and wants to see

---

[39] Trollope, says Michael Sadleir, was 'the supreme novelist of acquiescence' —*Commentary*, p. 367.

[40] As Colby explains, 'His fundamental argument for God's existence was based on his assumption of the priority, autonomy, and self-sufficiency of mind in creation'—*op. cit.*, p. 184.

evidence of creative passion. He cannot apply the maxim *ars est celare artem* in praise of Trollope's 'easy, sliding manner'.

In his discussion of the society-novelists in his long article on George Eliot, Hutton shows himself highly appreciative of their 'capacity for catching the under-tones and allusive complexity' of the upper ranges of society—an ability he finds comparatively lacking in George Eliot to date. (The article first appeared in 1860.) On the other hand, although George Eliot also works to a great extent 'from observation', she penetrates into the 'universal' passions and emotions. Her greater depth, Hutton thinks, is largely a function of her choice of social material, and hence of facts which obtain in the real world, too. In contrast to the 'drawing-room novelists', she observes 'the phases of a more natural and straightforward life':

> The English manners she delights in are chiefly of the simplest and most homely kind,—of the rural farmers and labourers,—of the half-educated portion of the country middle-class, who have learnt no educated reticence,—and of the resident country gentry and clergy in their relations with these rough-mannered neighbours. This is a world in which she could not but learn a direct style of treatment.[41]

Education is fundamental to the difference between the classes, and thus between the two types of novel as well:

> The habit of concealing, or at most of suggesting rather than down-right expressing, what is closest to our hearts, is, as we know, a result of education. It is quite foreign to the class of people whom George Eliot knows most thoroughly, and has drawn with the fullest power. All her deepest knowledge of human nature has probably been acquired among people who speak their thoughts with the directness, though not with the sharp metallic ring, of Miss Brontë's Yorkshire heroes.[42]

Because of the educated reticence of good society, some of the most striking moments in the works of the society-novelists occur when for once they run counter to 'the pervading principle of the society' by their 'direct treatment' of a character. This happens more commonly in Thackeray than in Trollope, says Hutton, because Thackeray starts his characterization in a basis of 'strong feeling', and his best moments are frequently disruptive of the social surface, while Trollope is normally stronger in the socially conventional:

> In Thackeray . . . in whom a vein of strong feeling, whether satiric or pathetic, is almost always the basis of delineation, the finest scenes are those in which the conventional strata are broken

[41] *Essays*, ii, 301 and 303.
[42] *Essays*, ii, 301.

through, such as that in which Becky half admires her husband for knocking down Lord Steyne, or Rawdon Crawley breaks out into tenderness over his little boy.[43]

When a few years after this was written, the *Spectator* finds just such a disruptive character in *Phineas Finn*, it comments on it with admiration, complimenting Trollope on achieving a sort of characterization normally beyond him. The vigour of Lord Chiltern's character in this novel is such that he breaks through the social conventions in a fashion reminiscent of Thackeray, for the essence of the character is sufficiently strong to disrupt the social surface. The critic's comments concern the nature of the personage portrayed as well as the author's chosen method of characterization,[44] since Chiltern's personality is so strong that it must be grasped in its entirety. In the same novel, the character of Robert Kennedy is brilliant for exactly the opposite reason, the critic says, for in him there is complete congruence between the inner and the outer life. Both these figures are particularly fine because they combine 'inward portraiture' with social reality and a typicality of their class.[45] The review is worth quoting at length:[46]

> Lord Chiltern's rather violent, not to say ferocious nature, pierces the crust of social *convenances* almost as the cone of a volcano is upheaved through the surface of the earth, and tells you more of what lies beneath than is told us in any other case. . . . [t]he Right Honourable Robert Kennedy . . . seems to us a great triumph of Mr. Trollope's art, less interesting and striking, indeed, but quite as perfect as the violent Lord Chiltern himself. The silent, stiff man, who is so taken by Lady Laura Standish's frank and eager manners before marriage, and so shocked by them after marriage; who makes such dull and persevering efforts to tame down his wife, and who gets so sullen when he finds her wits too many for him; . . . who would have no guests and no novels on Sunday, and would read aloud dull sermons in the evening after the double attendance in church; . . . studied, solemn, legal, decorous,

---

[43] Review of *Miss Mackenzie*, xxxviii, 4 Mar, 244–5. 1865. There is an ambiguity in this argument, because while the major part of it concerns the breaking of *social* conventions, the passage also suggests the breaking-down of the fixed lines of the characters as hitherto presented, or of the divisions between the types of character defined by literary convention.

[44] We should say the two amounted to the same thing.

[45] The critic's perception of the identity between Kennedy's Calvinism and his social life is particularly acute. In her review of *Ayala's Angel* (*Spectator* liv, 18 June 1881, 804–5), Miss Dillwyn commends Trollope, and particularly *The Way We Live Now*, for his 'knack of converting prevalent phases of thought and opinion into flesh and blood, so that in an individual may often be recognised the embodiment of some characteristic peculiarity of society'.

[46] xlii, 20 Mar. 1869, 356–7.

pious Mr. Kennedy, with his terrible unconscious tyrannies, and his 'suit for the restitution of conjugal rights' after his wife has deserted him, is as wonderful a picture as Mr. Trollope has yet drawn. . . . Mr. Trollope has never drawn any portrait more skilfully . . . [u]nless it be Lord Chiltern's. The savage and untamable element left in the English aristocracy . . . was never so finely caught . . . There is something marvellous in the ease and rapidity with which, in a few love scenes, a few scenes of stormy altercation with his father and his friend and rival, and a hunting scene or two, the man's nature is delineated so fully on such slender materials. . . . [J]ust as in the case of Mr. Kennedy, Lord Chiltern has scarcely uttered ten sentences before one becomes intimate with him,—in this case because the individual character breaks through all ordinary restrictions to express itself,—in Mr. Kennedy's case, because the individual character is identical with those restrictions, and is incarnate in them.

The violent image of Lord Chiltern as a volcano vividly contrasts with the images of inanimate objects Hutton usually associates with Trollope's characters, such as the mountain valley or the extensible telescope quoted above. The way this particular character breaks through the *convenances* can be contrasted with the usual restraint that manners impose, and the correspondingly different material the novelist has to deal with when restricting himself to the socially conventional:

> The manners of 'good society' are a kind of social costume or disguise, which is, in fact, much more effective in concealing how much of depth ordinary characters have, and in restraining the expression of universal human instincts and feelings, than in hiding the individualities, the distinguishing inclinations, talents, bias, and tastes of those who assume them. The slight restraints which are imposed by society upon the expression of individual bias are, in fact, only a new excitement to its more subtle and various, though less straightforward, development. Instead of speaking itself simply out, it gleams out in a hundred ways by the side-paths of a more elaborate medium.[47]

Social strategy and the language of manners

For Hutton, much of Trollope's 'secret charm' lies in his treatment of these socially imposed bounds, 'the truthfulness with which he assigns a fixed verge within which the natural restraints of society and habit confine the swing of the individual passion or impulse he delineates'.[48] The *Spectator*'s review of the *Small House* is an account of how, instead of developing his characters alone as individuals,

[47] 'The novels of George Eliot', *Essays*, ii, 303.
[48] *Spectator* review of *Orley Farm*.

Trollope takes the interaction between them within these restraints as his subject, using their 'complicated social strategy' as his means of characterization. This article, a most brilliant exposition of how Trollopian fiction works, analyses 'the moral "hooks and eyes" of life', and the 'social weapons' used in the 'moral engagements between the different characters'. Hutton is systematizing and generalizing from the fruits of Trollope's acute social observation, and in the process he arrives at results which are not only more penetrating than the remarks of most other Trollopian critics, but which achieve many of the insights of the modern psychology of interpersonal behaviour as well—a subject that has only got wide-spread recognition in the last two decades.[49] The reviewer quotes Trollope to show the importance of the setting of an interview to its outcome, of the special status conferred on a person by grief and misfortune, of the strategic use of 'perfect frigidity and utter heart-lessness', of the advantage of rank in the interaction of two people, the discomfort of being, in Trollope's words, 'enveloped in the fumes of an affectionate but somewhat contemptuous patronage', and the mechanism of 'social humiliation and despair'. Because Trollope depicts his people 'by their mode of wielding' these various 'social weapons', the critic says, his socially more sophisticated characters are better presented than a Johnny Eames, for example. As the *Spectator* puts it elsewhere, a character must be 'fully exposed to that pertinacious washing in the liquid atmosphere of Mr. Trollope's imagination, by which alone he can bring the figure vividly to the eyes of others', or 'the picture remains, as the photographers say, "undeveloped" '.[50]

The social development of a character is carried out through the multiple perspectives of the other characters' consciousnesses, or, in the *Spectator*'s words, 'the construction of the little circumstances, the variations of the angles of the little mental and moral reflectors in which we catch a new glimpse of his characters' nature and essence'.[51]

[49] Erving Goffman's influential monograph, *The Presentation of Self in EverydayLife*, Edinburgh 1956, analyses the sort of social behaviour that Trollope uses as the substance of his fiction; and the analysis is very similar to Hutton's. That the possibility of an artist's taking interpersonal behaviour as his subject is not yet automatically assumed, is proved by the following passage in the *TLS* review of Anthony Powell's *The Military Philosophers* (17 Oct. 1968, 1170): 'His talent is still entirely for the nuances of what is currently known as "interpersonal behaviour" . . . The fabric of social behaviour, not the fabric of society itself, is his theme; and there is little of "inwardness" with his characters . . . [but a] growing knowledge of men in their outward social roles . . .'—scarcely distinguishable from a review of *1868*.

[50] Review of *Tales of All Countries* (2nd series).
[51] Review of *Miss Mackenzie*.

In the case of Lady Mason, for example, '[t]here is certainly much art in the added vividness which her own sense of guilt takes the moment the pressure of constant concealment is removed, and she sees it reflected back from the minds of friends whom she reveres'.[52]

In the realm of social behaviour, Hutton regards Trollope as a great 'social microscopist' in his 'diagnosis of the true significance of various little *nuances* of social manners, and the influence which he assigns to them in the working-out of his story'.[53] 'The whole secret seems to be', the reviewer of *The Golden Lion of Granpere* suggests,

> that Mr. Trollope really knows what we may call the *natural history* of every kind of man or woman he seeks to sketch,—by which we mean not so much his or her interior thoughts and feelings, but the outward habits in which these thoughts and feelings are expressed, the local and professional peculiarities of manner and habit in every place and in every trade, nay more, the minutiæ of class demeanour, the value that is attached in particular situations to standing up rather than sitting down, to making a statement in one room rather than in another; in short, the characteristic dress in which the small diplomacies of all kinds of social life clothe themselves. . . . Mr. Trollope makes one feel how great a social naturalist he is.[54]

The 'outward habits' in which 'thoughts and feelings are expressed' constitute the 'kind of social costume' described in Hutton's George Eliot essay as 'a *medium* ready to [the society-novelists'] hand in which to trace the characteristic features of the natures they delineate'.[55] Trollope, concludes the reviewer of *Miss Mackenzie* in the *Spectator,* in a very modern-sounding phrase, 'paints those manners best which are almost an artificial language in themselves, which it almost takes an art to interpret'. In the word 'language' the critic fully recognizes the communicative function of conventional behaviour as well as its restraining effects, and in this 'language' of manners, he has identified a social substance worthy of a novelist who will pursue 'the study of man'.

The critic is not, of course, working unaided, because Trollope himself often explains the meaning or value of the social acts he presents. The *Spectator* does not quote any one particular passage of this sort to illustrate its thesis, but there are a number where Trollope describes the values related to an entire symbolic system of gestures. Chapter 25 of *The Belton Estate* is a case in point. Clara

[52] Review of *Orley Farm* by Hutton.
[53] Review of *Why Frau Frohmann Raised Her Prices and Other Stories,* lv, 1 Apr. 1882, 443 [by Hutton].
[54] xlv, 18 May 1872, 630–1. The novelist as 'natural historian' is a mid-Victorian critical commonplace.   [55] *Essays,* ii, 298.

Amedroz, arriving at Aylmer Park as the son's betrothed, expects to see Lady Aylmer in the hall. But, says the narrator,

> Lady Aylmer was too accurately acquainted with the weights and measures of society for any such movement as that. Had her son brought home Lady Emily to the house as his future bride, Lady Aylmer would probably have been in the hall when the arrival took place; and had Clara possessed ten thousand pounds of her own, she would probably have been met at the drawing-room door; but she had neither money nor title,—as she in fact brought with her no advantages of any sort,—Lady Aylmer was found stitching at a bit of worsted, as though she had expected no one to come to her. And Belinda Aylmer was stitching also,—by special order from her mother.[56]

Trollope reveals the secret of the system—reveals indeed implicitly that it *is* a semiological system—which Clara also, though imperfectly, understands: so that Hutton's achievement is to make the abstraction necessary to describe it *explicitly* in these terms, and to make the surprisingly modern equation of such a system with language.

The individual and society

About the time of Trollope's death, Bentley published a collected edition of Jane Austen, and Hutton took the opportunity to compare her novels with Trollope's in the pages of the *Spectator*.[57] He analyses the social differences between the fictional worlds of the two authors, and finds Trollope's world by far the more hectic, because even in the Barsetshire novels, social pressures are threatening and obtrusive, and people are unable to be themselves. The inner portions of Trollope's characters are invaded by the outside world, while Jane Austen's people are themselves alone.

> Everybody in Miss Austen, from the squires and doctors down to the lovers, is leisurely, giving one a great sense of perfect seclusion, ample opportunity, plenty of scope, and plenty of time. Everybody in Mr. Trollope is more or less under pressure, swayed hither and thither by opposite attractions, assailed on this side and on that by the strategy of rivals; everywhere someone's room is more wanted than his company; everywhere time is short.

Developing his account of the effect of social pressures on the individual, Hutton goes on to contrast Mr Collins in *Pride and Prejudice* with Mr Thumble in the *Last Chronicle*, seeing in the latter

> a clergyman almost as stupid as Mr. Collins, and quite as full of his own small affairs; but instead of seeing him, as you do Mr.

[56] World's Classics, pp. 323–4.
[57] 'From Miss Austen to Mr. Trollope', lv, 16 Dec. 1882, 1609–11.

Collins in 'Pride and Prejudice', swelling out like a shrivelled apple under an air-pump to its full size, and much more than its full importance, you see Mr. Thumble jostled and fidgetted by the impact of the world, and crumpled up, as it were, into the insignificant man he is. In Miss Austen's novel,—it is one of their chief attractions,—this is never so. Everybody is what he is by the natural force of his own nature and tastes. You hardly see the crush of the world on any one. The vain man's vanity sedately flowers; the dull man's dullness runs to seed; the proud man's pride strikes its roots deep; even the fidgettiness of the fidgetty persons appears to come from within, not from the irritation of external pressures. . . . Turn to Mr. Trollope, and everything is changed. The atmosphere of affairs is permanent. The Church or the world, or the flesh or the devil, seem always at work to keep men going, and prevent them from being themselves alone. Mr. Trollope's people are themselves so far as the circumstances of the day will allow them to be themselves, but very often are much distorted from their most natural selves.[58]

Hutton regards these changes in fiction as the result of actual social developments, and the vision of the individual crushed beneath the pressures of society, as reflecting accurately the state of modern life. The actual social change is from what he calls 'social home rule' for the counties, to a much tougher, faster-moving society, centred on London. It is relaxing to read about the former, for the latter reminds the reader too much of the strenuousness of real life. Thus Hutton's generation—he was then fifty-six—could use Jane Austen for escape, just as many people nowadays read Trollope nostalgically. Far from seeming in this respect *démodé* and irrelevant to Hutton, Trollope was felt to touch if anything too accurately on the anxieties of the age. Younger critics such as George Saintsbury undoubtedly thought otherwise.

Hutton is criticizing both Trollope and society together, and in describing Trollope's people, he is touching on one of the principal subjects of Victorian fiction—the examination of social stresses and the interdependence of individuals in a crowded world. The modern situation does not allow of characterization after the fashion of Jane Austen, whose people are the uninhibited flowering of an initial concept or essence, which precedes action—for by Trollope's time, Hutton is saying, the separation between the inner and the outer parts of personality is breaking down under the pressure of life. If, as Hutton claims in his obituary of Trollope, the author rarely 'takes us into the world of solitary feeling', we are forced to wonder from his

[58] R. M. Polhemus, in his *The Changing World of Anthony Trollope*, University of California Press, 1968, takes the change Hutton is talking about as his central theme.

description of the Trollopian universe whether it is possible for such a world any longer to exist. If this world is a *sanctum sanctorum*, uninvaded by the environment, then it is plainly absent in Trollope's people, who are constantly under the stress of circumstances. The Warden, Charley Tudor, Lady Mason, Burgo Fitzgerald and Dr Wortle, to name but a few, are examples of characters from all periods in Trollope's career, who must expend much of their energy on coming to terms with their situations. To get anywhere they would have to run twice as fast.

Unfortunately Hutton does not go on to give us examples of the distorted soul among Trollope's characters, and it is the inevitable weakness of his analysis that he has no space in a newspaper article to examine any text in detail, even if it would have occurred to him to do so. Yet his contemporary insight could lead to an important reassessment of Trollope's authorial techniques, and in particular his much misunderstood inclusion of frequent, lengthy passages where a character is alone with his thoughts. Hutton must normally have rejected these as not revealing the innermost depths of the character concerned, which, he would have argued, required the command of poetic utterance, while many later critics have assumed that these passages were mere summary, included as padding, or because Trollope was by nature slow and repetitive. They should, however, properly be regarded as a form of interior monologue, in which the character has running over in his mind—often quite obsessively—the particulars of the situation in which he finds himself. The logical extreme is found in *The Way We Live Now*, in which the people are totally deadened and emptied by the invasion of the material world.[59] An approach to Trollope through these monologues is indicated in the next and last chapter.

Masculine and feminine characterization

In one of his two last published articles on Trollope, 'Mr. Trollope as critic',[60] Hutton reiterates the opinion he has often expressed, that Trollope's women are far inferior to his men. This point of view—so different after all from Henry James's and Michael Sadleir's—rests not on mere personal preference, but on Hutton's diagnosis of the lack of 'inward portraiture' in Trollope, because, he thought, in depicting women it is imperative to grasp their characters from within. Hutton explains that '[t]he feminine essence is beyond the reach of men unless they be true poets, and never was there a man of great creative

[59] See P. A. Tanner, 'Trollope's *The Way We Live Now*: its modern significance', *Critical Quarterly* ix, Autumn 1967, 256–71.

[60] *Spectator* lvi, 27 Oct. 1883, 1373–4.

power who had less of the poet in him than Mr. Trollope'. The reviewer of *Sir Harry Hotspur of Humblethwaite* in the *Spectator* makes the same point, finding this novel to contain an excellent male character in Sir Harry himself, and a partial failure of a female character in Emily. 'Mr. Trollope', says the critic, 'can tell you what a girl of Emily Hotspur's passion of nature would *do*, and how she would do it, but he cannot tell you what she feels.' He does not even attempt the necessary 'intensiveness of style', for he lacks 'Thackeray's power of condensing passion into words'. 'He has drawn a nature which needed portraiture by the expression of feeling as much as by action, and has failed to portray the intensity of feeling of which he has given us the sign. . . . He needed the command of a "lyrical cry" in addition to the ordinary resource of a great novelist, and he had it not at his disposal.'[61]

In 'Mr. Trollope as critic, too, Hutton sees the failure as principally due to a shortcoming of style. Trollope has 'the style of a reporter hurrying on with the chronicle of matters which he has undertaken punctually to note down', so that his writing does not reflect 'any profound impression made on the feelings and imagination of the narrator'; and—the fallacy runs—the author-narrator must be moved by the emotions he is portraying, if he is to succeed at 'inward portraiture', which is an expressive art. Trollope's style is wholly unsuitable for presenting the 'female essence', which must be grasped and expressed directly; and his style is, by the same token, unsuitable for criticism as well, Hutton's main concern in this article.

Emily Hotspur, therefore, is not a total failure, because Trollope's style enables him to present her quite satisfactorily in the dramatic mode, the critic says, even if he cannot express her directly. Hence, the critic argues—falling even deeper into a well-known Victorian fallacy—she cannot be 'beyond his *conception*, but beyond the resources of his artistic style, to execute adequately'.[62] The shortcoming is due to the author's choice of a dramatic mode of characterization: 'It is', the reviewer says, 'like the attempt of a geometrician to solve by plane geometry a problem which requires geometry of three dimensions.'

[61] xliii, 26 Nov. 1870, 1415.
[62] *Ibid*. This gross intentionalism (universal in the period) derives from an unexamined assumption that once a fictional character has been in any way thought of, it then exists as a kind of real person, susceptible to any kind of presentation. A dramatic presentation would then be sufficient evidence of the 'existence' of the character, which would then be assumed to be available for some other kind of presentation. It remains a grotesque problem to see how any critic ever decided something was *beyond* the 'conception' of the artist when the 'execution' was inadequate.

On the other hand, the critic says, Trollope's normal method of characterization is admirably suited to the case of Sir Harry:

> Mr. Trollope's picture of the irresolution of the haughty and usually absolute old baronet, and the see-saw of policy into which this irresolution plunges him . . . is as good of its kind as any moral picture he has ever yet drawn for us. No subject ever suited Mr. Trollope better. He is, before all things, a man of the world, and as a man of the world he understands to the core every passion involved in this conflict, . . . and he delineates their [?][63] external effects with the most accurate and sure artistic touch.

The difference between the complete success of Sir Harry and the comparative failure of Emily is due to the distinction Hutton sees between male and female personality, as he expounds it in his essay on Browning in *Essays Theological and Literary*,[64] where he displays what we now regard as a typically Victorian attitude towards women:

> Educated *men's* characters are naturally *in position*, and most vigorous masculine characters of any kind have a defined bearing on the rest of the world, a characteristic attitude, a personal latitude and longitude on the map of human affairs, which an intellectual eye can seize and mark out at once. But it is not so usually with women's characters. They are best expressed not by attitude and outline, but by essence and indefinite tone. As an odour expresses and characterises a flower even better than its shape and colour, as the note of a bird is in some sense a more personal expression of it than its form and feathers; so there is something of vital essence in a great poet's delineations of women which is far more expressive than any outline or colour.[65]

In Hutton's eyes, Browning resembles Trollope very much although he nowhere compares the two directly. His discussion of Browning's 'intellectual' perception of character shows the same concern with the supposed limitations of portraiture from without:

> This marked genius of Mr. Browning for interpreting . . . character in *position*,—that is, in its most characteristic attitude towards the rest of the world—is probably the secret not only of his lyrical failures, but of his generally defective powers of poetical expression; for it implies an intellectual basis for his dramatic power, and suggests that Mr. Browning is rather a highly-intellectual interpreter of action . . . throwing out all his nervous perception into the defining outline and moral profile of his part, as a blind man will finger

---

[63] The original has 'these', which makes nonsense of the whole sentence; 'their', meaning 'of all these passions', seems to be the intended sense.

[64] ii, 190–247.

[65] *Ibid.*, ii, 205–6.

the contour of a face that is dear to him, to secure the image of the characteristic lines,—rather than that he works, like Shakespeare or Goethe, by intense sympathy from within, leaving the final outline to crystallise as it may, according to the internal law and nature of the life thus germinating in his imagination.[66]

In the highest literature of all, says Hutton, the essence of character precedes action, so that George Eliot is the greatest novelist in this respect, for 'what her characters *do* is always subordinate with her to what they *are*. This is the highest artistic power . . .'[67]

But as Dallas points out in *The Gay Science*,[68] the possibilities of action are severely limited for the respectable woman in Victorian fiction, so that, in Hutton's terms, only 'inward portraiture' can present the 'female essence', which must be grasped 'by intense sympathy from within', because a woman is not 'in position' with regard to her intellectual and moral environment as a male character is. This is why Sir Harry Hotspur's character can be presented by Trollope by virtue of the author's quality as 'man of the world', which leads also to his corresponding failure with the daughter. One of the other characters that Hutton most admires, and that he also describes in terms of 'personal latitude and longitude on the map of human affairs' is Robert Kennedy in *Phineas Finn*, whose character is 'identical' with his moral and religious stance. The alternative models of the mimetic process which Hutton uses for masculine and feminine characterization therefore depend ultimately on Victorian social facts. The limited scope that women have for positive action in the Victorian novel—restricted as they normally are to dealings with their lovers, and to domestic affairs—reflects the actual status of women in society, as discussed by Dr Hewitt in her article on Trollope's female characters in the *British Journal of Sociology* for 1963.[69] It seems likely that Trollope's interest in maturer and more active women, like Lady Mason, Mrs Woodward or Lady Carbury, was based on his fundamental preoccupation with character 'in position',

[66] *Ibid.*, pp. 204–5.
[67] 'The novels of George Eliot', *Essays*, ii, 336.
[68] See also p. 42 above.
[69] 'Anthony Trollope: historian and sociologist', *British Journal of Sociology* xiv, 1963, 226–39. George Eliot reports as much, when she says of Milly Barton, 'A loving woman's world lies within the four walls of her own home; and it is only through her husband that she is in any electric communication with the world beyond'–*Scenes from Clerical Life*, Blackwood's 'Standard Edition' [n.d.], i, 97.
Thackeray embodies the orthodoxy when he writes to Jane Shawe about his daughter Anny, 'I am afraid very much she is going to be a man of genius: I would far sooner have had her an amiable & affectionate woman . . .' —letter of July 1846, *The Letters and Private Papers*, ed. Ray, ii, 240.

or the 'moral physiognomy' of character, as Hugh Sykes Davies puts it.[70]

The imitation of character

Hutton, then, had two alternative models of the mimetic process: imagination from within and observation from without, belonging respectively to lyric poets and Charlotte Brontë on the one hand, and the 'school of society-novelists' on the other. The latter is mechanical, and expressed in metaphors of copying, printing, observing, and photography, and associated with static or mechanical images—the alpine valley, the diorama, the kaleidoscope, the extensible telescope—while the process at its best is seen as a probing or penetrating of character from without, or the sinking of a shaft. Such a reproductive view of mimesis descends directly from the age of Johnson, when 'the work of art continues to be regarded as a kind of reflector, though a selective one [and the] artist himself is often envisioned as the agent holding the mirror up to nature'.[71] Hutton's alternative model is expressive, and 'Romantic'. With 'imaginative' literature, Hutton associates the images of fire, spark, germ, organic growth, bird-song, and a flower's colour and perfume—the double sense of 'essence' is very useful—and the process is one of expressing, 'striking out', grasping, of 'natural' development and crystallization 'according to the internal law and nature of the life thus germinating in [the writer's] imagination', involving passion and 'imaginative travail' on his part. Obstetric imagery abounds.

As we have seen, many reviewers in the *Spectator* and elsewhere confirm the judgment of Trollope as 'unromantic', because lacking in imagination, and at least two quote Wordsworth to make their point:

> The light that never was on sea or land does not illuminate the writings of Mr. Trollope; but there is generally plenty of that other kind of light with which, after all, we are more familiar, and which not a few of us, perhaps, prefer to the transcendental lustre.[72]

and,

> 'Minds that have nothing to confer . . . find little to perceive, and the artist who places himself entirely at the mercy of his material, without the support of an independent invention, must discover

[70] H. S. Davies, *Trollope*, Longmans for British Council, 1960 (Writers and their Work, no. 118), p. 15.

[71] M. H. Abrams, *The Mirror and the Lamp: Romantic theory and the critical tradition*, N.Y., Norton, 1958, p. 42.

[72] Review of *Duke's Children*, *Spectator* liii, 12 June 1880, 755–6. This article reads quite unlike Hutton.

sooner or later that he is unable even to present a complete and vivid picture of the mere outward facts of life.[73]

The 'imaginative' artist is universally regarded as greater than the reproducer of reality, for the former alone is truly creative. To the mid-Victorian mind there is something too facile in the so-called rendering of observed reality.

Since the novel to Hutton ought to be 'the study of man' by the imitation of human nature, these two models of the mimetic process are always applied to an author's characterization. The two corresponding methods of imitating character each involve two stages of creation, so that a two-stage mimesis is common to Hutton's views of both types of artist.

The clearest statement of the expressive model is found in the *National Review* of 1857, where Hutton's brother-in-law, William Caldwell Roscoe, quotes with approval Mrs Gaskell's account of Charlotte Brontë's process of imitating character:

> Miss Brontë was struck by the force or peculiarity of the character of some one whom she knew; she studied it, and analysed it with subtle power; and having traced it to its germ, she took that germ as the nucleus of an imaginary character, and worked outwards; thus reversing the process of analysation and unconsciously reproducing the same external development.[74]

So her characters spring from an essence, which has been isolated from prototypes in the real world. Roscoe, while praising the 'body, reality, definiteness' of her characters, complains that they are 'too singular', because she is not one of those authors with 'a nature of very extended though not necessarily deep sympathies, which finds something in itself answering to all hints, and ready to gather up all clues', and it is these sympathies that make for the successful portrayal of external characteristics, or a whole phase of society.

Hutton has the same idea of the creative process in mind when in his volume in the *English Men of Letters* series he discusses Scott's lack of 'spiritual irony', which he attributes to the fact that Scott 'never even seemed so much as to contemplate that sundering of substance and form, that unclothing of the soul, in order that it might be more effectively clothed upon, which is at the heart of . . . spiritual irony'.[75] The passage contains the same assumptions about the mimetic

[73] Review of *Prime Minister, Saturday Review* xlii, 14 Oct. 1876, 481–2.

[74] 'Miss Brontë', *National Review* v, Jul. 1857, 127–64; repr. as 'The Miss Brontës', in his *Poems and Essays*, ed. R. H. Hutton, 2 vols, 1860, ii, 309–53. Like Hutton, Roscoe divides novelists into the deep portrayers of individual character, and the broad, superficial painters of society.

[75] *Sir Walter Scott*, 1902 (repr. 1907), pp. 120–1.

process as the earlier quotation from Mrs Gaskell. Character consists of an 'essence'—the 'germ' of Mrs Gaskell's passage—and an external appearance: and the two stages of mimesis correspond to these two parts. The first part is the isolation of the essence, and the second, its re-embodiment in a new outward form, so that the fiction stands at two removes from reality.

The case of Trollope's method of imitation is rather less clearcut, because as we have seen his contemporaries tended to attribute him with absolute 'truth to life', or to regard his characters as somehow having a real existence apart from his novels. In consequence, the critics often draw no distinct line between the fictional world and the real world, and beg the question of mimesis altogether, even when they admit that there is a degree of distortion in the fiction. Thus Trollope is denied the qualities of imagination and inventiveness because he 'sketches men chiefly as he sees them',[76] and 'contrives to give us the very *facsimile* of real life, but with an elastic feature here and there'.[77] Even his humour suffers from the same artistic limitations in the eyes of his contemporaries, and is 'rather a proper appreciation of the paradoxes of social life, than any very original faculty of his own'.[78] 'Mr. Trollope's humour', says Hutton in his obituary article, 'lay in his keen perception of the oddity of human motives, pursuits, and purposes, and his absolute truthfulness in painting them to the life. The humour . . . is not inventive, but perceptive.'

Hutton, however, sometimes goes far beyond the naïve assumption of direct copying from nature, as for example in his review of *Orley Farm*, where, recognizing the dangers of positing absolute reproduction of life, he says that Trollope may *seem* merely to observe the characters around him in society and point out their features to his readers; but, of course, 'this is more or less an illusion. Sir Peregrine Orme and Lady Mason, and Moulder and Kantwise, and the rest, whatever they may seem, *are* the creatures of Mr. Trollope's imagination and not the mere objects of his observing eye.' Yet, Hutton continues, they appear to be only reproductions from life because in origin 'they are not so much the offsprings [*sic*] of his heart, sentiment, and self-knowledge, as results of his alert, observing, and combining eye. No great novelist probably ever drew so little from the resources of his own visionary life,—so much from impromptu variations of the forms given by experience, as Mr. Trollope.' To regard Trollope as working from 'the forms given by experience', in this way, presupposes a two-stage process of imitation; but Hutton

[76] Review of *Last Chronicle*, *Spectator* xl, 13 Jul. 1867, 778–80.
[77] 'Mr. Trollope's caricature:—*Rachel Ray*', *Spectator* xxxvi, 24 Oct. 1863, 2660–1.   [78] *Ibid.*

goes further, and describes Trollope as having a working model of society in his head, which he can observe: 'In short, Mr. Trollope does not give us so much the impression of conceiving his own conceptions, as of very acutely observing them as they pass along the screen of some interior faculty.' The two stages in Trollope's mimesis, as Hutton sees it, are the setting up of a mental analogue of the real world, and then the transcription of that analogue.

The *Spectator* review of *Miss Mackenzie* also assumes that Trollope has his characters defined in his head before he starts to write, and that in writing he expends his effort chiefly on 'the construction of the little circumstances, the variations of the angles of the little mental and moral reflectors in which we catch a new glimpse of his characters' nature and essence':

> His characters themselves once conceived never vary . . . and always affect us as if they were data of Mr. Trollope's mind, the fixed, unalterable points on his chart of operations, as if all that his imagination really had to work at was to find out the little incidents which would best throw a variety of lights *upon* these fixed centres of his thought and on their relation to each other.

(Incidentally, Trollope himself says that Miss Mackenzie is one case where he did change his 'conception' of a character while writing a novel.[79]) The same assumption underlies the review of *Hunting Sketches*, when the critic says, 'Mr. Trollope has performed in these sketches the scientific operation of abstraction on the population of his memory and imagination. He has classified them, and found it an effort to do so.'[80]

The two models of the mimetic process underlie Hutton's whole discussion of the 'society-novelists' perfectly consistently, since the one is concerned with the isolation of an 'essence' as the basis of deep, individual characterization, while in the other the author works from the population of his mind, to depict a whole phase of society.[81] Thus these parallel models, the latter more or less Augustan, and the former Romantic, complete the logical structure of Hutton's theory of characterization.

[79] *Autobiography*, pp. 188–9.
[80] *Spectator* xxxviii, 27 May 1865, 587–8.
[81] The problem as to how the mental world is then transcribed is, of course, never faced, or even recognized.

6

TROLLOPE'S THEORY
AND PRACTICE OF
NOVEL-WRITING

Bradford Booth and Richard Stang both give sympathetic accounts, accurate as far as they go, of some important aspects of Trollope's theory of the novel.[1] His ideal of fiction as they convey it is broadly speaking 'a picture of common life enlivened by humour and sweetened by pathos',[2] which teaches wholesome moral lessons by means of fictional exemplars who are neither wholly good nor wholly evil. While both Professor Booth and Professor Stang admit the superiority of Trollope's practice over his theory, they nevertheless miss some of the most interesting features of the latter. Only such aspects as have hitherto been neglected or misrepresented will be dealt with here; but these will be found to be fundamental to Trollope's relation to his contemporaries, while contributing substantially to a new interpretation of his complete fictional output.

It is generally held that the publication of Trollope's *Autobiography* marked a distinct turning-point in his reputation, and that a new generation with more self-conscious aesthetic views, found in his account of his own career, the very ammunition it needed to attack him. In fact, as we have seen, his reputation with such people was already very low long before his death, and there was no longer any need for them to attack him. But it certainly is true that a number of Trollope's curiously self-depreciatory remarks have since been used and re-used for more or less honest purposes of disparagement; and even so, a certain amount of falsification has usually been wrought in the way of selective quotation. The *Autobiography* was completed in April 1876 when his sales and reputation had declined drastically, but the self-criticism in the work does not indicate a change in his view of his own fiction between the periods of his acknowledged

---

[1] Booth, *Anthony Trollope*, and 'Trollope on the novel'; Stang, *The Theory of the Novel in England*.
[2] *Autobiography*, p. 126.

popularity and success, and of his decline. He is not more apologetic in his authorial comments in his later novels than in his early ones. Nor do his damaging remarks in the *Autobiography* correspond to any radically new line of attack by his critics from 1870 onwards. The truth is surely that his falling sales may have been one impulse towards writing his apologia, but not the determining factor as to its contents.

The substance of the attacks Trollope suffered in the 1870s was little different from what the *Saturday Review* for one had been saying for years before. Only the emphasis was changed. Equally, the explicit attitude of Trollope's narrative persona to his own narrative remains remarkably constant. There can be changes in the choice of subject —so that (at the limits) the Barsetshire novels are predominantly county and clerical, and *The Way We Live Now* is almost entirely concerned with financial speculation in the metropolis; but the same rejection of suspense is expressed throughout, with the same disclaimers of narrative ability, the same choice of imperfect heroes, and the same partial sympathy for wrongdoers. From the revelation of Caroline Waddington's identity in *The Bertrams* (1859), to the disclosure of the Peacocke's bigamy in *Dr. Wortle's School* (1881), from the too human Mark Robarts in *Framley Parsonage* (1860–61) to John Caldigate (1878–79), from the sympathetic criminal, Lady Mason, in *Orley Farm* (1861–62), to the pathetic wrongdoer, Cousin Henry (1879), we find the same rejection of the conventions of fiction, and a number of authorial apologies and explanations associated with each case. These deliberate and acknowledged ruptures of convention (or 'subtilising of a literary platitude', as Cockshut calls the process)[3] represent a continued, lifelong effort, first to establish and then to defend, a particular form of everyday truth-to-life, or Trollopian realism, as I have called it in the foregoing chapters.

Trollope's disclaimers of narrative ability, however, are often a serious flaw in his novels, and the *Saturday* is surely right to object to his purposeless admission that he cannot solve the problems presented by the plot of *Doctor Thorne*.[4] This is one of a number of serious 'slaps at credulity', as Henry James calls them,[5] like that which opens the last chapter of *Ayala's Angel*, where the narrator discusses the arrangement of his story, admitting that it is fictional, and may be manipulated at will. Even though this could be damaging to the integrity of the novel, it nevertheless fits into Trollope's whole programme of disturbing the conventions—this time that of the happy ending: for the narrator says, 'Infinite trouble has been taken not only in arranging these marriages but in joining like to like,—so

[3] *Anthony Trollope*, p. 164.
[4] See p. 11 above. [5] *House of Fiction*, p. 102.

that, if not happiness, at any rate sympathetic unhappiness, might be produced.' Thus, though he is only very slightly straining the convention, he is still declaring his interest in potentially unhappy marriage as a 'true' fictional subject. So although some 'intrusions' by the narrator are very damaging to the fiction, and others not, most of them have the deliberate purpose of furthering Trollopian realism. His disclaimers of greatness in the *Autobiography*[6] may be disbelieved, but his own low estimate of himself can be seen from his belief that he had to apologize for every slight deviation from the conventions of sentimental fiction. Undoubtedly he misjudged himself, and though a nearly great novelist, had the instincts of a mediocrity.

These narrative comments or apologies taken together constitute his defence of his literary methods. Similarly we misread the *Autobiography* if we look at the 'self-accusations' it contains as merely illustrating his psychology, or exemplifying his critical naïvety. The book contains a strong element of attack on the literary fashions of the age, and of counterattack on his critics, all expressed through a sarcasm so quiet, and an irony so unobtrusive, as to be largely overlooked. In fact the *Autobiography* misfires as polemic, and was decidedly unsuited to touch the age which followed. The impression that has lasted and has affected our reading of it ever since, is of critical naïvety and a unique mixture of philistinism, thin-skinnedness, honesty, pride and self-effacement.

The 'Autobiography'

It is impossible not to feel at times that his disclaimers of high literary merit are overdone, and that he is trying to protect himself by anticipating possible adverse criticsm. Yet this is by no means the whole story, as the notorious comparison of the novelist's work to the shoemaker's will illustrate. As we have seen, he was constantly attacked throughout his career for 'mechanical' work, and as early as 1860 the *Saturday Review* accused him of making a novel 'just as he might make a pair of shoes',[7] while at about the same time he was using a similar comparison himself in letters and conversation, to convey the need for hard work in writing.[8] The key passage, however, occurs in chapter seven of the *Autobiography*, and as usually quoted, reads:

> There are those who would be ashamed to subject themselves to such a taskmaster [as Trollope's working tables], and who think that the man who works with his imagination should allow himself to wait till—inspiration moves him. When I have heard such

[6] e.g. *Autobiography*, p. 120.
[7] ix, 19 May 1860, 643-4.   [8] See p. 55 above.

doctrine preached, I have hardly been able to repress my scorn. To me it would not be more absurd if the shoemaker were to wait for inspiration . . .[9]

The first thing to point out is that these sentences refer to the labour of writing in the sense of getting down on paper something which the author has already worked out in great detail. However fallacious his ideas may sound with reference to modern theories of language, Trollope always made a sharp distinction between the work of 'conception' and the 'writing' of his fiction. His whole defence against the charge of mechanical writing (examined in greater detail later in this chapter), is based upon this division. He claims that it is the 'conception' which requires the hardest and most important effort of creation, and that while his 'writing' may have been fast and disciplined, his work of 'conception' had always been thorough.

More significant still is the sarcastic tone of the passage, where all the scorn he can hardly repress is condensed into the single dash half-way through the quotation: '. . . till—inspiration moves him.' His attack is directed against those who, like Victor Hugo, 'this sententious French Radical', would claim 'exemption from punctuality . . . if not on the score still with the conviction of intellectual superiority'.[10] The conclusion of the 'shoemaker' passage confirms the impression of sarcasm: 'To me', it reads, 'it would not be more absurd if the shoemaker were to wait for inspiration, or the tallow-chandler for the divine moment of melting.' The humorous intention is clear, although the second image is normally omitted, to give a greater prominence to the notorious 'shoemaker'. But the passage cannot be read without it, since he is obviously—and quite wittily—attacking a pseudo-'Romantic' view of literary work.

Another important section of the *Autobiography* where the tone of a key passage has been overlooked is in Trollope's discussion of 'sensational' and 'anti-sensational' novels:

Among English novels of the present day, and among English novelists, a great division is made. There are sensational novels and anti-sensational, sensational novelists and anti-sensational; sensational readers and anti-sensational. The novelists who are considered to be anti-sensational are generally called realistic. I am realistic. My friend Wilkie Collins is generally supposed to be sensational. The readers who prefer the one are supposed to take delight in the elucidation of character. They who hold by the other are charmed by the construction and gradual development of a plot. All this is, I think, a mistake,—which mistake arises from the inability of the imperfect artist to be at the same time realistic and sensational. A good novel should be both, and both in the highest degree.[11]

This passage is polemical, and its whole point lies in its style. It is not a case of extreme critical naïvety. Trollope had good reason to attack the standard classification of novels in his own day, considering the abuse he suffered throughout his career for his extreme realism, and for his choice of shocking subjects. He often remained unappreciated too, because his critics had the wrong expectations from his fiction. An example which he cites from his own work as combining sensation and realism is 'Lady Mason, as she makes her confession at the feet of Sir Peregrine Orme'[12] in *Orley Farm*, which was one novel whose principal story contrived to please all his most demanding critics. In the passage quoted, the reiteration of 'sensational . . . and anti-sensational', and the deliberate shortness of the sentences, do not show any weakness in his command of language, but are his way of mocking the naïvety of the views he is attacking, while the reiteration itself produces a humorous crescendo from the acceptable sensational novels', through the extension 'sensational novelists', to the absurdity of 'sensational readers', with a comma between the first two terms, and a longer pause before the climax. The choice of words for this effect is careful throughout: for example, 'a *great* division'; 'novelists *who are considered to be* anti-sensational *are generally called* realistic'; 'readers . . . *are supposed* to take delight', and so on. Hence, too, the sometimes ridiculously simple sentences, such as 'I am realistic. My friend Wilkie Collins is generally supposed to be sensational.' There is an absurdity in claiming to be 'realistic', and an equal absurdity in suggesting that one might have a 'sensational' friend. At the end of the passage the tone changes suddenly away from the factitiousness of 'They who hold by the other are charmed by the construction and gradual development of a plot', to the forthrightness of 'All this is, I think, a mistake . . .'—a deliberate understatement in view of the mockery of the prevalent orthodoxy that has come before. Certainly his positive critical notions, once he develops them, are thin, but his statements of point of view can be quietly most compelling.

If more energy has been expended on these passages than they alone seem to deserve, it is because Trollope's style is largely neglected —so that even the perceptive Cockshut can call it 'nondescript'[13]— and consequently most of his stylistic successes are held to be mistakes

---

[11] *Autobiography*, pp. 226–7.   [12] *Ibid.*, p. 227.
[13] *Anthony Trollope*, p. 31. But see H. S. Davies, 'Trollope and his style', *Review of English Literature* i, Oct. 1960, 73–85; G. Tillotson, 'Trollope's style', in G. Tillotson and K. Tillotson, *Mid-Victorian Studies*, Athlone Press, 1965, pp. 56–61,

or lucky chances, and exceptions to the rule of pedestrian dullness, so much does the power of expectation guide the reader's understanding. And nowhere is this more true than in the *Autobiography*, where the gentle irony is overlooked because it does not rise to epigram or wit. What he says is often not strikingly original, and his power of marshalling facts and ideas in an argument is not impressive. We must pay constant attention to his style, both in the *Autobiography* and in the novels, or we miss what is one of the most important values of his work—the point and bias in what he says, which derives from his quiet but sometimes brilliant deployment of his linguistic resources.

Trollope on the creative process

Trollope makes a very clear distinction between the work of 'conception' and of writing; and his account of his own creative process is very close to the two-stage mimetic model Hutton assumes.[14] The two stages of composition for Trollope too are the setting up of a set of characters in a mental world, where they become to him as friends, and the almost mechanical writing-down of the story which springs from his consideration of the characters.

Conception

In the *Autobiography*, Trollope speaks of

> that work of observation and reception from which [comes the novelist's] power, without which his power cannot be continued,— which work should be going on not only when he is at his desk, but in all his walks abroad, in all his movements through the world, in all his intercourse with his fellow-creatures. He has become a novelist, as another has become a poet, because in those walks abroad he has, unconsciously for the most part, been drawing in matter from all that he has seen and heard. But this has not been done without labour, even when the labour has been unconscious.[15]

This, he says, is 'that portion of a novelist's work which is of all most essential to success'. And it is also so much the most demanding part of his work that a decline in a novelist's power is caused not by a failing ability to write—for 'a man to whom writing well has become a habit may write well though he be fatigued'—but by a loss of interest in the world around him, if 'there comes a time when he shuts his eyes and shuts his ears . . .', and 'woodenness' results.

This work of 'conception'—and Trollope uses the word in this

[14] See chapter 5 above.   [15] pp. 230–1.

sense[16] was not a matter of directly copying characters met with in real life, but of training his 'moral consciousness', and picking up 'as I went along whatever I might know or pretend to know'—about clergymen, for *The Warden*,[17] for example. Thus he built a fictitious world, which stood at one remove from the real world, and was a sort of analogue of it, produced by 'that work of observation and reception', very much like the society Hutton speaks of as built up by the novelist's 'alert, observing and combining eye'.[18]

At all stages in his life Trollope led a vivid imaginary life, and Hugh Sykes Davies points out the relevance of his early indulgence in fantasy to his later writing. 'I never became a king, or a duke' Trollope says,

> . . . a learned man, nor even a philosopher. But I was a very clever person, and beautiful young women used to be fond of me. And I strove to be kind of heart, and open of hand, and noble in thought, despising mean things; and altogether I was a very much better fellow than I have ever succeeded in being since. . . . I learned in this way to maintain an interest in a fictitious story, to dwell on a work created by my own imagination, and to live in a world altogether outside the world of my own material life.[19]

Mr Davies comments: 'This passionate and genuinely imaginative concern with moral existence was the essence of his approach to the novel, from *The Warden* on.'[20] Later in life he continued to lead an active inner life, but now in the fictional world of the novels he was engaged upon, which he implicitly likens to the real world, and shows that, while all the novels take place, as it were, in the same country, with the same social laws, he had no tendency to confuse one story or set of characters with another:

> Many of us live in different circles; and when we go from our friends in town to our friends in the country, we do not usually fail to remember the little details of the one life or the other. . . . In our lives we are always weaving novels, and we manage to keep the different tales distinct. A man does, in truth, remember that which it interests him to remember . . .[21]

Thus, even when writing *Castle Richmond* and *Framley Parsonage* together, he was able to proceed without any confusion of the two.

[16] *Autobiography*, p. 175.
[17] *Ibid.*, p. 93.
[18] Review of *Orley Farm* in the *Spectator*; see p. 124 above.
[19] *Autobiography*, p. 43.
[20] *Trollope*, pp. 14–15. A similar observation is made in a review of the *Autobiography*, *Westminster Review* (ns) lxv, Jan. 1884, 83–115, pp. 104–5.
[21] *Autobiography*, pp. 155–6.

He had an inner world, of which the world of each novel was, as it were, a sub-world; or rather, he set up a mental model of society, of which the world of each novel was a sub-model.

The inner world

It was mid-Victorian orthodoxy to assert that a novelist had to have an 'affectionate intimacy with his creations', as Alexander Shand expressed it,[22] and Trollope himself says that he lived with his characters 'in the full reality of established intimacy'.[23] A novelist's characters, he goes on, 'must be with him as he lies down to sleep, and as he wakes from his dreams. He must learn to hate them and to love them. He must argue with them, quarrel with them, forgive them, and even submit to them.' And this he must do in the dimension of time as well, noting the effect of all the events of life on them: 'On the last day of each month recorded, every person in his novel should be a month older than on the first. . . . It is so that I have lived with my characters, and thence has come whatever success I have attained.' Of his ambitious scheme to carry the same set of characters through all the Palliser novels, he says, 'I . . . found myself so frequently allured back to my old friends. So much of my inner life was passed in their company, that I was continually asking myself how this woman would act when this or that event had passed over her head, or how that man would carry himself when his youth had become manhood, or his manhood declined into old age.'[24] The story was determined by the characters, and such speculations as these about them.[25]

He knew the places just as intimately:

I had [Barsetshire] all in my mind,— its roads and railroads, its towns and parishes, its members of Parliament, and the different hunts which rode over it. I knew all the great lords and their castles, the squires and their parks, the rectors and their churches. . . . Throughout these stories there has been no name given to a fictitious site which does not represent to me a spot of which I know all the accessories, as though I had lived and wandered there.[26]

So indelibly implanted were these persons and places in his mind, that: 'Had I left *Framley Parsonage* or *Castle Richmond* half-finished fifteen years ago, I think I could complete the tales now with very little trouble. I have not looked at *Castle Richmond* since it was pub-

[22] 'The literary life of Anthony Trollope', *Edinburgh Review* clix, Jan. 1884, 186–212, p. 201. Walter Besant makes the same point (more diffusely) in his *The Art of Fiction*, 1884—a lecture, which suffers, like many of Trollope's pronouncements, from being designed as advice to youthful aspirants.

[23] *Autobiography*, p. 233.   [24] *Ibid.*, p. 319.

[25] See Booth, 'Trollope on the novel', *loc. cit.*, for more on this subject.

[26] *Autobiography*, p. 154.

lished; and poor as the work is, I remember all the incidents.'[27] The
vigour and reality to him of his mental creations cannot be doubted.

While the *Spectator* speaks of Trollope's characters as figures in a
'diorama', or as passing along 'the screen of some interior faculty'.
Trollope himself talks of his 'gallery' of characters, from which he
could summon them up at will, and in which he knew each individual,
visually and socially: '. . . of all in that gallery I may say that I know
the tone of the voice, and the colour of the hair, every flame of the
eye, and the very clothes they wear. Of each man I could assert
whether he would have said these or other words; of every woman,
whether she would then have smiled or so have frowned.'[28] Hutton's
idea of the author observing an interior world of his own is very close
to Trollope's own.

Hutton considered that an author had need of what, quoting
Forster's *Life of Dickens*, he called a ' "city of the mind" for inward
consolation',[29] and Trollope too suggests that he derived some sort of
'consolation' from the mental world of the Palliser novels (just as he
had from his youthful fantasies), when he says that 'in the perform-
ance of the work I had much gratification, and was enabled from
time to time to have in this way that fling at the political doings of
the day which every man likes to take, if not in one fashion then in
another'.[30] His failure at the Beverley election was very poignant to
him, and he speaks with unusual passion and even bitterness about his
ambition to enter Parliament.

The 'telling' of the tale

Having set up his mental model, and thoroughly immersed himself in
his fictitious world, Trollope set off writing at high speed, using his
characters as the basis of the action, and relying very little on a pre-
conceived plot: '[W]ith nothing settled in my brain as to the final
development of events, with no capacity of settling anything, but
with a most distinct conception of some character or characters, I
have rushed at the work as a rider rushes at a fence which he does
not see.'[31] He defends his fast writing by maintaining that his
'execution' or 'telling' may be rapid, but the work of 'conception' has
been thorough.

> When my work has been quickest done, . . . the rapidity has been
> achieved by hot pressure, not in conception, but in the telling of
> the story. . . . I have trebled my usual average, and have done

---

[27] *Autobiography*, p. 156.   [28] *Ibid.*, p. 233.
[29] 'The genius of Dickens', repr. from the *Spectator* of 1874, in his *Criticisms on Contemporary Thought and Thinkers*, 2 vols, 1894, i, 87–93, p. 91.
[30] *Autobiography*, p. 184. See p. 29 above.   [31] *Ibid.*, p. 175.

so in circumstances which have enabled me to give up all my thoughts for the time to the book I have been writing. This has generally been done at some quiet spot among the mountains . . . At such times I have been able to imbue myself thoroughly with the characters I have had in hand. I have wandered alone among the rocks and woods, crying at their grief, laughing at their absurdities, and thoroughly enjoying their joy. I have been impregnated with my own creations till it has been my only excitement to sit with the pen in hand, and drive my team before me at as quick a pace as I could make them travel.[32]

The division into 'conception' and 'telling' is almost absolute, with the work of cogitation as by far the harder part. In this way he was able to let his story develop as it went along—he mentions elsewhere a story's need 'to tell itself'[33]—while keeping in his characters the feeling of 'speaking, moving, living, human creatures'.[34] 'Forethought', he says in *Thackeray*, 'is the elbow-grease which the novelist . . . requires.' 'The arrangement of the words is as though you were walking simply along a road. The arrangement of your story is as though you were carrying a sack of flour while you walked.'[35]

In 1879, three years after finishing his *Autobiography*, and about the same time as his *Thackeray*, Trollope published an article entitled ' A Walk in a Wood' in *Good Words*,[36] in which he describes his methods of work at greater length, and helps to bridge the gap between the 'conception' of his characters, and the writing down of his story. It is an unusually lyrical piece of writing for him, and may possibly help to dispel the impression of him as a passionless dullard. He recounts how he must walk alone in a wood to order his thoughts before sitting down to write, and he lists his best-loved haunts, such as Devonshire, where 'there are still some sweet woodland nooks, shaws and holts, and pleasant spinneys, through which clear water brooks run, and the birds sing sweetly, and the primroses bloom early, and the red earth pressing up here and there gives a glow of colour'. Equally, 'the chestnut groves of Lucca, and the oak woods of Tuscany are delightful, where the autumnal leaves of Vallombrosa lie thick' ; but he finally settles on the Black Forest as his favourite 'hunting ground for my thoughts'. The article gives a more complete idea of just how far everything was prepared in his mind before his 'stint' of writing began:

If I can find myself here of an afternoon when there shall be another two hours for me, safe before the sun shall set, with my stick in my

[32] *Ibid.*, pp. 175–6.   [33] *Letters*, p. 265.
[34] *Autobiography*, p. 232.   [35] pp. 122–3.
[36] Sept. 1879, pp. 595–600.

hand, and my story half-conceived in my mind, with some blotch of a character or two, just daubed out roughly on the canvas, then if ever I can go to work, and decide how he, how she, and they shall do their work. . . . Gradually as I walk, or stop, as I seat myself on a bank, or lean against a tree, perhaps as I hurry on waving my stick above my head till with my quick motion the sweat-drops come out upon my brow, the scene forms itself for me. . . . [Then] words are weighed which shall suit, but do no more than suit, the greatness or the smallness of the occasion.

To Trollope, then, the writing itself was the least of the novelist's problems, as long as like Trollope himself, he was blest with robust health, and did not wish to 'twist his work to curl-papers'.[37] He is very insistent on the need to learn a clear, correct and pleasing style, which nobody can do 'without much labour',[38] but once this has been achieved, the fitting of the words to the thoughts is almost automatic, almost a matter of reflex: '[The novelist's] language must come from him as music comes from the rapid touch of the great performer's fingers; as words come from the mouth of the indignant orator; as letters fly from the fingers of the trained compositor; as the syllables tinkled out by little bells form themselves to the ear of the tele-graphist.'[39] He speaks as though there were words which fitted exactly what he wanted to say, standing in direct correspondence with his mental images, like the relation between the telegraphic code and normal written English—an exceedingly naïve view of language, but one which confirms his own careful mental preparation, and his complete mastery of a style that could express very easily all he wished to say by it. The best language, he says, 'should be as ready and as efficient a conductor of the mind of the writer to the mind of the reader as is the electric spark which passes from one battery to [another] battery'.[40] What he wants to say is already rehearsed, like the music the performer is interpreting; and he is powerfully urged to write by the vividness of his 'conception', which motivates him as strongly as indignation does an orator. Finally, the energy and exhilaration of writing are expressed in his image of driving his team as fast as possible, or riding—as, literally, the myopic Trollope must often have done[41]—at a fence he cannot see.

The most unsatisfactory aspect of Trollope's account, and of Hutton's, too, is this utterly reproductive view of language. Yet Trollope would make a most interesting subject for a stylistic study,

---

[37] William Hardman considered 'Meredith writes so much better when he has not time to finish, rewrite, and (as Anthony Trollope says) twist his work to curl-papers.'—*The Hardman Papers*, ed. Ellis, Constable, 1930, p. 175.

[38] *Autobiography*, p. 177. See also *Thackeray*, pp. 184-7 and 196-7.

[39] *Autobiography*, p. 177.   [40] *Autobiography*, p. 235.

[41] *Ibid.*, pp. 171-2.

because we know a great deal of his habits of work. Louis Milic, a computer stylistician who largely approves of Hugh Sykes Davies's article 'Trollope and his style', is correct but slightly unfair when he says 'Davies works hard to defend his author against a charge that could have been dismissed as absurd, that Trollope's style had no individuality'.[42] But Milic underestimates the resistance of some of Trollope's critics to self-evident truths. The story that Trollope is virtually 'without' a style has persisted for a long time, and it is time it was finally demolished.

Trollopian realism

As well as providing a large amount of evidence about Trollope's use and extension or rejection of the novel-writing conventions of his age, and about mid-Victorian literary expectations, the examination of contemporary attitudes *vis-à-vis* his work—of (in a broad sense) the critical language of the day—has opened up some other important new approaches to his fiction. From the evidence of the *Autobiography*, and from the advance layouts of his novels, such as those of *Sir Harry Hotspur* and *The Way We Live Now* reproduced by Sadleir in his *Commentary*, we must take it as given that Trollope's fiction is based on sets of characters, who precede the action and largely determine it. As long as we do not follow Bradford Booth's example, and conclude from this that it is the characters themselves that must be discussed, the primacy of character can be seen as the key to his whole theory and practice of the novel.

In his *Anthony Trollope*, Professor Booth says, 'Normally one approaches the work of a novelist from the point of view of the ideas that are developed or from the point of view of the techniques that are employed. But Trollope's novels do not deal primarily with ideas, and the technique is elementary' (p. ix). Despite this view of the matter, Professor Booth goes on to write a considerable volume on the ideas and techniques displayed in Trollope's novels. As the 'technique' is difficult for the critic to recognize, since he ignores all questions of language, he says very little new on the subject, and falls into the fallacy of believing he can examine the 'content' of the novels without regard to their form or medium.[43] He pays no attention

---

[42] 'The computer approach to style' in G. Levine and W. Madden, ed., *The Art of Victorian Prose*, N.Y., Oxford University Press, 1968, pp. 338–61. p. 343.

[43] On the matter of content Professor Booth is like a man who thinks he is examining the contents of a Klein bottle (a Klein bottle being a topological figure consisting of a surface so disposed as to appear to enclose a space, although in fact the 'inside' and the 'outside' are topologically the same space).

whatsoever to Trollope's style beyond attributing 'solecisms' to him, where none are to be found.[44] (Like many Victorians, too, Professor Booth apparently believed 'higher than her' to be ungrammatical.) In fact he even falls into Michael Sadleir's way of expressing extravagant affection for various Trollopian heroines, and can go so far as to waste words enthusing over Trollope's feeblest production, *The Two Heroines of Plumplington*. In any case he does nothing to rescue Trollopian criticism from mere 'appreciation', and from the mania for ranking the novels and characters in order of merit.[45]

Because of the very powerful quality of illusion in Trollope's novels, the critic must be particularly vigilant not to fall into Nathaniel Hawthorne's way of thinking about them as a great lump of earth hewn out and put on display.[46] Once there is thought to be some specially intimate relationship between the world of a Trollope novel and the real world, it follows that the work of art itself disappears from view, becoming, as it were, totally transparent.[47] One of the contradictions central to most critical readings of Trollope's novels is that he seems to 'intrude' drastically into his fiction, even at times admitting that it is fiction, and yet he is so unusually self-effacing in terms of style, that his work seems more strikingly transparent than almost any other. And this 'transparency' in turn aggravates the offence of his 'intrusions'. Thus his work has often been regarded as a kind of crystal with local impurities, through which an independent 'content' is seen, like the lump of earth with its inhabitants that is put on exhibition under glass in Hawthorne's description of the early novels.

Any description of Trollopian realism must account for a central paradox in his novels: that of all novels they are the most 'social', in the sense of depending on the interaction of sets of persons, and of creating a supremely convincing illusion of a functioning fictional community; and yet that an examination of any of the novels will show how very significant a proportion of the book concerns the situation of a single character, alone, so that such portions must either be irrelevant to the rest of the novel, or much of the action must take

[44] *Anthony Trollope*, p. 227.

[45] Although the most important long work we have since Sadleir's, much of Booth's volume is old-fashioned 'Trollopology' rather than criticism.

[46] In a letter of 11 Feb. 1860, quoted by Trollope in his *Autobiography*, p. 144.

[47] Sadleir can be seen falling into the fallacy of the transparent or disappearing novel in 'Anthony Trollope' in his *Things Past*, Constable, 1944, pp. 16–53, p. 21.

place at the level of the individual and not society. A second paradox emerges during an examination of the first, and that is that the compelling illusion of reality is produced not by a specially intimate connection with the world the reader inhabits, but by a technique of including as many of the rules of operation of the fictional world as possible in the novel itself, to obviate the necessity of constant and disturbing reference to a world outside it. There is in fact less need for reference from the world of a Trollope novel to the real world, than from much other fiction.

One of the basic assumptions underlying Trollopian realism is that for the sake of 'truth to life', fictional characters should be neither wholly good nor wholly bad, but always 'mixed'. Trollope justified this type of character on moral grounds, arguing that its didactic effect was greater.[48] His interest in 'mixed' characters is not particularly original, nor does it display in origin any specially profound psychological insight; but this does not prevent it from forming the basis of an exceedingly interesting fiction, of great social significance. The choice of imperfect heroes, sympathetic villains, and all manner of characters neither purely good nor bad has been so extensively documented for over a century now, that there is no need to demonstrate it again here. Certain of its implications, however, have been largely ignored.

The first of these implications (already indicated)[49] is that 'natural justice' is now possible without theotechny, both on the social level, and within the individual character, who having (except in the cases of Mr Harding, Lizzie Eustace, and some of the characters in *The Way We Live Now*) conflicting impulses and standards, frequently judges himself, and condemns himself to mental torture, as Mark Robarts, Lady Mason, Julia Brabazon, Cousin Henry and John Caldigate do, to name but a few. Even Trollope's 'social justice' can operate better on mixed characters, who have something to lose, such as Julia Brabazon, again.[50]

The second and more important consequence of the mixed character is that much of the important action in a novel—which always in Trollope depends on moral decision and dilemma—is automatically played out at two levels, parallel to those on which 'natural justice' works—the social level of interaction between persons, and the private

[48] e.g. *Ralph the Heir*, chapter 56, World's Classics 1939, 2 vols, ii, 337: '... the faults of a Ralph Newton, and not the vices of a Varney or a Barry Lyndon, are the evils against which men should in these days be taught to guard themselves;—which women also should be made to hate. Such is the writer's apology for his very indifferent hero, Ralph the Heir.'

[49] pp. 39–40 and 69 above.

[50] See *Spectator* and *Saturday* reviews of *The Claverings*, pp. 39–40 above (Julia Brabazon becomes Lady Ongar); see also *Autobiography*, pp 197–8.

level of solitary debate with the self. The former has often been discussed, but nowhere better than in the *Spectator* reviews discussed in the last chapter, and especially that of *The Small House at Allington*.[51] The private level has been curiously neglected, and we have seen how Hutton complained that Trollope did not take us 'into the world of solitary feeling at all'.[52] Most of this mental action takes place in internal monologues, consisting mainly of narrative report, which from time to time slips into direct speech, reported speech, or *erlebte Rede*. As these monologues always concern an individual's dilemma *vis-à-vis* a situation which has already been fully presented in narrative or summary, and as the individual's thoughts are therefore limited to these facts already known to the reader—usually events which have occurred within the action of the novel itself, and not even before the start of the first chapter—the reader can easily mistake the often long passages of internal debate for repetitive summary; although this is to mistake their function and structural importance. They can be long—several pages is not exceptional, or even half a chapter—and hence Trollope has been accused of tedious and unscrupulous padding. It is true that many of these passages are far less entertaining than his dialogue—there is less humour, for example, to enliven them—and if Trollope lacks any stylistic resource that his fiction seems to demand, it is a method of presenting these internal debates without slowness or repetition. He has a problem which the modern writer would probably solve by a 'stream of consciousness' technique.

There are various interesting narrative words used when a character is thinking in this way, to present his 'ideas, as expressed to himself in these long unspoken soliloquies'.[53] In her review of *Ayala's Angel* in the *Spectator*, Miss Dillwyn (herself a novelist) complains of 'Mr. Trollope's fondness for making people "tell," "teach," "encourage," or "bring" themselves to think this, that, or the other'; and she comments: 'It is a mode of expression which is excellent and effective in suitable places, but which loses its force, and becomes a mere mannerism, if constantly used where the various tenses of the verb "to think" would do equally well, without any "teaching," "telling," "educating," or "bringing." '[54] While accepting Miss Dillwyn's observation, I cannot agree with her adverse judgment, for in *Ayala's Angel* as elsewhere, these words are essential to Trollope's presentation of his characters' internal conflicts.

---

[51] xxxvii, 9 Apr. 1864, 421–3; repr. *Critical Heritage*, pp. 197–201. See pp. 113–14 above.
[52] *Spectator* obituary, lv, 9 Dec. 1882, 1573–4.
[53] *He Knew He was Right*, chapter 84, World's Classics, p. 787.
[54] liv, 18 June 1881, 804–5.

In the first half of *The Small House at Allington* (vol. i of the World's Classics edition), 'to teach oneself' occurs ten times, and 'to tell oneself' and its synonyms at least twenty, while such expressions as 'he argued the matter . . . within his own mind'[55] are found some thirteen times in the same thirty chapters. There are in addition at least twenty-seven cases of characters deciding to control their own thoughts, and they or the narrator use intentional words to express this resolve. For example, after Crosbie has announced to Lily the need to delay their marriage for two years, she says to her sister, 'Don't talk to me, Bell . . . I'm trying to make myself quiet, and I half feel that I should get childish if I went on talking. I have almost more to think of than I know how to manage.' Then the narrator reports on her mental activity on going to bed:

> And she had great matter for thinking; so great, that many hours sounded in her ears from the clock on the stairs before she brought her thoughts to a shape that satisfied herself. She did so bring them at last, and then she slept. She did so bring them, toiling over her work with tears that made her pillow wet, with heart-burning and almost with heart-breaking, with much doubting, and many anxious, eager inquiries within her own bosom as to that which she ought to do, and that which she could endure to do. But at last her resolve was taken, and then she slept.[56]

This mental action is just as central to the whole action of the book as Lily's actual offer to set Crosbie free, later in the chapter, and is also essential to her characterization, since so much depends on her strong-minded resolves.

Again, a few chapters later, Crosbie has just completed a letter to Lily:

> As he had waxed warm with his writing he had forced himself to be affectionate, and, as he flattered himself, frank and candid. Nevertheless, he was partly conscious that he was preparing for himself a mode of escape . . . I do not intend to say that he wrote with a premeditated intention of thus using his words [as an escape at some future time]; but as he wrote them he could not keep himself from reflecting that they might be used in that way.[57]

Here, in a passage of typically Trollopian insight, we find the language of self-persuasion ('forced himself', 'flattered himself', 'could not keep himself from reflecting') associated with semi-conscious motivation, which is described in almost Freudian terms. There are numerous cases of such unconscious or semi-conscious motivation in Trollope, frequently connected with the writing of letters, as though the act of letter-writing allowed the narrator more time to analyse such things

[55] World's Classics i, 151.   [56] i, 198–9.   [57] i, 250.

than the fleeting act of speech did. The most striking example of all occurs in *Castle Richmond*, when Lady Desmond has written to her daughter, while subconsciously remembering how she had renounced all hope of Owen Fitzgerald's love so that her daughter might have him:

> 'My anxiety has been only for your welfare, [she writes] to further which I have been willing to make any possible sacrifice.' Clara when she read this did not know what sacrifice had been made, nor had the countess thought as she wrote the words what had been the sacrifice to which she had thus alluded, though her heart was ever conscious of it, unconsciously.[58]

But of all the novels, *The Small House* is one of those most occupied with mental struggles, and is thus most rich in striking examples of internal debates, mainly belonging to Lily, Johnny and Crosbie.

There is an analysis of one element in the style of these 'unspoken soliloquies' in Liza Glauser's *Die erlebte Rede im englischen Roman des 19. Jahrhunderts*.[59] Analysing *Rachel Ray*, for example, she finds *erlebte Rede* used in internal monologues with different frequencies for the different characters, as a means of characterization.[60] Out of over sixty examples of *erlebte Rede* in *Reflexion* (as she calls it), only five belong to Luke, for his is the active driving-force in the novel, while the reflective nature is Rachel's, who has over twenty examples of *erlebte Rede* in her thought. Mrs Ray has fourteen examples, always embedded in narrative report (*Bericht*), to depict her apprehensions, while her other daughter, Mrs Prime, has seven examples, mainly connected with her moral judgments over her mother's and sister's worldliness.

Thus Trollope's concern with internal monologue not only has an important structural function, in providing a double plane of action, but has definite stylistic consequences as well, which deserve further investigation elsewhere.

A feature of Trollope's narrative which is almost necessarily connected with his use of internal monologue is the usually very simple chronology of the events recounted, by which nothing can feature in a character's thoughts which has not already been narrated before, so far is Trollope from using these monologues for narrative 'flashback'. Nearly everything a character thinks about is composed of events which have been part of the action of the novel, and everything else from an earlier past has been filled in as each character has been introduced, so that in this sense the novels are strictly unidirectional

---

[58] *Castle Richmond*, chapter 43.
[59] Bern, 1948 (*Schweizer Anglistische Arbeiten*, 20).
[60] *Ibid.*, pp. 101–3.

and self-enclosed. 'I would wish to have no guessing, and shall therefore proceed to tell all about it'[61] might be taken as Trollope's rule
for more than just the avoidance of surprises, for it is his normal
rule deliberately and openly to provide every particle of information
that the reader needs in order to understand the events of the novel,
and the interactions, conversations and thoughts of the characters, as
they occur; and, in recounting things chronologically, he keeps the
horse strictly before the cart, as he puts it in *The Duke's Children*.[62]
As a result, to fulfil both these conditions, he must start off his novels
with summary accounts of the past lives and so on of the chief
characters, and every time he introduces a new person, he pauses to
fill in the newcomer's background, sometimes, as with Mr Arabin in
Barchester Towers, taking a full chapter to do so. These accounts
partake very much of the nature of definitions, and very frequently
end with a sentence like 'Such was Mr. Arabin, the new vicar of
St. Ewald, who is going to stay with the Grantlys, at Plumstead
Episcopi.'[63] Similar sentences are found in most of the novels, right
up to *The Landleaguers*, and signal the switch back from description
to action again, once the process of making the character 'stand before
the reader's eye' is complete.[64] At this point the reader is in a position
to understand all the future conduct, speech and thought of the
character in question, so that a reading of the novel follows the
same logical order as its composition, beginning with fully formed
characters, which precede the action.

Writing from a vivid mental picture of a number of characters,
whose personalities and interactions largely determine the course of
the story, Trollope finally arrives at a working model of society; but
it is not a total model. Sabine Nathan condemns Trollope for not
recognizing the truths of economic exploitation, and (although she
does not phrase it this way) wanting to maintain the old vertical
divisions of society into interest-groups, rather than recognize the
existence of classes:[65] and he is indeed staunch in his support of the
interdependence of the gentry, their tenants and labourers, and the
local tradespeople too, because this is the basis of the traditional rural
society as he likes to see it. He omits industrial towns almost entirely
from his model, and shows only a very small part of the life and work
of the numerous class of servants who enable the lives of the gentry
and aristocracy to be maintained. The tip of the iceberg that we can

---

[61] *The Bertrams*, opening to chapter 13.
[62] *Duke's Children*, chapter 9, The Oxford Trollope, i, 83.
[63] World's Classics, p. 174.
[64] *Ibid.*, p. 167.
[65] 'The Popularity and Literary Value of Anthony Trollope's Barsetshire
Series Related to the Literary and Critical Standards of the Nineteenth
Century', unpubl. thesis, Humboldt Univ., Berlin, 1962.

see consists of the interactions between master and servant, usually in matters outside daily routine, at times of crisis and so on, as well as the role of the servant class in conveying information, and retailing rumour: that is, servants as objects of the social perceptions of the higher classes, as the machinery whereby certain specific ends are achieved, and as an indication of the standing, prosperity and reputation of a family or individual. But in general they are seen very little in their own family lives.

It is not necessary, on the other hand, to prove at length the remarkable accuracy of the picture of upper- and middle-class society that Trollope conveys. This has been shown many times before, but it cannot be better demonstrated than with reference to F. M. L. Thompson's *English Landed Society in the Nineteenth Century*.[66] The reader of Trollope who opens this excellent study is struck by what Henry James called 'the surprise of recognition'. With everything that Thompson describes, the reader of Trollope is already familiar: the country estates, the location of the seats, the wealthy magnates, the less opulent squires, the parvenus of various ranks, the methods of estate management, the great aristocratic entertainments, the sale of land, the problems of entail and inheritance, and the striving for social status through land-ownership—all these things are in Trollope with an accuracy that is startling when one considers that he was an observer within the society, not a disinterested student of it from without. The fact that on reading Thompson one need not change the picture of nineteenth-century landed society that one has gathered from Trollope, or even very much alter the relative stress and emphasis given to each fact, is surely proof of the adequacy of Trollope's model of that social area.

The question that has interested Trollope's critics most, both in his own day and now, concerns how his novels work so well, and without any apparent fuss create such a perfect illusion of reality. Underlying this perplexity, I suspect, there is an important but unspoken assumption about the relationship of Trollope's novels—or, rather, the fictional worlds of Trollope's novels—to the real world. Because the illusion is so perfect, and—at the social level at least—the involvement of the reader so inexplicably complete, it has been assumed that therefore the world of a given novel is not only equivalent to reality in some way, but that it exists at a level particularly close to 'objective reality', or in a particularly close relationship to the real world. It is not sufficient to point out Trollope's factual accuracy on specific points. The phenomena of his fictional world are in one–one corre-

---

[66] Routledge, 1963. This work is chosen for comparison since it contains not a single reference to the novel for its evidence, but is drawn entirely from perfectly factual evidence such as estate records and account books.

spondence with those of the real world, and organized in much the same way as the phenomena of the real world can be organized—indeed, rather in the way in which we normally do order the facts of our worlds (taught in this partly by our literature). But this correspondence does not imply that the fictional world is any the less an artistic construct, although the illusion of reality has usually directed attention away from one of the most important features of Trollopian realism—its independence, or autarky: in the sense that all the rules by which the fictional world runs, and the rules by which the reader can make moral and other judgments on the events of that world, are built into the book itself. Because these rules are in both cases generally valid in the readers' real worlds as well (or were, a hundred years ago) Trollope is a realist. We find his novels very substantial and comprehensible even in their presentation of, say, moral dilemmas we no longer share or fully understand, because we are taught by the narrator how to interpret what is happening.

The result is that the narrative presence of Trollope's persona in the novels is essential to their illusion, and not damaging to it. (It would in any case be absurd to discuss a Trollope novel without the narrator.) There is certainly one sort of authorial intrusion which does ruin the coherence of the work by admitting that it is fiction, but there are fewer of these harmful intrusions than is often supposed. They are different in kind from the narrative comments and that constant narrative presence which provide the stability and completeness of the fictional world, by stopping the reader going outside the book for his terms of reference. The narrative comments are often overtly didactic, but should not be seen as a moral additive, nor as the 'philosophic pill' which the fiction has to gild. They may sometimes be imperfectly fitted into the flow of the narrative, or even at times badly written, and can on occasion lead Trollope far away from his subject (as in the case of the essays on travelling in *The Bertrams*, which originally are relevant to the story, but expand eventually quite away from it). Yet they are not only an integral part of each novel, but are essential to its unity as well. And they mediate between the reader and the fiction, which they in fact establish as 'realistic'.

The essential thing about Trollopian autarky is that it gives a complete scheme of social and moral standards, by which to judge the characters and situations as each novel progresses. If the narrator gave us a judgment alone, we should be forced to go outside to whatever we knew of 'the Victorian way of thought' in order to understand its implications. As it is, the narrator usually does two things: he discusses the character or situation in concrete terms, using only that data which the reader already has at his disposal through the earlier part of the novel, and he writes short 'essays' (or makes even shorter passing comments) which put the problem in a wider perspective, and mediate between the fictional construct and the world of the reader.

Take questions of money, for example. In *Framley Parsonage* we know exactly the amount of Mark Robarts's income, and we know the precise amount he pays for his hunter, how much he signs a bill for, how much he eventually pays on it, and even how much his brother inherits from their father. Because we are given everybody's income and the prices of so many things, from houses to mutton, we have a good idea of what these sums mean. Moreoever, the narrator often explains just what a character can and cannot expect to afford in terms of servants, carriages and horses of a given income, in the West End, St John's Wood, or the country. The account of Crosbie setting up house in *The Small House at Allington* is a wonderfully detailed and humorous example of this.[67] In contrast, consider Thackeray's treatment of money in *Pendennis*. It is impossible to imagine Trollope leaving unknown the details of Pen's Oxbridge income, the amount of Major Pendennis's half-pay, and the size of the debt the Major settled for Captain Costigan, while the reader does not even know how much 'Arthur's Educational Fund' amounted to. Instead, Thackeray explains without giving precise figures, that Pen was living beyond his means, so that the reader must accept the narrator's judgment on trust—as is consonant with moral, satirical purpose. Trollope's narrator, on the other hand, includes all the necessary data for guiding the reader's judgment, in order to create his illusion. Trollopian realism does not work by referring outside itself to another world, but by absorbing the necessary facts and relationships of the world into the fiction itself.

Two more examples will suffice to illustrate this point, of which the first can be the system of status-determined greetings that Lady Aylmer uses in *The Belton Estate*.[68] The second is embedded in the first paragraph of *The Claverings*:

> The gardens of Clavering Park were removed some three hundred yards from the large, square, sombre-looking stone mansion which was the country-house of Sir Hugh Clavering, the eleventh baronet of that name; and in these gardens, which had but little of beauty to recommend them, I will introduce my readers to two of the personages with whom I wish to make them acquainted in the following story. It was now the end of August, and the parterres, beds, and bits of lawn were dry, disfigured, and almost ugly, from the effects of a long drought. In gardens to which care and labour are given abundantly, flower-beds will be pretty, and grass will be

[67] Chapter 40, 'Preparations for the Wedding', World's Classics, ii, 127–46.
[68] See pp. 115–16 above.

green, let the weather be what it may; but care and labour were scantily bestowed on the Clavering Gardens, and everything was yellow, adust, harsh, and dry. Over the burnt turf, towards a gate that led to the house, a lady was walking, and by her side there walked a gentleman.

The narrator is explicitly addressing his reader, and introducing him to the persons and places—significantly, not them to him. First describing the unattractive state of the gardens, he proceeds to explain its significance in general terms, telling what abundant care and labour will effect; and then, pivoting his sentence expressively about a semicolon and a Trollopian 'but',[69] he particularizes on the Clavering Gardens, leaving the reader to draw his own conclusions—as he now must unambiguously—as to the quality of Sir Hugh's solicitude for his family seat, and hence as to his character. It is significant that this paragraph should be equally understandable by someone unacquainted with English gardens, or a dry English August. Next, the description concentrates on the burnt turf, and then the part of the turf near the gate on the house side, before finally focusing suddenly down on to the two walking figures to round off the paragraph. From the stylistic point of view it is worth noting the deceptively quiet precision of the last dozen words: 'a lady was walking, and by her side there walked a gentleman'. This is an exact statement of the situation where, it turns out, she is dismissing him, but he is succeeding in obtaining a final interview. It is also characteristic of Harry Clavering's life, for he is largely passive, and the decisions are all made by his womenfolk. Then the narrator disappears completely, and a long dramatic conversation takes over. This apparently simple paragraph, then, illustrates some of the fundamentals of Trollopian realism. So much meaning and development in a mere 170 words should help to banish the myth of Trollope's narrative dullness and inexpressiveness.[70]

Having established the characteristics of Trollopian realism, and the twin levels of action—social interaction and internal monologue—it is now possible to see clearly what is the social significance of Trollope's vision of the world, by setting up a correspondence between his fiction and his society more satisfactory than the mere congruence

[69] See Davies, 'Trollope and his style', *loc. cit.*

[70] It is possible that the general lack of awareness of Trollope's style stems in part from the lack of good editions of his work. Fortunately many of his novels have been available in the World's Classics (though now largely out of print), but the area covered in the World's Classics edition by the paragraph just analysed is approximately that of four special-issue postage stamps.

of certain facts: that is, a correspondence between his views of society and his fictional method.

His vision of society shows human ties of love and respect in danger, and being replaced by money, ambition and power, while everybody is nonetheless tied together, willy-nilly, in a vast web of interdependence. Social pressures, even in the world of Barsetshire, deform individuals, as Hutton says, 'from their natural selves'.[71] The world of *The Way We Live Now*, with its all-involving title, is the ultimate fictional realization of this state. This novel is central to Trollope's whole corpus of work in that it is the purest embodiment of an idea which runs through all his fiction: a vision of modern life in which each man is an unwilling dependant on his fellows, and victim of all manner of social forces, inextricably part of society, yet increasingly cut off from his neighbours. So, in the midst of a crowded world, the individual is in the last analysis alone. In his novels, Anthony Trollope recognizes this as a central contradiction in modern existence, and his artistic methods correspond exactly to this important social observation.

[71] 'From Miss Austen to Mr Trollope', *loc. cit.*; see pp. 116–18 above. See also G.–M. Tracy's comments on social 'cadres déformants', in his otherwise thin 'L'œuvre de Trollope—ou le paradis perdu', *Mercure de France*, cccviii, Mar. 1950, 434–45.

APPENDIX I

Notes on Some Uses of the Word 'Realism' in mid-Victorian Criticism of the Novel

'Le mot *réalisme* . . . est un de ces termes équivoques qui se prêtent à toutes sortes d'emplois et peuvent servir à la fois de couronne de laurier ou de couronne de choux.'

Champfleury, *Le réalisme*, 1857

1. The widest sense distinguishes the novel of modern life, such as the *Chronicles of Barsetshire*, Mrs Oliphant's *Chronicles of Carling-ford*, Bulwer Lytton's *The Caxtons* and most of Thackeray's novels— see review of the *Last Chronicle* in the *Examiner*, repr. *Critical Heritage*, p. 297.

2. Referring to fiction written in accordance with certain theoretical standards, such as those put forward by G. H. Lewes, whereby 'realism' is its own justification, ennobling a 'low' subject and best treating a 'high' one. Lewes maintains that 'Realism' is as 'imaginative' as 'Idealism'.—See pp. 51–6 above.

3. Referring (often approvingly) to (Trollope's) restriction of his fiction to probable everyday persons and events:

. . . realism seems to have reached its limits. Confining himself to actual life in England, and relying implicitly upon his power to inspire interest by the accuracy of his descriptions and the complete verisimilitude of his sketches, Mr. Trollope scorns and rejects all extraneous aid whatever. [He will] not travel afield in search of startling incidents or dramatic surprises . . . In *The Claverings* it is necessary to remove two characters . . . No manner . . . can be found more convenient than that of drowning them at sea. . . . But lest the shipwreck should assume the shape of a dramatic surprise, the reader is prepared for it beforehand with care that becomes almost ostentatious.

—J. Knight, *Fortnightly Review* (ns) i, 1 Jan. 1867, 770–2.

4. Hence 'realistic' as the opposite of 'sensational' and 'sentimental':

[T]he realist in fiction is careless about plot. His sole object is to describe men's lives as they really are; and real life is fragmentary and unmethodical.
—A. S. Kinnear, *North British Review* (ns) i, May 1864, 372.

Mr. Trollope makes light of one of those sentimental fictions which originate with the romantic school of novelists . . . This is the idea that a man can love but once in his lifetime.
—J. Knight, *loc. cit.*

Trollope makes fun of the distinction in *Autobiography*, pp. 226–7. See pp. 129–30 above.

5. 'Realistic' as the opposite of 'elevated' or 'idealized' (humour being a form of 'idealization'):

Trollope has made a noteworthy attempt to understand and admire Hawthorne, and in so doing has afforded a charming illustration of the fact that between the realist and the idealist there is a great gulf fixed . . .
—*University Magazine* iv, Oct. 1879, 437.

It is Thackeray's aim to represent life as it is actually and historically . . . Dickens . . . is more light and poetic . . . He has characters of ideal perfection and beauty . . . Even his situations and scenery often lie in a region beyond the margin of everyday life.
—David Masson on 'real' and 'ideal' fiction, in *British Novelists and their Styles*, 1859, pp. 248–9.

There are two classes of novelists . . . and Mr. Meredith is of the *humourist* class, which draws its presentment of mankind in a large degree from its inner consciousness, while the other class paints life phenomenally, as the majority would see it.
—*The Times* 14 Oct. 1859, 5; repr. Forman, ed, *George Meredith Some Early Appreciations*, 1909, p. 52.

Between realism and idealism there is no natural conflict. This completes that. Realism is the basis of good composition . . . A great genius must necessarily employ ideal means, for a vast conception cannot be placed bodily before the eye, and remains to be suggested. Idealism is as an atmosphere whose effects of grandeur are wrought out through a series of illusions, that are illusions to the sense within us only when divorced from the groundwork of the real.
—George Meredith in a letter of 1864, *Letters* ed. W. M. Meredith 1912, vol. I, p. 156.

6. 'Realism' as a type of description, especially involving attention to (needless) minutiae:

> . . . one is rather impressed by [Trollope's] realism, than attracted by the realities . . .
> —*Dublin Review* (ns) xix, Oct. 1872, 393–430.

> The directness and verisimilitude of [Trollope's] manner, and the absence of any attempt at fine writing, enables him to be far more really pathetic [in 'The Spotted Dog'] than the professed dealers in this kind of sentiment. . . . The story . . . exemplifies the legitimate use of a good realistic description.
> —*Saturday Review* xxx, 13 Aug. 1870, 211–12.

7. 'Realism' as a limited or offensive choice of subject: J. H. Stack complains of its limitations to everyday social and domestic life, and wants 'something higher, nobler' (*Fortnightly Review* (ns) v, 1 Feb. 1869, 188–98); while A. S. Kinnear says, 'That such things are . . . [is] no sufficient reason for describing them in a novel'—see p. 84 above.

8. 'Realism' as a vague term of abuse, and the opposite of 'imaginative'. Indicating dullness, or a combination of dullness and sordidness. For example, T. H. S. Escott contrasts Disraeli's treatment of politics with that of 'a realistic dullard' (*Fraser's Magazine* (ns), ix, Apr. 1874, 521), while the *Saturday* accuses Trollope of holding 'a crude half-considered notion of realism' in *The Belton Estate*—see pp. 55–6 above.

It must be noted that 'fidelity to nature' is not in general a synonym for 'truth to life', or 'realism' in any of the above senses (except no. 2). As used by the *Spectator* in its review of *An Editor's Tales*, 'fidelity to nature' means fidelity to 'human nature', in explicit contrast to 'superficial' truth, which does not aim at knowledge of 'the universal self' in fictional character (*Spectator* xliii, 8 Oct. 1870, 1203, and p. 108 above). Richard Stang misses the distinction at one point, when he quotes the *Saturday Review* of 1861: ' "The highest art is the nearest approach to nature", and the best novelists are those who "draw from life, having studied human nature, in all its varieties, as it is, and not through the distorting medium of their own fanciful conceptions." ' Professor Stang misleadingly includes this under the heading of an 'extreme kind of realism, which almost seems to preclude any sort of selection on the part of the artist or any artistic shaping'.[1] It is in fact an attack on false conventionalism.

Because Trollope has never received much attention in Scandinavia, it is interesting to note an unidentified Dane writing about him in 1885 under the name 'L. Kornelius', and making a distinction between 'good' and 'bad' realism, parallel to that existing in English:

> Han er i Ordets gode Betydning Realist, forsaavidt som han ikke griber til Umuligheder eller Usandsynligheder, ligesaalidt som han driver Realiteten ud i den yderlige Grad af Detail og Smagløshed, der er moderne i den nyere franske Litteratur, og som har fundet saa talrige Efterlignere ogsaa hos os.

> (He is a realist in the good sense of the word, inasmuch as he does not grasp at improbable or impossible things, any more than he pushes reality to the uttermost degree of detail and tastelessness, which is modern in recent French literature, and which has found such numerous imitators in this country.)

> —'L. Kornelius', in the introduction to *Skizzer og Novelletter*, Copenhagen 1885—a translation of the Tachnitz volume *Alice Dugdale and other Stories*. (My translation.)

[1] *The Theory of the Novel in England 1850–1870*, 1959, p. 150.

APPENDIX II

Bibliography of Contemporary British Articles on Trollope

A review of a single book is indicated by the title of that book, unless the heading of the article is of special significance. Attributions of anonymous articles are put in square brackets, followed by the source of information, except where the source of all the attributions for a given journal is put at the head of the list.

BIBLIOGRAPHY

Allibone, S. A. *A Critical Dictionary of English Literature and British and American Authors Living and Deceased*, 3 vols, Philadelphia 1859–71. With a Supplement by J. F. Kirk, 2 vols, Philadelphia 1891.
Houghton, W. E. 'British Periodicals of the Victorian Age: Bibliographies and Indexes'—*Library Trends* vii, Apr. 1959, 554–65.
Houghton, W. E., ed. *The Wellesley Index to Victorian Periodicals 1824–1900*, vol. i, 1966.
Irwin, M. L. *Trollope: a Bibliography*, New York 1926.
Poole's Index to Periodical Literature 1802–81, 1853–82.
Smalley, D., ed. *Trollope: the Critical Heritage*, Routledge 1969.

PERIODICALS

The Academy

Phineas Redux, v, 7 Feb. 1874, 141–3. Edith Simcox.
Lady Anna, v, 2 May 1874, 482. George Saintsbury.
Harry Heathcote of Gangoil, vi, 19 Dec. 1874, 652. George Saintsbury.
        do.   vii, 17 Apr. 1875, 396. F. M. Owen.
Prime Minister, x, 29 Jul. 1876, 106–7. R. F. Littledale.
The American Senator, xii, 24 Nov. 1877, 487–8. T. W. Crawley.
South Africa, xiii, 6 Apr. 1878, 294–6. Coutts Trotter.
Is He Popenjoy?, xiii, 8 June 1878, 505. R. F. Littledale.
An Eye for an Eye, xv, 8 Feb. 1879, 117. R. F. Littledale.
Thackeray, xv, 21 June 1879, 533. T. H. Ward.
John Caldigate, xvi, 5 Jul. 1879, 5. E. Purcell.
Cousin Henry, xvi, 1 Nov. 1879, 316. William Wallace.
The Life of Cicero, xix, 5 Feb. 1881, 91–2. W. Warde Fowler.
Why Frau Frohmann Raised Her Prices and Other Stories, xxi, 7 Jan. 1882, 5. Arthur Barker.

Lord Palmerston, xxii, 5 Aug. 1882, 98–9. (anon.)
Kept in the Dark, xxii, 25 Nov. 1882, 377–8. W. E. Henley.
Obituary, xxii, 16 Dec. 1882, 433. R. F. Littledale.
Mr Scarborough's Family, xxiii, 19 May 1883, 344. William Wallace.
An Autobiography, xxiv, 27 Oct. 1883, 273–4. R. F. Littledale.
The Landleaguers, xxiv, 17 Nov. 1883, 328. E. Purcell.
An Old Man's Love, xxv, 29 Mar. 1884, 220. C. E. Dawkins.

The Athenaeum

All attributions from the editors' marked file. I am grateful to the proprietors and editor of the *New Statesman* for permission to consult this file.

The Macdermots of Ballycloran, no. 1020, 15 May 1847, 517 [Chorley].
The Kellys and the O'Kellys, no. 1081, 15 Jul. 1848, 701 [Chorley].
La Vendée, no. 1184, 6 Jul. 1850, 708 [Chorley].
The Warden, no. 1422, 27 Jan. 1855, 107–8 [Jewsbury].
Barchester Towers, no. 1544, 30 May 1857, 689–90 [H. St John].
The Three Clerks, no. 1574, 26 Dec. 1857, 1621 [Jewsb[ury]].
Doctor Thorne, no. 1597, 5 June 1858, 719 [Jewsbury].
The Bertrams, no. 1639, 26 Mar. 1859, 420 [Jewsbury].
The West Indies and the Spanish Main, no. 1671, 5 Nov. 1859, 591–3 [H. St John].
Castle Richmond, no. 1699, 19 May 1860, 681 [Jewsbury].
Orley Farm (part one), no. 1741, 9 Mar. 1861, 319–20 [Dixon].
Framley Parsonage, no. 1747, 20 Apr. 1861, 528 [Dixon].
North America, no. 1804, 24 May 1862, 685–7 [Dixon].
Orley Farm, no. 1823, 4 Oct. 1862, 425–6 [Dixon].
Rachel Ray, no. 1877, 17 Oct. 1863, 492–4 [Jeaffreson].
The Small House at Allington, no. 1900, 26 Mar. 1864, 437–8 [[Je]affreson].
Miss Mackenzie, no. 1953, 1 Apr. 1865, 455 [Jewsbury].
Can You Forgive Her?, no. 1975, 2 Sept. 1865, 305–6 [Jewsbury].
The Belton Estate, no. 1997, 3 Feb. 1866, 166 [Wilberforce].
Nina Balatka, no. 2053, 2 Mar. 1867, 288 [Chorley].
The Claverings, no. 2068, 15 June 1867, 783 [Jewsbury].
The Last Chronicle of Barset, no. 2075, 3 Aug. 1867, 141 [Jewsbury].
Lotta Schmidt and Other Stories, no. 2091, 23 Nov. 1867, 683–4 [Jewsbury].
Linda Tressel, no. 2117, 23 May 1868, 724–5 [Jeaffreson].
The Vicar of Bullhampton, no. 2218, 30 Apr. 1870, 574 [Collyer].
The Commentaries of Caesar, no. 2224, 11 June 1870, 771 [Rumsey].
An Editor's Tales, no. 2230, 23 Jul. 1870, 112 [Doran].
Sir Harry Hotspur of Humblethwaite, no. 2247, 19 Nov. 1870, 654 [Editor: i.e. Norman MacColl].
Ralph the Heir, no. 2268, 15 Apr. 1871, 456 [Collyer].
The Golden Lion of Granpere, no. 2326, 25 May 1872, 652–3 [Collyer].
The Eustace Diamonds, no. 2348, 26 Oct. 1872, 527–8 [Collyer].

Australia and New Zealand, no. 2366, 1 Mar. 1873, 276 [Dilke].

Phineas Redux, no. 2411, 10 Jan. 1874, 53 [Collyer].

The Way We Live Now (part one), no. 2418, 28 Feb. 1874, 291 [Editor: i.e. MacColl].

Lady Anna, no. 2424, 11 Apr. 1874, 485 [Editor: i.e. MacColl].

Harry Heathcote of Gangoil, no. 2454, 7 Nov. 1874, 606 [Collyer].

The Way We Live Now, no. 2487, 26 June 1875, 851 [Editor: i.e. MacColl].

The Prime Minister (part one), no. 2512, 18 Dec. 1875, 829 [do].

The Prime Minister, no. 2540, 1 Jul. 1876, 15 [do.]

The American Senator, no. 2590, 16 June 1877, 766–7 [Cook].

South Africa, no. 2625, 16 Feb. 1878, 211–12 [Chesson (?)].

Is He Popenjoy?, no. 2636, 4 May 1878, 567 [Collyer].

An Eye for an Eye, no. 2672, 11 Jan. 1879, 47 [Collyer].

Thackeray, no. 2694, 14 June 1879, 749–50 [Minto].

John Caldigate, no. 2694, 14 June 1879, 755 [Sergeant].

Cousin Henry, no. 2712, 18 Oct. 1879, 495 [Collyer].

The Duke's Children, no. 2744, 29 May 1880, 694–5 [Cook].

Dr. Wortle's School, no. 2777, 15 Jan. 1881, 93 [Collyer].

Ayala's Angel, no. 2795, 21 May 1881, 686 [Cook].

The Life of Cicero, no. 2806, 6 Aug. 1881, 170–71 [Piele].

Why Frau Frohmann Raised Her Prices and Other Stories, no. 2829, 14 Jan. 1882, 54 [Collyer].

The Fixed Period, no. 2837, 11 Mar. 1882, 314–15 [Collyer].

Marion Fay, no. 2852, 24 June 1882, 793–4 [Collyer].

Lord Palmerston, no. 2864, 16 Sept. 1882, 367 [Fox Bourne].

Kept in the Dark, no. 2873, 18 Nov. 1882, 658 [Collyer].

Obituary, no. 2876, 9 Dec. 1882, 772–3 [Fox Bourne].

Mr. Scarborough's Family, no. 2898, 12 May 1883, 600 [Collyer].

An Autobiography, no. 2920, 13 Oct. 1883, 457–9 [Cook].

The Landleaguers, no. 2926, 24 Nov. 1883, 666 [Collyer].

An Old Man's Love, no. 2945, 5 Apr. 1884, 438 [Collyer].

Bentley's Quarterly Review

The Bertrams, i, Jul. 1859, 456–62.

Blackwood's Magazine

All attributions from the *Wellesley Index*.

North America, xcii, Sept. 1862, 372–90 [E. B. Hamley].

The Claverings and The Last Chronicle of Barset, cii, Sept. 1867, 275–8 [Mrs Oliphant].

The Vicar of Bullhampton and He Knew He Was Right, cvii, May 1870, 647–8 [Mrs Oliphant].

South Africa, cxxiv, Jul. 1878, 100 [Henry Brackenbury].

Life of Cicero, cxxix, Feb. 1881, 211–28 [W. Lucas Collins].

'Anthony Trollope', cxxxiii, Feb. 1883, 316–20 [Cecilia E. Meetkerke].

An Autobiography, cxxxiv, Nov. 1883, 577–96 [W. Lucas Collins].

British Quarterly Review

The West Indies and the Spanish Main, xxxi, Jan. 1860, 263.
    do.   xxxii, Jul. 1860, 98–122.
Castle Richmond, xxxii, Jul. 1860, 233–4.
Framley Parsonage, xxxiv, Jul. 1861, 263.
North America, xxxvi, Oct. 1862, 477.
The Last Chronicle of Barset, and Lotta Schmidt and Other Stories, xlvi,
  Oct. 1867, 557–60.
Linda Tressel, xlviii, Jul. 1868, 281.
He Knew He Was Right, l, Jul. 1869, 263–4.
An Editor's Tales, lii, Oct. 1870, 542.
The Struggles of Brown, Jones, and Robinson: by One of the Firm, liii,
  Jan. 1871, 261–2.
Ralph the Heir, liv, Jul. 1871, 240–2.
Australia and New Zealand, lvii, Apr. 1873, 528–31.
Harry Heathcote of Gangoil, lxi, Jan. 1875, 250.
    do.   lxii, Jul. 1875, 282.
South Africa, lxvii, Oct. 1878, 556–7.
Thackeray, lxx, Jul. 1879, 247.
Lord Palmerston, lxxvi, Oct. 1882, 450–1.
Kept in the Dark, lxxvii, Jan. 1883, 220–1.
Mr Scarborough's Family, lxxviii, Jul. 1883, 233.
An Autobiography, lxxix, Jan. 1884, 165–8.
An Old Man's Love, lxxx, Jul. 1884, 210–11.

Church Quarterly Review

In 'The World of Fiction', iv, Apr. 1877, 136–62.
South Africa, vii, Oct. 1878, 236–40.

Contemporary Review

Attributions from the *Wellesley Index*.

'Mr. Anthony Trollope and the English Clergy' (*Clerical Sketches*), ii,
  Jun. 1866, 240–62 [Henry Alford].
Phineas Finn, xii, Jan. 1870, 142–3 (sgd) 'M.B.' ['Matthew Browne',
  pseud. of W. B. Rands].
The Commentaries of Caesar, xv, Sept. 1870, 314 (sgd) 'J.D.' ['probably'
  James Davies].
An Editor's Tales, xv, Sept. 1870, 319 (sgd) 'M. B.' ['Matthew Browne',
  pseud. of W. B. Rands].
Australia and New Zealand, xxii, Oct. 1873, 699–730 (sgd) R. H. Horne.
Thackeray, xxxv, Jul. 1879, 768–9. In 'Contemporary Books. IV . . .
  (Under the direction of Matthew Browne)' [W. B. Rands].
An Autobiography, xliv, Nov. 1883, 787 [authorship unknown to *Wellesley*
  Index].
An Old Man's Love, xlvi, Jul. 1884, 149–51 (sgd) Julia Wedgwood.

Cope's Tobacco Plant

Thackeray, ii, Jul. 1880, 504 [James Thomson—bibliography of J. T.'s writings in W. D. Schaefer, *James Thomson (B.V.) beyond 'The City'*, University of California Press 1965].

Cornhill Magazine
Attributions from the *Wellesley Index*.

North America, vi, Jul. 1862, 105–7 [G. H. Lewes or Frederick Greenwood].
Orley Farm, vi, Nov. 1862, 702–4 [G. H. Lewes, or (possibly) J. F. W. Herschel or J. W. Kaye].

Dublin Review
The Dublin Review, 1836–1936. Complete list of Articles Published between May 1836 and April 1936. 1936.
'Mr. Trollope's Last Irish Novel' (in part a review of Phineas Finn), (ns) xiii, Oct. 1869, 361–77.
'The Novels of Mr. Anthony Trollope', (ns) xix, Oct. 1872, 393–430.
'The Character of Julius Caesar' (The Commentaries of Caesar, and 3 other works), (ns) xxviii, Jan. 1877, 127–41.
'The Novels of Anthony Trollope' (3rd ser.) ix, Apr. 1883, 314–34.

Dublin University Magazine
Framley Parsonage, lix, Apr. 1862, 405–6.
North America, lx, Jul. 1862, 75–82.
Orley Farm, lxi, Apr. 1863, 437.
Miss Mackenzie, lxv, May 1865, 576.
　　Continued as *The University Magazine* (q.v.)

Edinburgh Review
'Mr. Anthony Trollope's Novels', cxlvi, Oct. 1877, 455–88 [A. I. Shand—*Wellesley Index*].
'The Literary Life of Anthony Trollope' (An Autobiography), clix, Jan. 1884, 186–212 [A. I. Shand—*Wellesley Index*].

Fortnightly Review
Hunting Sketches, i, 1 Aug. 1865, 765–7 (sgd) Charles Stewart.
The Claverings, (ns) i, 1 June 1867, 770–72 (sgd) J. Knight.
'Mr. Anthony Trollope's Novels', (ns) v, 1 Feb. 1869, 188–98 (sgd) J. Herbert Stack.
Australia and New Zealand, (ns) xiii, May 1873, 662–3 [the last of nine notices, of which this is one, is signed Edith Simcox].
An Autobiography, in 'Theories and Practice of Modern Fiction', (ns) xxxiv, Dec. 1883, 870–86, pp. 870–1 (sgd) Henry Norman.

Fraser's Magazine
North America, lxvi, Aug. 1862, 256–64.
Thackeray, (ns) xx, Aug. 1879, 264–70.

Home and Foreign Review

North America, i, Jul. 1862, 111–28 [D. C. Lathbury(?)—*Wellesley Index*].

Orley Farm, ii, Jan. 1863, 291–4 [authorship unknown to *Wellesley Index*].

The Leader

The Warden, vi, 17 Feb. 1855, 164–5.
Barchester Towers, viii, 23 May 1857, 497.
The Three Clerks, viii, 19 Dec. 1857, 1218.
Doctor Thorne, ix, 29 May 1858, 519–20.
The Bertrams, x, 2 Apr. 1859, 431.

Macmillan's Magazine

'Anthony Trollope', xlvii, Jan. 1883, 236–40 (sgd) Edward A. Freeman.
'Anthony Trollope' (An Autobiography), xlix, Nov. 1883, 47–56 [John Morley and Mary Augusta Ward—*Wellesley Index*].

National Review

'Mr. Trollope's Novels' (The Warden, Barchester Towers, The Three Clerks, Doctor Thorne), vii, Oct. 1858, 416–35.
The Bertrams, ix, Jul. 1859, 187–99.
Orley Farm, xvi, Jan. 1863, 27–40.
Tales of All Countries (2nd series), xvi, Apr. 1863, 522–5.

Nineteenth Century

The Duke's Children, viii, Aug. 1880, 340.
John Caldigate   do.
       (two brief, separate, unsigned notices)

North British Review

Attributions from the *Wellesley Index*.

Orley Farm, in 'Novels and Novelists of the Day', xxxviii, Feb. 1863, 168–90, pp. 185–8 [Alexander Smith].
'Mr. Trollope's Novels', (ns) i, May 1864, 369–401 [A. S. Kinnear].

Quarterly Review

'The Confederate Struggle and Recognition' (North America, and 5 other works), cxii, Oct. 1862, 535–70 [Robert Cecil—*Wellesley Index*].

The Reader

Tales of All Countries (2nd series), i, 28 Feb. 1863, 224.
Rachel Ray, ii, 17 Oct. 1863, 437–8 'E.D.' [E. Dicey (?)—E. Dicey is listed among 'Contributors to Volume I'].
The Small House at Allington, iii, 2 Apr. 1864, 418–19.
Miss Mackenzie, v, 27 May 1865, 596.

'The Fortnightly Review' (contains an attack on Trollope's article 'On Anonymous Literature', *FR* i, 1 Jul. 1865, 491–9), vi, 8 Jul. 1865, 35.

Hunting Sketches, vi, 26 Aug. 1865, 233.

Saturday Review

Barchester Towers, iii, 30 May 1857, 503–4.

The Three Clerks, iv, 5 Dec. 1857, 517–18.

Doctor Thorne, v, 12 June 1858, 618–19.

The Bertrams, vii, 26 Mar. 1859, 368–9.

'Trollope's West Indies', viii, 26 Nov. 1859, 643–5.

'Mr. Trollope on Central America', viii, 3 Dec. 1859, 675–6.

Castle Richmond, ix, 19 May 1860, 643–4.

Framley Parsonage, xi, 4 May 1861, 451–2.

Tales of All Countries (1st series), xii, 7 Dec. 1861, 587–8.

North America, xiii, 31 May 1862, 625–6.

Orley Farm, xiv, 11 Oct. 1862, 444–5.

Tales of All Countries (2nd series), xv, 28 Feb. 1863, 276–8.

Rachel Ray, xvi, 24 Oct. 1863, 554–5.

The Small House at Allington, xvii, 14 May 1864, 595–6.

Miss Mackenzie, xix, 4 Mar. 1865, 263–5.

'Mistaken Estimates of Self' (attacks Trollope for publishing a letter on Lincoln's assassination, *Pall Mall Gazette*, 5 May 1865, 4), xix, 13 May 1865, 564.

Can You Forgive Her?, xx, 19 Aug. 1865, 240–2.

'An Amateur Theologian' (on Trollope's article 'The Fourth Commandment', *Fortnightly Review* iii, 15 Jan. 1866, 529–38), xxi, 3 Feb. 1866, 131–3.

The Belton Estate, xxi, 3 Feb. 1866, 140–2.

The Claverings, xxiii, 18 May 1867, 638–9.

Lotta Schmidt and Other Stories, xxiv, 21 Sept. 1867, 381–2.

Phineas Finn, xxvii, 27 Mar. 1869, 431–2.

He Knew He Was Right, xxvii, 5 June 1869, 751–3.

British Sports and Pastimes, xxviii, 13 Nov. 1869, 652–4.

The Vicar of Bullhampton, xxix, 14 May 1870, 646–7.

An Editor's Tales, xxx, 13 Aug. 1870, 211–12.

Sir Harry Hotspur of Humblethwaite, xxx, 10 Dec. 1870, 753–5.

Ralph the Heir, xxxi, 29 Apr. 1871, 537–8.

The Golden Lion of Granpere, xxxiii, 29 June 1872, 833–5.

The Eustace Diamonds, xxxiv, 16 Nov. 1872, 637–8.

Australia and New Zealand, xxxv, 26 Apr. 1873, 554–5.

Phineas Redux, xxxvii, 7 Feb. 1874, 186–7.

Lady Anna, xxxvii, 9 May 1874, 598–9.

Harry Heathcote of Gangoil, xxxviii, 7 Nov. 1874, 609–10.

The Way We Live Now, xl, 17 Jul. 1875, 88–9.

The Prime Minister, xlii, 14 Oct. 1876, 481–2.

The American Senator, xliii, 30 June 1877, 803–4.

South Africa, xlv, 23 Feb. 1887, 241–3.

Is He Popenjoy?, xlv, 1 June 1878, 695–6.
An Eye for an Eye, xlvii, 29 Mar. 1879, 410–11.
John Caldigate, xlviii, 16 Aug. 1879, 216–17.
Cousin Henry, xlviii, 25 Oct. 1879, 515–16.
The Duke's Children, xlix, 12 June 1880, 767–8.
Dr. Wortle's School, li, 22 Jan. 1881, 121–2.
The Life of Cicero, li, 26 Feb. 1881, 279–80.
Ayala's Angel, li, 11 June 1881, 756–7.
Why Frau Frohmann Raised Her Prices and Other Stories, liii, 11 Mar.
    1882, 305–6.
The Fixed Period, liii, 8 Apr. 1882, 434–5.
Marion Fay, liv, 8 Jul. 1882, 64–5.
Lord Palmerston, liv, 5 Aug. 1882, 182–3.
Obituary, liv, 9 Dec. 1882, 755–6.
Mr. Scarborough's Family, lv, 19 May 1883, 642–3.
'Anthony Trollope' (An Autobiography), lvi, 20 Oct. 1883, 505–6.
The Landleaguers, lvii, 12 Jan. 1884, 53–4.
An Old Man's Love, lvii, 29 Mar. 1884, 414–15.

The Spectator

Many attributions from the *Spectator* editorial records, largely in Hutton's
own hand. Abbreviated to 'RHH'. I am grateful to the Editor of the
Spectator for permission to consult these records.
    —described by R. H. Tener, 'The *Spectator* Records 1874–1897',
    Victorian Newsletter 17 (Spring 1960), 33–6.

See also:

Skilton, D. J. 'The *Spectator*'s attack on Trollope's *Prime Minister*:
    a mistaken attribution', *Notes and Queries* (ns) xv, Nov. 1968,
    420–1.
Tener, R. H. 'More articles by R. H. Hutton', *Bulletin of the New York
    Public Library* lxvi, Jan. 1962, 58–62.
Tener, R. H. 'A clue for some R. H. Hutton attributions', *Notes and
    Queries* (ns) xiv, Oct. 1867, 382–3.

The Macdermots of Ballycloran, xx, 8 May 1847, 449.
The Warden, xxviii, 6 Jan. 1855, 27–8.
Barchester Towers, xxx, 16 May 1857, 525–6.
The Three Clerks, xxx, 12 Dec. 1857, 1300–1.
Doctor Thorne, xxxi, 29 May 1858, 577–8.
The West Indies and the Spanish Main, xxxii, 12 Nov. 1859, 1166–7.
Castle Richmond, xxxiii, 19 May 1860, 477.
Orley Farm (volume one), xxxv, 4 Jan. 1862, 5.
Tales of All Countries (1st series), xxxv, 18 Jan. 1862, 80.
North America, xxxv, 7 June 1862, 635–6.
Orley Farm, xxxv, 11 Oct. 1862, 1136–8 [R. H. Hutton—Tener, 'A clue
    for some R. H. Hutton attributions'; on satisfying stylistic grounds].

Tales of All Countries (2nd series), xxxvi, 7 Mar. 1863, suppl. to no. 1810, 20–1.

'Mr. Trollope's Caricature:—Rachel Ray', xxxvi, 24 Oct. 1863, 2660–1.

The Small House at Allington, xxxvii, 9 Apr. 1864, 421–3.

Miss Mackenzie, xxxviii, 4 Mar. 1865, 244–5.

Hunting Sketches, xxxviii, 27 May 1865, 587–8.

Can You Forgive Her?, xxxviii, 9 Sept. 1865, 978–9.

The Belton Estate, xxxix, 27 Jan. 1866, 103.

Nina Balatka, xl, 23 Mar. 1867, 329–30 [R. H. Hutton (?)—Trollope's *Autobiography*, p. 205. Trollope's word is not rigorous evidence, but Tener concedes that the article is probably Hutton's: 'More articles by R. H. Hutton'].

The Claverings, xl, 4 May 1867, 498–9.

The Last Chronicle of Barset, xl, 13 Jul. 1867, 778–80.

Lotta Schmidt and Other Stories, xl, 21 Sept. 1867, 1062–3.

'Mr. Trollope's New Magazine' (Saint Paul's Magazine), xl, 5 Oct. 1867, 1120–1.

Linda Tressel, xli, 9 May 1868, 562–3.

British Sports and Pastimes, xlii, 2 Jan. 1869, 16–17.

Phineas Finn, xlii, 20 Mar. 1869, 356–7.

He Knew He Was Right, xlii, 12 June 1869, 706–8.

The Commentaries of Caesar, xliii, 18 June 1870, 757–8.

An Editor's Tales, xliii, 8 Oct. 1870, 1203.

Sir Harry Hotspur of Humblethwaite, xliii, 26 Nov. 1870, 1415.

Ralph the Heir, xliv, 15 Apr. 1871, 450–2.

The Golden Lion of Granpere, xlv, 18 May 1872, 630–1.

The Eustace Diamonds, xlv, 26 Oct. 1872, 1365–6.

Australia and New Zealand, xlvi, 10 May 1873, 607–8.

      do.   xlvi, 17 May 1873, 640.

Phineas Redux, xlvii, 3 Jan. 1874, 36–7.

Harry Heathcote of Gangoil, xlviii, 20 Feb. 1875, 247–8 [R. H. Hutton —RHH].

The Way We Live Now, xlviii, 26 June 1875, 825–6 [Meredith Townsend —RHH].

The Prime Minister, xlix, 22 Jul. 1876, 922–3 [Meredith Townsend— RHH].

South Africa, li, 6 Apr. 1878, 445.

The American Senator, li, 31 Aug. 1878, 1101–2.

Is He Popenjoy?, li, 5 Oct. 1878, 1243–4.

'Mr. Trollope on the Moral Effect of Novel-Reading' (on Trollope's article 'Novel-Reading', *Nineteenth Century* vi, Jan. 1879, 24–43), lii, 4 Jan. 1879, 9–10.

An Eye for an Eye, lii, 15 Feb. 1879, 210–11.

John Caldigate, lii, 19 Jul. 1879, 916–17.

Thackeray, lii, 6 Sept. 1879, 1130–2.

Cousin Henry, lii, 18 Oct. 1879, 1319–21.

The Duke's Children, liii, 12 June 1880, 755–6.

The Life of Cicero, liv, 12 Mar. 1881, 353–4 [J. Clayton—RHH].

Ayala's Angel, liv, 18 June 1881, 804–5 [Miss Dillwyn—RHH].

The Fixed Period, lv, 18 Mar. 1882, 360–1 [R. H. Hutton—RHH].

Why Frau Frohmann Raised Her Prices and Other Stories, lv, 1 Apr.
1882, 443 [R. H. Hutton—RHH].

Marion Fay, lv, 19 Aug. 1882, 1088–9 [Miss Lock—RHH].

Obituary, lv, 9 Dec. 1882, 1573–4 [R. H. Hutton—RHH].

'From Miss Austen to Mr. Trollope', lv, 16 Dec. 1882, 1609–11 [R. H.
Hutton—RHH].

Kept in the Dark, lvi, 20 Jan. 1883, 88–9 [Miss Lock—RHH].

Mr. Scarborough's Family, lvi, 12 May 1883, 612–14 [Meredith
Townsend—RHH].

'The Boyhood of Anthony Trollope' (An Autobiography), lvi, 20 Oct.
1883, 1343–4 [Meredith Townsend—RHH].

'Mr. Trollope as Critic' (An Autobiography), lvi, 27 Oct. 1883, 1373–4
[R. H. Hutton—RHH].

'Anthony Trollope's Autobiography', lvi, 27 Oct. 1883, 1377–9 [R. H.
Hutton—RHH].

The Landleaguers, lvi, 15 Dec. 1883, 1627 [Rev A. J. Church—RHH].

The Times

All attributions from *The Times* Editorial Diaries. I am very grateful to
Mr J. Gordon Phillips, Archivist of *The Times*, for his kind assistance
in finding these attributions for me.

The Kellys and the O'Kellys, 7 Sept. 1848, 6 [Diary Missing].

Barchester Towers, 13 Aug. 1857, 5 [E. S. Dallas].

'Anthony Trollope' (The Bertrams), 23 May 1859, 12 [E. S. Dallas].

'The West Indies', 6 Jan. 1860, 4 [E. S. Dallas].

'Trollope's Travels' (The West Indies and the Spanish Main, 2nd notice),
18 Jan. 1860, 12 [E. S. Dallas].

North America, 11 June 1862, 6 [S. Lucas].

Orley Farm, 26 Dec. 1862, 5 [E. S. Dallas].

Rachel Ray, 25 Dec. 1863, 4 [E. S. Dallas].

Miss Mackenzie, 23 Aug. 1865, 12 [E. S. Dallas].

He Knew He Was Right, 26 Aug. 1869, 4 [F. N. Broome].

Vicar of Bullhampton, 3 June 1870, 4 ['Edward Halfacre': i.e. George
Dasent].

Sir Harry Hotspur of Humblethwaite, 16 Nov. 1870, 4 [do.].

Ralph the Heir, 17 Apr. 1871, 6 [Dasent].

The Eustace Diamonds, 30 Oct. 1872, 4 [Broome].

Australia and New Zealand, 12 Apr. 1873, 7 [Broome].

Lady Anna, 24 June 1874, 5 [Dasent].

The Way We Live Now, 24 Aug. 1875, 4 [Lady Barker: wife of
F. N. Broome].

The Prime Minister, 18 Aug. 1876, 4 [Alexander Innes Shand].

The American Senator, 10 Aug. 1877, 3 [Shand].

South Africa, 18 Apr. 1878, 7 [authorship unknown].

Is He Popenjoy?, 14 Sept. 1878, 4 [Shand].

John Caldigate, 8 Aug. 1879, 3 [Shand].
Cousin Henry, 6 Nov. 1879, 6 [Shand].
Dr. Wortle's School, 16 Apr. 1881, 10 [Shand].
Ayala's Angel, 16 July 1881, 5 [Shand].
The Fixed Period, 12 Apr. 1882, 3–4 [Shand].
Obituary, 7 Dec. 1882, 9 [Mrs Ward].
An Autobiography (a 'paragraph' on the appearance of the book),
    28 Sept. 1883, 3 [Diary missing].
An Autobiography, 'First Article', 12 Oct. 1883, 10 [Diary missing].
An Autobiography, 'Second and Concluding Article', 13 Oct. 1883, 8
    [Diary missing].
An Old Man's Love, 14 Apr. 1884, 3 [Shand].

University Magazine (successor to *Dublin University Magazine*)

'Polar opposites in fiction' (on Nathaniel Hawthorne and A. T., and
    A. T.'s 'The Genius of Nathaniel Hawthorne', *North American
    Review* cxxxix, Sept. 1879, 203–22, iv, Oct. 1879, 437–42.

Westminster Review

Barchester Towers, (ns) xii, Oct. 1857, 594–6 [George Meredith—see
    G. S. Haight, 'George Meredith and the "Westminster Review"',
    Modern Language Review liii, Jan. 1958, 1–16].
Framley Parsonage, (ns) xx, Jul. 1861, 282–4.
Rachel Ray, (ns) xxv, Jan. 1864, 291–3.
The Small House at Allington, (ns) xxvi, Jul. 1864, 251–2.
Miss Mackenzie, and Can You Forgive Her? (volume one), (ns) xxviii,
    Jul. 1865, 283–5.
The Struggle of Brown, Jones, and Robinson: by One of the Firm, (ns)
    xxxix, Apr. 1871, 574–5.
Harry Heathcote of Gangoil, (ns) xlvii, Apr. 1875, 558.
The Way We Live Now, (ns) xlviii, Oct. 1875, 529–30.
Thackeray, (ns) lvi, Jul. 1879, 258.
The Duke's Children, (ns) lviii, Oct. 1880, 574.
The Life of Cicero, (ns) lix, Apr. 1881, 605–6.
Dr. Wortle's School, (ns) lx, Jul. 1881, 283–4.
Ayala's Angel, (ns) lx, Oct. 1881, 566–7.
Fixed Period, (ns) lxii, Jul. 1882, 285–6.
Lord Palmerston, (ns) lxii, Oct. 1882, 566.
Kept in the Dark, (ns) lxiii, Jan. 1883, 287.
Mr. Scarborough's Family, (ns) lxiv, Jul. 1883, 301.
An Autobiography, (ns) lxv, Jan. 1884, 83–115.
The Landleaguers, (ns) lxv, Jan. 1884, 276–7.
An Old Man's Love, (ns) lxvi, Jul. 1884, 305.

INDEX

Characters in Trollope's fiction are distinguished by an asterisk.